Ordinary People, Extraordinary Profits

Founded in 1807, John Wiley & Sons is the oldest independent publishing company in the United States. With offices in North America, Europe, Australia, and Asia, Wiley is globally committed to developing and marketing print and electronic products and services for our customers' professional and personal knowledge and understanding.

The Wiley Trading series features books by traders who have survived the market's ever-changing temperament and have prospered—some by reinventing systems, others by getting back to basics. Whether you are a novice trader, professional, or somewhere in between, these books provide the advice and strategies you need to prosper today and well into the future.

For a list of available titles, visit our web site at www.WileyFinance.com.

Ordinary People, Extraordinary Profits

How to Make a Living as an
Independent Stock, Options,
and Futures Trader

DAVID S. NASSAR

WILEY

John Wiley & Sons, Inc.

Published by John Wiley & Sons, Inc., Hoboken, New Jersey.
Published simultaneously in Canada.

Library of Congress Cataloging-in-Publication Data:

Nassar, David S.
    Ordinary people, extraordinary profits : how to make a living as an independent stock, options, and
futures trader / David Nassar.
        p.   cm.—(Wiley finance series)
    Includes bibliographical references and index.
    ISBN-13: 978-0-471-71236-7 (cloth/dvd)
    ISBN-10: 0-471-71236-1 (cloth/dvd)
    ISBN-13: 978-0-471-72399-8 (cloth)
    ISBN-10: 0-471-72399-1 (cloth)
    1. Investment analysis.   2. Portfolio management.   3. Risk management.   4. Investments.   I.
Title.   II. Series.
  HG4529.N372   2005
  332.6—dc22
                                                                                        2005010210

Printed in the United States of America

10   9   8   7   6   5   4   3   2   1

Contents

Preface

A WORD ABOUT RISK . . .

Investing and trading—in anything, be it real estate, raw land, oil, gas, securities, futures, options—has associated risks. You must understand, face, and embrace them before you act.

What are the risk factors for stocks, options, and futures?

First, they are all speculative in nature, but what isn't? Will you live 5 more years? 10? 20? 50? Who knows? Yet you endure day in and day out with this uncertainty. We all understand that at some point our life, as we know it, ceases. What happens next has been debated without a consensus since humans learned to talk.

Investing and trading are no different. You can do all the fundamental research in the world about a particular investment, only to watch it melt like a block of ice in the parking lot on a hot summer's day. Or, you can be the top technical trader and execute the perfect trade only to be whipsawed by an erratic market.

Life does not offer a money-back guarantee—why should you expect any more from the stock, futures, or options markets?

Nevertheless, educating yourself about the markets you plan to trade gives you an edge. Although it is not huge, I hope that edge will make you a net winner instead of a net loser. But I cannot guarantee it because there are too many uncontrollable factors in the win-lose equation. In any trade or investment, think about the elements you have absolute control over—the specific entity you decide to trade, the side (long or short) you decide to enter on, the size of your position, and the length of time you hold the position.

But the most important factors you face are totally unpredictable! Is your market headed higher or lower? How fast is it moving? What new information will influence the market for or against your position without warning? Will you have time and the will to exit, if you enter your position on the wrong side?

I cannot train you to know which direction the market you are trading is going to go. What I do in *Ordinary People, Extraordinary Profits* is teach foundational analysis that will—if you employ it properly—tell you what the market *should* do next. Then I explain how you can protect yourself if the market does not do what it should do. That is the edge you can take away from this book. I intend to teach you to make good decisions and place protective stops in case the decision is incorrect. The ancient axiom, "Let your profits run; cut your loses short!" sums it all up.

Specific risks are associated with the various types of trading and investing discussed in the following chapters. The philosophy of the long-term investor is to mitigate the risk of owning stocks by holding them for a long time. The *should* process is that eventually stocks will rise, if they are held long enough. The fallacy of this approach has to do with timing and the amount of gain earned while waiting. There have been periods in the history of the stock market when long-term investors have held securities for decades with little or no gain. If you were an owner of such stocks during those periods and needed income or capital gains for retirement or other needs, you were out of luck.

Short-term traders attempt to deal with the risk of holding positions for long periods by entering and exiting positions quickly. They want to be long when stocks are rising and short when they are falling. That is the idea, which is seldom, if ever, achieved all the time. Since these participants trade frequently, they often spend a lot of money on brokerage commissions.

Timing of trades, no matter if they are long or short in duration, is critical, and it is impossible for anyone to be always right. Being on the right side and for the right amount of time only half the time or less can result in success—especially if the losers are cut before they grow unmanageable.

What about the futures and options traders? Do they fare any better?

If you trade futures, you face the dreaded limit up or limit down trading sessions when the price of the futures contract opens at the limit up or limit down price. The price of the contract can move against, or in your favor, for the specified limit amount without any trading taking place. Sometimes a limit move continues for several days. If it is against your position, you are losing substantial amounts of money and there is nothing you can do to relieve your suffering.

Or what about the options traders who buy a put or a call? They pay the premium and will never face a margin call. The downside is that the options will eventually expire. If the underlying entity does not move in their favor or they do not offset the position before expiration, they lose 100 percent of their investment—the premium and transaction cost. Option writers face a theoretical, unlimited risk if the position moves massively against them.

No matter what you do to protect yourself—trade fast, trade slow, trade small, trade big, trade stocks, futures, options, and so on—you still risk losing your capital. I cannot guarantee your success. My goal in the following pages is to share the information and experience of our teaching-trading staff to help you assess what the market you wish to trade should do next and how to protect yourself if it does not.

Trade Wise!

DAVID S. NASSAR

Acknowledgments

There are many people who have contributed to this course book, but first let me categorically thank all the great people I have worked with at MarketWise, TerraNova Trading, and RealTick, both past and present. In particular, we would like to acknowledge the following contributors to the book: All the people listed have helped to compile, write and format the work, and without their support and efforts, this course would not have been possible.

A special thanks to Brian Shannon. Brian co-created this course with me and if it were up to me, his name would also appear on the cover as co-author. Brian is an outstanding writer, trader, and most importantly—friend. He has been a part of MarketWise since 1999 and has been a true leader within our organization.

To Kevin Ward for his contributions that are too numerous to define here. Kevin has been part of MarketWise since inception (10 years) and has been simply an outstanding asset to the team.

To Eric Erickson for his continued efforts in writing, creating charts, and a multitude of tasks that truly go "above and beyond."

Walter Wood, for his contribution and genius in creating the "Profiler Technology." Walter is a true gentlemen and friend to everyone within MarketWise.

Craig Bradley, Walter Phipps, and Alex Pasek, thank you for the outstanding work in the DVD and website. This is a very talented and creative team!

I would like to extend appreciation to my partners, MarrGwen Townsend, Stuart Townsend, Jerry Putnam, Jack Whitehouse, and Chris Doubek. I do not want to forget Chris Myers, president of Traders Library who initiated this project. Finally, and most importantly, I want to recognize my family, Tracy, Zachary, and Weston Nassar.

D. S. N.

Introduction

The Inner Game

You are about to embark on one of the most exciting journeys of your career. . . . *Ordinary People, Extraordinary Profits* shows you the way to care for and nurture your investment capital.

This book is an outgrowth of information that I have presented to many aspiring traders and investors to help them improve their trading and investment decisions. With study and application, you will find that it can help you, too.

No one cares more about your money than you do. Even qualified investment planners and stockbrokers seldom have the time to focus on your account as intently as you do. Taking complete responsibility for your financial future is one of the wisest decisions you can make.

Your money provides you and your family with a certain lifestyle. Just as you paint your home and change the oil in your car, it is prudent to learn how to preserve your capital and work toward its growth.

In the bull market in stocks that soared to an apogee at the end of the past century, many people made huge profits. The year 2000, however, ushered in a bear market that, in just a few years, erased $7 trillion in investment gains. The tumbling market most heavily punished the investors who clung to the traditional buy-and-hold methodology. It is essential to have alternative ways for making—and securing—stock market profits against events like those that began March 2000. That disaster is a recent example, but history provides many others. Herein lies the foundation of what you are about to learn: History repeats itself because human nature rarely changes. We can state it another way: Market psychology is the study of aggregated human nature as manifested on the

1

charts and prices of securities. Astute traders have known this for many years.

Investors have learned that techniques employed by traders can protect gains and minimize losses. If you are, or want to be, a short-term investor or trader in the stock market, I congratulate you for choosing this book. I have designed it to be the most comprehensive and state-of-the-art course in the industry.

TRADE THE PROFESSIONAL WAY

By adopting the skills of professional traders, you will learn how to enter and stay on the right side of a trend—be it minutes or weeks in duration—and, most importantly, how to gauge when that trend may be flattening or about to end. (Those who held on to their Enron shares all the way up, and then all the way down, undoubtedly could have used that knowledge.)

Consistently profitable trading is related to the probability theory, which says the more possible outcomes there are, the greater the chance for success. This is also known as expectancy theory, and it works like this: There are no secrets, only statistical probabilities that markets will act and trend in a certain manner (bullish, bearish, market neutral, strong, or weak). The probabilities are quantifiable (based on market psychology) and use a model that statistically evaluates more winning trades than losing trades. When winners are found, profits are left to run using tools such as trailing stops; losers are quickly identified and covered (based on discipline). If this is a secret, then it is, by far, the most valuable one a trader can learn. After all, casinos have learned this lesson and build billion-dollar hotels in the desert with only an epsilon of an edge. The trader can gain better odds with this approach.

As the first step, you must see the market with an indifferent, instead of a positive (bullish) or negative (bearish) predisposition. With the proper techniques, you can make money in all market conditions, even directionless markets. You are best served by viewing the market for what it is, without a bias about direction. Said another way, "Trade what you observe, not what you believe."

Mutual fund managers are often guilty of ignoring this rule. Most mutual funds only make money *if* the market goes up (the manager can enter only long positions), whereas hedge funds can make money in multiple directions, including sideways. It makes sense that increasing your strategies and opportunities to make money improves your odds of profiting. At

MarketWise (www.marketwise.com), we attempt to take profits out of any market setting, no matter what direction that may be.

RIDE THE STATISTICAL EDGE . . . LIKE BETTING SEVEN IN CRAPS

It is no accident that the number seven is the magic number in craps (see Table I.1). The number seven simply has more statistical opportunities than any other number when throwing a pair of dice; therefore, it is the one that, when thrown after the initial roll, signifies that the roller has lost. This is a statistical fact and reality; it is not based on "feel" or heightened emotions. The casino knows that the amateur gambler will bet emotionally when he or she throws the dice. Additionally, the house has a statistical edge.

Casinos do not change the rules in the middle of a game of craps; they systematically trade the odds. Conversely, amateur gamblers drink alcohol while playing and make arbitrary bets that are anything but systematic. The combined statistical edge of seven showing up more than any other number, along with the greed and fear emotions of the amateur gambler, creates an awesome advantage that builds pyramids in the desert. Trade the odds . . . be the smart money!

As you read this book, you will discover how to look for high-probability setups and entries prior to taking a position. You will learn how to calculate your risk on each position *before* you enter, and ascertain exactly where you want to exit if the trade goes against you. You will identify which stop-loss exit is best for your trading methodology and why.

TABLE I.1 Expectionary theory reference table.

Dice Total		Chance	Odds
2	1–1	One	6 to 1
3	1–2, 2–1	Two	3 to 1
4	1–3, 3–1, 2–2	Three	2 to 1
5	1–4, 4–1, 2–3, 3–2	Four	3 to 2
6	1–5, 5–1, 2–4, 4–2, 3–3	Five	6 to 5
7	1–6, 6–1, 2–5, 5–2, 3–4, 4–3	Six	Even
8	2–6, 6–2, 3–5, 5–3, 4–4	Five	6 to 5
9	3–6, 6–3, 4–5, 5–4	Four	3 to 2
10	4–6, 6–4, 5–5	Three	2 to 1
11	5–6, 6–5	Two	3 to 1
12	6–6	One	6 to 1

You will also learn how to calculate your profit target. With a firm plan in place, you can determine exactly how to manage your trade at all times.

Perhaps the most important skill you can possess as a trader is the proper mind-set. When you enter a position, you are not—in the short term—trading a stock or financial instrument. Instead, you are trading people and their emotions of greed and fear on every level of the spectrum that creates the momentum that, in turn, moves price.

MASTER THE INNER GAME

Once you learn the skills and strategies of trading, your continued success depends on your attitude and mind-set—how you play the inner game.

One way to approach this is to consider the technique used by method actors. They play the role of the character assigned to them by "getting inside" that character and "becoming" that person. Just so, you must get inside, understand, and acquire the disciplined confidence of professional traders, who know the stock market cannot hurt them unless they allow it to do so. When you know—*and you know you know*—you can operate with knowledge and self-assurance within the market's ebb and flow—your self-assurance will replace fear and anxiety.

Before you start trading, it is wise to perform self-discovery and personal motivational analysis to target your particular strengths and challenges as they apply to trading. You can have 10 monitors lined up on your desk and purchase the most sophisticated software. You can execute with lightning-quick rapidity. You can read and absorb every book written on trading and attend every class. Yet, if you don't attain the unique mentality that a trader must have, your road to trading success is likely to be an extremely challenging one.

Finally, the mastery of trading competence is a journey that never ends. The skill-set of trading has many components, from a workable knowledge of technical analysis, order execution, and market psychology, to the broader scope of market machinations and money management. You will have to dedicate your time toward learning, researching, and doing your homework. You will need to commit money to your trading account, and you must make sure it is not "scared money" (money that, if lost, would alter your lifestyle or that of your family). You must also delve inward and assess personal psychological traits that you may need to alter—or strengthen.

This journey is an exciting and worthwhile expedition. Go slowly, study, and craft your skills diligently. To paraphrase a popular adage, "Trading is not a sprint; it is a marathon."

CHAPTER 1

Foundational Analysis

I like to use the analogy of the human body—in a purely physical sense——to describe your needs as an investor/trader (I/T). Just as your body needs quality food to survive and thrive, you need quality information to build and maintain healthy investments. Most "market food" has already been digested by the market (reflected in price) before the average person gets it. Like any other digested food, it no longer has nutritional value. People get market information from the media only after its value has been exhausted. The question is, why then do so many people still rely on this information to make decisions?

On our journey, we will hunt for quality information that is still nutritious and full of value so that our investments can flourish from it before its value is digested. This information will not come from the media reports, which are based on news from brokerage firms and corporations. Too many people are enamored with these reports, which is why most participants lose their money in the market. Our food comes from the art of tracking market psychology in the form of greed and fear. This is where you will find the best market food.

The difficult lesson to convey here is that those who have brilliant success in the stock market employ the simplest methods. Indeed, it is the shock market's simplicity that is its greatest disguise. For, in the end, what causes stocks to go up and down is not some diabolical force that lies beyond human intelligence, but instead the interaction of basic emotions. It is only when we learn to distance our emotions from market analysis that we begin to understand the fundamental simplicity of the stock market and to trust that, at any level, the game is neither mysterious nor unbeatable.

In this chapter, I describe specific tools that you can use to simplify reading the stock market's vital signs. These tools all fall within the rubric of *foundational analysis*, a discipline that uses only a few variables to fully reveal the essence of stock-price fluctuations. The four key variables of foundational analysis are *price, volume, time,* and *velocity*. In combination, they can tell us nearly all we need to know to profit as traders. Including more variables will only complicate the task by increasing our bias and making us susceptible to subjective factors as well as to emotional swings.

Emotions are a trader's worst enemy. The skills that you must learn to succeed can develop only when you focus on what is real and available in the market and ignore the extraneous, mystical, and subjective. In this book, I discuss ways to quantify such observations using foundational variables, but you must first be aware that knowledge of these variables cannot ensure successful trading, for no trading signal works all the time. Diligent traders monitor real-time market data derived from price, volume, time, and velocity, as well as from historical trends; but they do not apply this data in the same way with every trade, since the markets are constantly changing. Thus, mastery of the stock market is more of an art than a science.

The array of information at our disposal can be bewildering: Pictograms, heat maps, histograms, and oscillators produce a never-ending stream of bullish and bearish signals. But all of it is useless unless you incorporate sound principles of risk management as well as a perspective that wisely takes the past into account. Even then, the most valuable tool—experience—is something that can only come with time. Books or seminars cannot fully explain or replicate experience, no matter how thorough the curriculum. As a trader, you should rely on *Ordinary People, Extraordinary Profits* for valuable guidance, while interpreting the material in terms of your own experience.

You should view foundational analysis as a tool to structure and organize your market observations so that you can apply them systematically toward the goal of profitable trading. As you read this book, keep in mind that you want to learn and hone a systematic approach to the market, not to perfect a trading system per se. As you absorb the lessons of the various chapters, the differences will become apparent, but in practical terms this approach means that you will be seeking to develop an edge over other traders rather than a guaranteed lock on profits. Holding an edge requires learning from others who are successful, keeping an open mind, and never succumbing to the belief that any one method or technique will work forever.

Because the markets never stop mutating, the best traders know that the only thing that works over time is to constantly embrace change. How we made money yesterday is not always going to be the same way we will make money today or tomorrow. Many traders learned this the hard way when the raging bull market of the late 1990s abruptly turned into a hostile bear market. Not only did the temper of the market change, but the rules changed as well, including a move to decimal prices. This action tightened spreads between bids and offers, effectively eliminating a successful arbitrage tactic of easier money. What did not change when the bear market came marauding in March of 2000 were the foundational variables with which we interpret the market's underlying dynamics. To understand this is to survive. Our steadfastness in adhering to bedrock principles of the market is why we have endured long enough to share with you the means for duplicating our success.

It takes discipline and courage to confront the psychological challenges that the stock market throws before you each day. In the end, the market is all about the unknown—what we might call the far-right edge of the chart. This is an undeniable truth. The far-right edge could be applied to life itself. Every time you get in your car, you do not know if you will have a good day or a bad day. So on any given day, you cannot know in advance if the market is going to go with you or against you. That is the reality of life. Harsh? Probably. Realistic? Absolutely.

Trading is about gaining whatever small edge exists to predict the very near-term future. This concept builds on common sense, and applying it to the market relies on the principle that the most recent past will have the greatest influence on the near-term future. The further you try to project a trend out into the future, the farther back in time you must look.

CHARTS

Before examining the key components of foundational analysis, it is necessary to understand the charts that are used to record price, time, volume and velocity. The dedicated chartist will say that all the information needed to predict what a stock will do is contained in charts showing what the stock has already done. Some might scoff at this claim, but charts are the best indicator of what a stock is about to do and what it has just done. Before exploring why this is so, we are going to look at several types of charts that appear in this book. Figure 1.1 is a simple bar chart.

In Figure 1.2 we examine just a piece of the chart in Figure 1.1 under a magnifying glass. Notice that these bars are not simple sticks, but they have tiny tick marks protruding from their sides. The tick mark on the left side indicates the opening price; the one on the right side shows the closing price. The high point of the bar is the highest price that was traded

Daily **XYZ Corp**

RealTick Graphics used with permission
of Townsend Analytics, Ltd.

FIGURE 1.1   The price activity of a particular stock over a period of five months, from October to February. Time is shown on the horizontal axis, with monthly intervals noted at the bottom. The vertical axis shows price. In this example, the stock has fluctuated from a low of about $18 in early October to a high just above $45 in mid-February. There are many facts on the chart in which we could also say the stock fluctuated between $30 and $35 between late November and early January. We could also say that the stock rallied steeply between mid-January and February. This last statement relates to velocity, one of our four key foundational variables.

during that particular period and the low point is the lowest price traded within the period.

Analyzing a stock on a chart should not be limited to just one dimension of time; rather, we combine multiple time frames to gain further clarity about the stocks' behavior. It is common to begin our analysis with a study of daily data (Figure 1.1) and then magnify that period of time by use of an intraday time frame (Figure 1.2). The shorter-term time frame allows us to get more precise in our entry orders as well as to manage the trade with carefully placed exit orders.

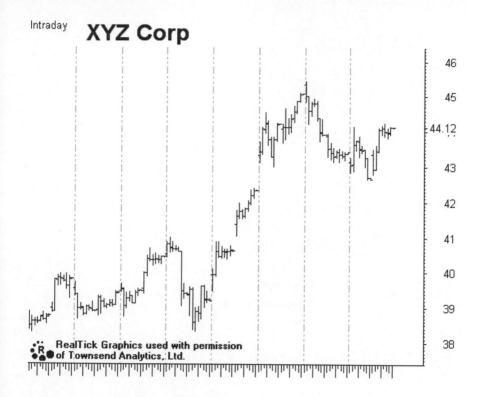

FIGURE 1.2   This intraday chart shows a more detailed view of the last 14 days in Figure 1.1. Vertical lines separate the data into two-day increments of time.

Figure 1.3 shows the chart of a stock with the foundational variable of volume displayed beneath it. Volume shows how many shares of a stock have traded hands for a particular period.

Thus, we can summarize a stock's price history merely by glancing at its chart. In the preceding examples, price, time, and volume are all explicit whereas the remaining foundational variable, velocity, must be inferred. The quantification of velocity is discussed later in this chapter, but for now simply think of velocity as the rate at which a stock's price changes over a given interval.

Another type of chart that offers an especially concise summary of a stock's price history is called a *candlestick* chart (see Figure 1.4). Here the XYZ chart is rendered with price represented in candlestick form. The bars are shaped like wax tapers, and most have "wicks" sticking out of the top and the bottom. Candlestick charts date back to seventeenth-century Japan, where a rice broker named Munehisa Homma is said to have been

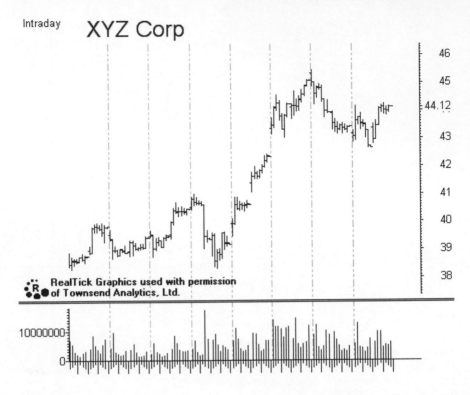

FIGURE 1.3 Nearly identical to Figure 1.2, this chart also contains volume bars that tell us how many shares of XYZ stock traded for each intraday period.

one the first traders to use price history to predict price future. His theories and rules form the basis of the candlestick charting methods in use today. In Figure 1.4, each candlestick represents a single day's price action, with open, high, low, and closing all noted.

The highs and lows are intuitively obvious because they are marked, respectively, by the tops and bottoms of each wick, or shadow. For instance, if you look closely at the spike higher near mid-January, you will see that the candlestick bar's shadows extend from approximately 35 to 37. That was the stock's price range on that day. But also observe that the "bodies" of some candlesticks are clear (they would be green if shown in color) whereas others are black (or red, if in color). The detailed diagram in Figure 1.5 summarizes the basic candlestick. If the rectangle or real body is clear (or green), the stock closed *above* its opening price. When the real body is black (or red), the stock closed *below* its opening price. If the body does not exist, it means the stock opened and closed at the same price, even though it may have traded over a wider range for the period being measured.

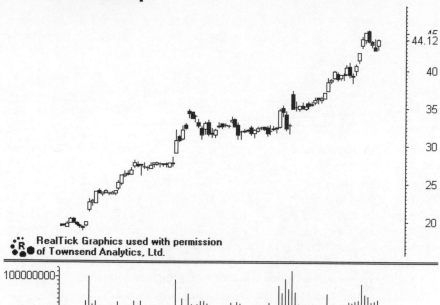

Daily **XYZ Corp**

RealTick Graphics used with permission
of Townsend Analytics, Ltd.

FIGURE 1.4 The same information as the daily chart in Figure 1.1, but the open, high, low, and close are shown as candlesticks.

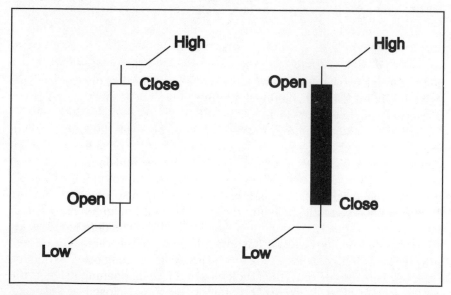

FIGURE 1.5 The white candles indicate a period of time where the stock closed above the price it opened during the period. The dark candles show a period where the close was below the open. When illustrated in color we could expect green and red respectively.

An advantageous aspect of candlesticks is that they tell us at a glance whether the close was positive or negative. Also, those of us who stare at charts for hours at a time find candlesticks are easy on the eyes.

TWO TYPES OF ANALYSIS

Now that you have a basic understanding of price charts, you need to decide how to analyze them. Active traders must have a method for deciding when to enter trades and, more importantly, when to exit them. How do you plan to do that? When will you know a stock, index, option, or futures contract is at a specific price or a price level that provides an acceptable risk-to-reward ratio? Once in a trade, how will you know when the trade is working for you, when it is not working, or when you should exit because the risk-reward ratio is no longer in your favor? As an active trader, you must have a system that allows you to react quickly, not one that requires extensive fundamental research.

On the broadest level, you only have two choices: fundamental or technical analysis. Most traders who come from a background that emphasizes investing for the long-term are familiar with fundamental analysis. In its most basic form, it uses earnings per share of a stock to evaluate whether the stock is a buy (undervalued) or a sell (overvalued). In reality, the analyst may examine all the information that is fundamental to the entity (stock, commodity, etc.) to evaluate the chances that it will gain or lose value. The fundamentals for a stock include any factors that will help or hurt the company's chances of making money: actual and projected earnings, market share, product sales performance, management expertise, industry performance, micro- and macroeconomic outlook, government regulations, news, public relations announcements, and so on.

For physical commodities like corn or silver, the fundamental analysis is often oriented to actual supply-and-demand data. The fundamental analyst wants to know how much of the commodity is left over from previous years (carryover), how much is in the supply line (storage), and how much will be produced (grown, mined, refined, etc.) in the near-term, mid-term, and long-term. Then they look at demand, usually worldwide, for that commodity. Is it strong or weak? Is the world overflowing in that commodity or is it scarce? What and where are the stocks. Does any event loom on the horizon (e.g., drought, war) that would affect supply or demand? The analyst needs to know whether the price of the commodity being evaluated is elastic or inelastic: How responsive is the price to changes in supply and demand? Will demand dry up for a commodity if the price gets too high? Do chocolate addicts worry about the price of cocoa when supplies tighten and prices soar? Not likely. But will cattle feeders switch from feeding corn to feeding wheat if wheat is substantially cheaper than corn? Yes—thus the difference between elastic and inelastic.

Finding, gathering, analyzing, and evaluating all the fundamental factors influencing the price of a stock or other entity takes time and is often subjective. Likewise, many of these factors take a long time to show their impact. Negative news or a poor earnings report could knock $10 off the per share price of a stock. Nevertheless, investors may know that the company behind that stock is fundamentally sound—well run, progressive, and a good buy for the long-term. If they are planning on holding the stock for months, quarters, or even years, it is probably a good buy at the depressed price.

But as a trader, should you buy? Traders think short-term; they buy and sell over a period of several weeks, days, and even hours and minutes. Traders think income; the objective of investors is building wealth. The income from trading may be used to create the wealth. The only interest traders may have in the stock in question is to sell the stock short it if it continues to show weakness, or to reverse and go long when the stock shows signs of strength again.

If you come to trading from an investing background, you need to make a substantial mental adjustment. Traders live in the here and now, not the future. Where a day means almost nothing to a long-term investor, it can be the entire lifetime of a trade. For some traders, it could easily be the lifetime of 5, 10, 25, 50, or more in a single day. Executing dozens of trades a day is common for active traders. There have been times when the markets were as hot as a summer in Phoenix and traders racked up a hundred or more trades a day, but this is not our focus.

Active traders generally do not depend on fundamental analysis on a daily basis for selecting stocks and picking entry and exit points. It simply takes too long to do the analysis or to wait for major price-influencers to take hold. Instead, active traders like to do what they call "keeping the wind at their back." They want to look at the fundamentals to learn the overall trend. They feel more comfortable trading from the long side in bull markets and from the short side when the bear rules, particularly if the trend is strong.

Deep fundamental analysis has another drawback for the active trader; it is not self-correcting. If a stock appears to be a good buy at $20 per share based on fundamental analysis, it must look twice as good at $10. Obviously, if you purchased 1000 shares at $20 and it is now $10, it might not seem to be such a good idea.

Technical analysis solves these problems. It can quickly alert traders to opportunities, it marks specific entry and exit price levels, and corrects itself when it is wrong. This last capability may be its most important characteristic—the difference between a long and successful career as a trader and a short and unhappy one.

There are only five possible outcomes for any trade. It can be a big winner or loser, a small winner or loser, or break even. You can survive with any of these outcomes except being a big loser. Winners are always welcome, whatever the size. Losers are inevitable. They are as common to active traders as strikeouts are to major league baseball players. Ballplayers who can't deal with striking out or traders who become depressed by repeated losses are doomed to the bush league. Worse yet, those who don't learn to avoid big losses get thrown out of the game altogether.

Technical analysis is an ideal tool for the active trader, but it is no panacea. You can go broke using technical analysis just as you can with any trading or investing system. Its greatest strength—its ability to self-correct—also can be its most frustrating feature. When you set up a trade using most any type of technical analysis, one of the key elements is selecting a price point that confirms the trade is *not* working. This is known as the *stop-loss* price. Let's say the stock you are trading is in an uptrend. You decide to stay in that trade until the stock breaks through the uptrend line drawn on a price chart by connecting all the closing prices. Once the trend is broken, you close the trade.

Trading the uptrend and exiting when it is broken is a legitimate trading approach that self-corrects. But what if, as soon as the trend is broken and you exit the trade, the price of the stock reverses again and heads higher? You exited too early and missed some additional profit, or even lost money. This is known as being *whipsawed* by the market. Although it can be frustrating, it is a part of trading you must accept and avoid losing discipline over. The worst thing you can do is to start second-guessing your stop-loss level by arbitrarily staying in some trades and exiting others when they hit your stop-loss price. This is how to set yourself up for a major loss.

If used properly, technical analysis prevents major losses and provides a framework for selecting trades with acceptable risk-reward ratios.

WHAT EXACTLY IS TECHNICAL ANALYSIS?

Technical analysis is a method of evaluating stocks, futures contracts, options, and other securities. It relies on the assumption that market data, such as price, volume, volatility, open interest, and other quantitative facts, can be used separately or in combination to predict future (usually short-term) price movements or trends. Unlike fundamental analysts, technical analysts do not even consider the intrinsic value of the entity being evaluated. They believe that they can accurately predict the future price movement by looking at its historical price activity and related statistics. They assume market psychology is reflected in the technical data allowing them to anticipate when an entity's price will rise or fall and when price movement or trends will start, stall, or reverse. Many technical analysts tend to be market timers, who believe that technical analysis can be applied to the market as a whole—to market sectors, indexes, and individual stocks, futures contracts, or options.

Literally thousands of technical studies are available. Some are simple and straightforward; others are complicated and esoteric. Here is a short list of subjects of well-known studies:

- Advance/decline line
- Moving average
- Point-and-figure charts
- Resistance and support
- Descending tops and bottoms
- Breath-of-market theory
- Breakouts and breakdowns
- Price chart formations—cup and handle, saucer, flag, pennant, double bottom, head and shoulders, and double tops
- Elliott wave theory
- High-low index
- Momentum indicator
- MACD
- On-balance volume
- Overbought/oversold indicators
- Tape reading
- Relative strength
- Arms index
- Bollinger bands
- Stochastics
- TRIN
- Turnover ratio
- Volatility index
- Regression analysis
- Money flow
- ADX

Technical analysis is a smorgasbord. It is a giant feast, set for anyone hungry for ideas, information, and an edge on the market. The problem is that there is often too much to enjoy, and too many traders want to start at the dessert-end of the table. They want the softest, gooiest, sweetest, and easiest trade first. In other words, just pass them a technical system that is foolproof and 100 percent effective. Junk food for the mind.

Such a system does not exist. If it did, would any of us be reading (or writing) this book? The next thing to understand is that technical analysis uses both art and science. The latter part occurs when the technician develops the quantitative part of the trading system. All the commonly used methods are computerized on trading platforms (e.g., RealTick®), making it simpler to get started. Visit www.realtick.com for more information.

The former part, the art of technical analysis, refers to the trader's interpretation of the data or signals that the system generates. When is a signal a signal? This may sound strange now, but once you begin to trade you will understand exactly what I am saying here. For example, you are set to enter a long position when a certain price is hit, but what do you do if that price is immediately exceeded by a few pennies or is hit and immediately retraces? Do you go long or wait? What if volume spikes or flat lines at the same time? What if extremely good or bad news, or a rumor, sweeps the trading pits? Even the best technical systems cannot take all the market fluctuations into consideration. You, as a trader, must often make a decision with conflicting or imperfect information.

The art of trading evolves from experience. You cannot learn to trade without trading. For this reason, I recommend that you start out small, trading a hundred or so shares using a simple system. The objective is to learn how to execute good trades. Is a good trade one that makes money? Often it is, but not exclusively. A good trade is one in which you have absolute control and you exercise that control with ironclad discipline. You may lose some money, but you do it on your own terms, not at the whim of the market. Or it could be a trade that you exited based on your system, but too early—leaving money on the table. You don't want to do that on a regular basis, but you do always want to be in control. You pick the trade. You enter it at your price. You exit at your price or at your stop-loss limit. You are calling the shots. Even if a call results in a loss, you are acting on the market, rather than reacting to the market's gyrations. Acquiring the control that you want to get from the use of technical analysis is neither easy nor automatic; it requires cool headedness and discipline. Nevertheless, making every trade a perfect trade is your goal.

You may have a trading system that you feel fits the criteria I have described. If not, this book provides a simple and reliable one. Once you master it, you will probably begin to modify it to better suit your needs and personality (this is the art of trading coming to the surface). Before going any further, it is useful to learn how and why technical analysis works.

Four foundations or principles support technical analysis. The first is *market action discounts everything*. This means that everything known to the market is reflected in the current price. Stocks trade for what they are worth and the current price reflects all the supply and demand factors. Some market participants get news and act on it before the general public can do so, but astute technicians can spot this activity by monitoring charts and volume data. Recognizing what traders are doing doesn't tell us why they are doing what they are doing.

A chart illustrates what all the participants are doing. It represents the collective psychology of thousands of decision makers. The stock market is known as a discounting mechanism because it attempts to factor future events into current prices. It is important to recognize that decisions to buy and sell stocks are often based on what is expected to happen. Much of what moves stock prices is the anticipation of future events. It is here that fundamental analysis plays a role in the development of long-term trends. Because perceptions about the worth of a stock continually change, prices are in flux. The catalyst for a change in perception is often a fundamental development, but technical events can also lead to a move higher or lower, especially in the short-term time frames that are so important to active traders.

Price moves in trends is the second principle of technical analysis. A trend once established is more likely to continue than reverse, Sir Isaac Newton's First Law of Motion states: Every object in a state of uniform motion tends to remain in that state of motion unless an external force is applied to it.

Stocks are no exception to this rule. A stock that is moving higher continues to do so until it reaches a level that motivates sellers, an external force, to offer enough stock to overwhelm the buyers, thus halting an advance. Stated in another way, as long as demand exceeds supply, prices rise. That only makes sense because publicly traded securities represent the largest auction markets in the world, and all markets are ruled by the basic laws of supply and demand.

Likewise, a stock will continue to drop in price until the perception of value has changed enough to motivate buyers to overcome the supply of stock being offered by the sellers, thus halting a decline. Simply stated, as long as supply exceeds demand, prices drop. It is important to point out the use of the word *perception*, because the markets move based on perception, not necessarily on fact, common sense, or even fundamentals.

It is said that the collective intelligence of the market sinks to the level of the least informed participant. That is a scary thought, but understanding it allows you to put your feelings aside and observe market action on its own merits, rather than on what may appear to be the logical scenario.

The third principle of technical analysis is *history repeats itself.* An often-repeated phrase goes something like this: "Those who forget the past are condemned to repeat it." A study of previous market action provides significant insight into the way it trades. There is no doubt that certain patterns repeat themselves on different charts at different times. These patterns merely reflect the sum of the hopes, fears, and expectations of all market participants. Because people are often emotional decision makers, they tend to react to certain events in predictable ways, especially when it comes to investing in the stock market. These emotions are the only true constant in the perpetually changing market mechanism. By understanding human psychology and what motivates the buy and sell decisions, you can often position yourself ahead of the action and anticipate profitable trade setups. When you are looking at a chart, keep in mind that you are actually looking at the collective psychology of the market participants.

The final principle of technical analysis is *always have a backup plan*. Trading is an art, not an exact science, and your analysis will not always be on target. Put harshly, the market does not care what you think. Your opinion as a trader does not count, unless it is correct. When the final bell rings, only the right votes count. Once you have done your analysis and come up with a plan of action for a trade, your work is just beginning. Successful traders know that they will be wrong many times, and they prepare for those situations with predetermined stop losses that help avoid large losses. If you can eliminate large losses, your account will be able to handle the unpleasant, but inevitable, string of small losses that most traders experience before hitting it big.

No one initiates a trade with the intent of losing money, but even the best traders do stupid trades occasionally. What separates the good traders from the excellent ones is the ability to take losses unemotionally at predetermined levels. These levels are based on time-proven money management strategies. A backup plan is part of an intelligent approach to trading that recognizes that no one is a perfect trader.

Now that we have discussed the four principles of technical analysis, let's explore how stocks are actually supposed to trade. Most traders have heard of the *Random Walk Theory*, which was made popular in Burton Makkiel's book *The Random Character of Stock Market Prices* (1964). According to this theory based on stock prices trading randomly around their intrinsic value, the best strategy is simply to buy and hold stocks. Well, anyone who bought stocks based on this theory during the bear market of 2000 to 2003 and is still holding them today would likely disagree with the theory. There is a lot of randomness in the day-to-day movement of stock prices, but being able to recognize trends and developing a strategy for selling based on the discontinuation of a trend allows you to be in cash or to sell short during volatile and uncertain markets like those of 2000 through 2003. The Random Walk Theory also states that price movement is random and unpredictable. Although it is true that stock price movement cannot be accurately predicted all the time, it is also irrefutable that prices often move in trends. You will not always enter a stock at the right time so you must protect your capital through the intelligent employment of stop-loss orders. If you are going to have any faith in technical analysis, or even in trading, you need to forget the Random Walk Theory right now.

The only true constant in the market is that humans tend to act, react, and overact in similar ways to certain situations and this behavior repeats over and over in the market. This is why technical analysis has merit; you are merely looking at emotions reflected on a chart to gain insight into how the crowd may act in a future similar situation.

THE FOUR-STAGE THEORY

Four distinct stages or phases govern the movement of stock prices:

1. Accumulation
2. Markup
3. Distribution
4. Decline

Each phase can be viewed and accurately interpreted on all time frames from 1-month charts all the way down to 1-minute charts (see Figure 1.6). For traders, it is important to make sure that the trend is the same on various time frames; you want the long-, intermediate-, and short-term trends to be sending the same message. Inconsistency among the time

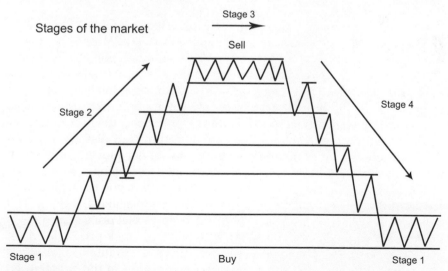

FIGURE 1.6 This Illustration could represent the action of a stock over a 10-year time frame, a 1-year time frame, 45 days, 10 days, or even 30 minutes. Regardless of the time being studied, these cycles are repeated over and over. To understand what action to take in each of these stages, first we need to break down each stage.

frames diminishes the probability of a winning trade. An alignment of a trend across time frames greatly increases the odds of a successful trade, provided, of course, that you make the proper entry and have a favorable risk-reward ratio.

In this book, three time frames—daily, 60-minute, and 10-minute—are covered for each security to ensure that the short-term trends are not in conflict with larger, more powerful, trends on long-term charts. These time frames are the ones we consider most important for swing trading decisions (1 to 10 days). This is an excellent way to find candidates for short-term price movement as opposed to looking solely at the short-term time frames to time day or swing trades. The daily chart (where each bar or candle represents one day of trading data) is the first time frame to examine to verify the overall trend and to determine its maturity (see Figure 1.7). This is also the time frame that our "Profiler" scanning technology uses consistently to find the best trading and investing ideas each day (see Figure 1.11).

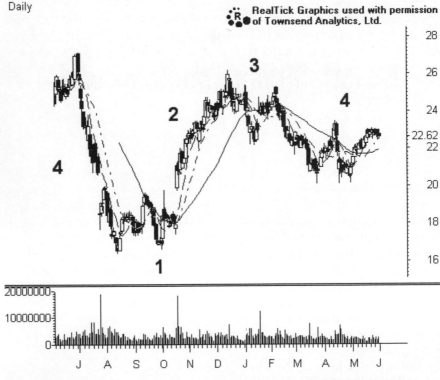

FIGURE 1.7 All four stages of stock movement for a given stock over the course of approximately one year. Each candle represents the trading activity for one day.

Intraday (60-Min)

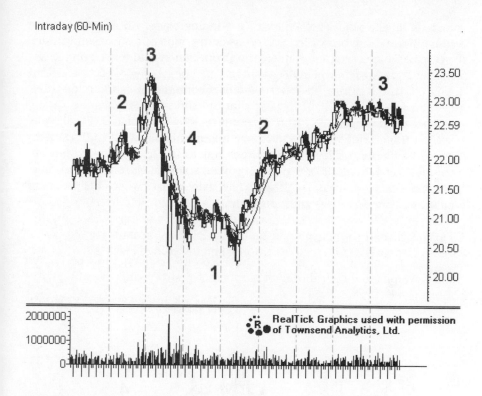

FIGURE 1.8 Shares of the same stock as in Figure 1.7 on the hourly time frame, showing the four stages of a stocks' life on the most meaningful time frame for swing traders.

The hourly chart (each candle represents 60 minutes of trading) is the next and probably the most important period for swing traders to study (see Figure 1.8). It is the time frame for planning the trade, which is based on a risk-reward ratio of at least 1:3. A 1:3 risk-reward ratio means that for every dollar at risk, there should be a potential to make three dollars. The risk reward ratio is best planned for on the hourly time frame because this is where we can most easily recognize important levels of support and resistance that form the trends. Having a favorable risk-reward ratio allows for the occasional small losses everyone experiences, while the winners will make up for those losses with less than a 50 percent win-loss ratio. When you eliminate the large losses, you can increase your probability of overall success.

For a closer look at the action, the 10-minute chart (each bar represents 10 minutes of trade data) should be studied next. On this time frame, you can become more detailed in your analysis and identify short-term levels of support and resistance. This allows you to manage risk with tight stop-loss levels within the context of the longer-term trend, where the profit potential can be significant (see Figure 1.9).

Using these three time frames together in a consistent, disciplined approach to trading lets you take advantage of short-term movements within the larger trends during all four stages of accumulation, markup, distribution, and decline.

These four stages are found over and over for all stocks, regardless of the time frame. One of the keys to success in the market is to trade with the prevailing trend, which is why you purchase stocks in Stage 2: Markup; you sell short in Stage 4: Decline and you avoid trend less stocks in Stage 1: Accumulation or Stage 3: Distribution, when fluctuations tend to be small and trading opportunities are inconsistent.

Stage 1: Accumulation

In Stage 1, bullish participants acquire stock in anticipation of higher prices, which will occur during Stage 2. These participants are able to ac-

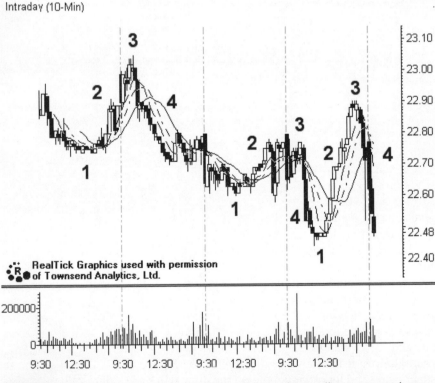

FIGURE 1.9 Moving down to an even shorter time frame allows you to observe how the four stages are repeated over and over for all securities. Your objective for time in a trade dictates which time frames to use to focus your cycle analysis.

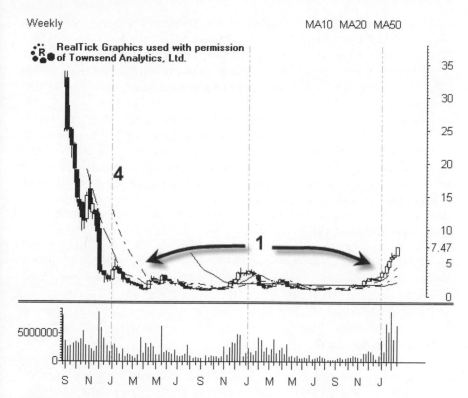

FIGURE 1.10   The Accumulation stage can sometimes last years; participating in these stocks can unnecessarily tie up your capital in a stagnant position.

cumulate shares of a stock without moving the price higher because this phase usually follows a large decline. There are still many sellers of the stock looking to reduce or eliminate positions. During this period, there is a fierce battle between the bullish buyers who are trying to establish a long position and the bearish sellers of the stock who are still getting out of positions they may have ridden down in price.

So who is doing all this accumulating? And who is selling them the stock? A Stage 1 stock is usually viewed as a major reversal pattern that can take up to a couple of months to complete on a daily chart. There usually isn't much downside risk in purchasing in this phase. The risk here is time. Your capital may be tied up in a stagnant position for months while other stocks could be experiencing powerful Stage 2 uptrends—this is opportunity cost. Why wait for the stock to move, when it could take months, if not years, before it is ready to go higher? (See Figure 1.10.) This is a time to stand aside and let other people do the dirty work of ridding sellers of their supply. The objective of short-term trading is to keep your money in the stocks that are moving *now*, and Stage 1 stocks do not advance that goal of consistent profitability. The only time it may make sense to purchase a stock in this phase is if it pays a decent cash dividend; then you must rely on fundamental analysis to determine whether the dividend is safe.

Think of a large institution, mutual fund, or major retirement fund wanting to build a substantial position in a stock. A stock in this phase is the perfect opportunity to buy large (sometimes as much as tens of millions of shares) positions without moving the stock higher. Buying a stock during Stage 1 allows an institutional investor to minimize the market impact cost (the amount that their buying moves the stock higher). *Value players* (whose strategy is to buy stocks that trade for less than their intrinsic value) are some of the most patient people on the planet. They do all kinds of forward-looking fundamental analysis on an industry or company, and buy millions of shares from the less astute growth fund managers, who may have ridden the stock lower during its decline and believe they are holding damaged goods in their portfolios. There is a saying that warns, "If they don't scare you out, they'll wear you out!" It applies to all the people who rode a stock down waiting for "just one more rally" that never materialized. Now they are tired of seeing that stock on their statements because it reminds them how stupid they were not to sell earlier, so they sell at this point. This sale is known as moving the stock from "weak hands into strong hands."

The volume and moving averages (MAs) are of little value while a stock is in the actual healing process of back-and-forth action, but they can provide some clues as to when the stock may be ready to advance to Stage 2: Markup. The best time that volume can provide clues about the action to come is when a period of sustained high volume occurs after the stock has been trading in a tight range that may last up to nine months. This pick up in volume is often a sign that the buyers are getting more aggressive, which sets the stock up for the Markup phase and higher prices. Moving averages, discussed later in this chapter, are of little value for generating trading ideas while a market is not trending, and the price usually stays below the longer-term MAs during the healing process. Short-term MAs display a lot of back-and-forth action as the stock price rises above and falls back below these MAs, which give numerous and conflicting signals. After the stock has recovered for some time, the longer-term MAs will slowly begin to flatten out. Until the longer-term MA flattens out, purchases should be avoided and the stock should be considered "guilty until proven innocent."

The Profiler developed at MarketWise breaks down each of the four stages into three substages. Stage 1, for example, has these substages: 1-1 (early Accumulation), 1-2 (mid-Accumulation) and 1-2 (late Accumulation). This information is unique to the Profiler and has valuable uses. Suppose the overall market has been in the Accumulation phase for quite awhile and it suddenly breaks out to a strong uptrend (Stage 2-1). In this environment, investors can customize a scan in the Profiler that searches out the stocks in Stage 1-3 (late Accumulation). The stocks in this stage are often the next ones to break out into an uptrend and follow the market higher. Although there is no sure way of knowing when or even if these candidates will move higher, investors can concentrate their analysis on the fundamentals that may lead to the uptrend. A company that may not yet be profitable but is reporting strong sales growth may be just around the corner from reporting earnings that could provide the catalyst for a sustained upward movement. And because it is unlikely that all the stocks in this stage will move higher, taking a quick look at fundamentals allows us to discard weak companies and focus only on the candidates with the greatest potential to move higher. You might be thinking that the Profiler may give you hundreds of Stage 1-3 stocks to choose from because if the market is just beginning an ascent, many stocks will be in that phase. The Profiler doesn't just scan for stages, however; it also allows users to customize their search by exchange, as well as by number of days in the stage, average daily volume minimums and maximums, and minimum and maximum prices. The more customized the user makes the scan, the fewer results there are to scrutinize (see Figure 1.11).

Stage 2: Markup

Stage 2 is where most people want to be involved in a stock's cycle (see Figure 1.12). If you are bullish, it is where you make money. Markup begins where Accumulation ends. The charts have characteristics that make it easy to identify the transition from Accumulation to Markup. Presumably while the risks were higher because of uncertainty about the trend, participants who are bullish on the stock's future built large positions at low levels. Now they are ready to participate in the upside as the stock advances. The continuous buying in Stage 1 has taken half of the supply-and-demand equation out of the picture; supply has been reduced. Buyers depleted supply from the previous large owners while the stock was in the Accumulation phase, and anyone still long the stock will hold out for higher prices before selling. The perception of what the stock is worth is changing at this point, and in the markets, perception is reality. If you are an investor, the breakout into Stage 2-1 (strong Markup) is the perfect opportunity to buy your stock near the beginning of a strong move; then your work gets easy. In this phase of a stock's cycle, there are substantial gains, and your job is to monitor the strength of the stock using all the tools you are learning about to determine when to exit based on a discontinuation of the primary trend. If you are a trader, this stock will be one that you can trade over and over again to the upside as the stock continues to move higher throughout the strong (2-1), mid (2-2), and weakening (2-3) stages of the uptrend. For

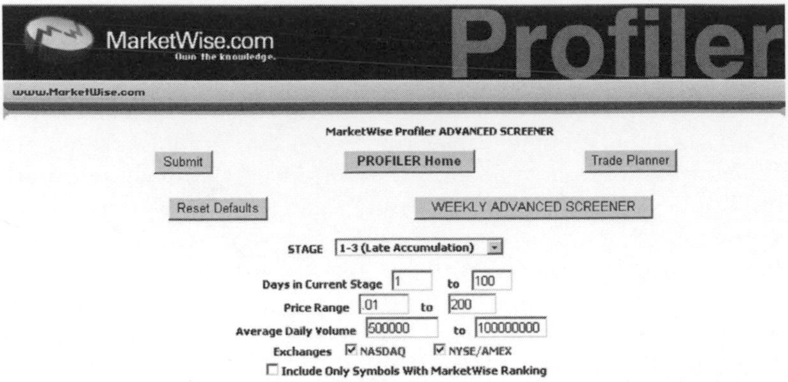

102 Ticker Symbols Found with this Criteria Symbols Only

1 2 3 4 5

MW Rank	Ticker Symbol	Company Name	Latest Close	Stage	Days In Stage	Avg. Volume	Exchange
144	MERQ	Mercury Interactive Corp	45.41	1-3	7	2,479,985	NASDAQ
146	NILE	Blue Nile	28.95	1-3	7	550,515	NASDAQ
149	CHIR	Chiron Corp	33.58	1-3	5	1,744,205	NASDAQ
153	SRNA	Serena Software Inc	22.31	1-3	9	542,920	NASDAQ
158	ISIL	Intersil Holding Corp	16.39	1-3	4	1,940,400	NASDAQ
160	ASCL	Ascential Software Corp	15.09	1-3	4	912,815	NASDAQ
161	SLAB	Silicon Laboratories Inc	34.59	1-3	4	1,699,530	NASDAQ
162	NVLS	Novellus Systems Inc	28.58	1-3	3	4,158,430	NASDAQ
163	INTC	Intel Corp	23.76	1-3	3	73,307,955	NASDAQ
165	ENDP	Endo Pharmaceuticals Hld	21.32	1-3	4	687,780	NASDAQ
166	INFY	Infosys Technologies Ads	72.24	1-3	3	524,745	NASDAQ
167	LLTC	Linear Technology Corp	38.1	1-3	5	4,125,675	NASDAQ

FIGURE 1.11 (Top) The Advanced Screener feature of the Profiler allows user-defined searches of over 6,800 individual stocks and exchange-traded funded to find the opportunities that make sense for your trading style. This screen allows the user to search out that stocks that are late in the Accumulation stage. Perhaps the results will show stocks that are ready to break out into the Stage 2 uptrend. (Bottom) This is how these results of the scan are displayed. The stocks that meet the specified criteria are ranked by MW Rank—the result of our internal *M*arket*W*ise algorithms that sort for the best trading setups in each category. The display of screened stocks can be further sorted by clicking on any of the column headings such as company name alphabetically, by closing price or volume.

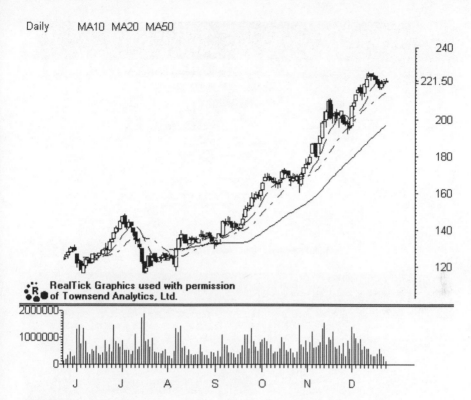

Daily MA10 MA20 MA50

FIGURE 1.12 Once this stock cleared 150, it experienced a large volume breakout above the rising 10-, 20-, and 50-day moving averages. In early September, the stock was considered to be in a strong uptrend (Stage 2-1). This stage represents the highest probability for further upside to come. Note that the solid line represents the 50-day MA, the short dashed line—the 20-day MA, and the long dashed line—the 10-day MA.

investors who may have missed the original opportunity to get in at the beginning of the trend, the continuation patterns through the substages of the Markup offer a low-risk point to get in and participate in significant gains with risk minimization techniques that are found on shorter time frames. Although we will not explore each of the continuation patterns in uptrends, we will study the reason (which is more important) for continuation and how to determine when the stock has a low-risk/high-profit potential to continue the advance.

For bullish traders interested in finding stocks that are moving now, the Profiler allows customized screening of 6,800 different stocks to search out the stocks in each of the three substages of Markup: strong (2-1), mid (2-2), and weakening (2-3). Each of these substages can be further screened by days in the stage, price and volume ranges, and exchange preference (see Figure 1.13).

MarketWise.com
Own the knowledge.
www.MarketWise.com

MarketWise Profiler ADVANCED SCREENER

| Submit | | PROFILER Home | | Trade Planner |

| Reset Defaults | | WEEKLY ADVANCED SCREENER |

STAGE 2-1 (Strong Mark-Up) ▾

Days in Current Stage	1	to	100
Price Range	.01	to	200
Average Daily Volume	500000	to	100000000

Exchanges ☑ NASDAQ ☑ NYSE/AMEX
☐ Include Only Symbols With MarketWise Ranking

161 Ticker Symbols Found with this Criteria

Symbols Only

1 2 3 4 5 6 7

MW Rank	Ticker Symbol	Company Name	Latest Close	Stage	Days In Stage	Avg. Volume	Exchange
3	SNDK	Sandisk Corp	25.54	2-1	6	6,979,345	NASDAQ
4	GRU	Gurunet Corporation	22.32	2-1	2	1,664,540	AMEX
5	XXIA	Ixia	17.86	2-1	2	1,130,495	NASDAQ
6	QLGC	Qlogic Corp	42	2-1	19	3,120,315	NASDAQ
7	AAPL	Apple Computer Inc	85.29	2-1	28	19,255,080	NASDAQ
9	PGH	Pengrowth Energy Tr	22.58	2-1	1	634,845	NYSE
11	LZ	Lubrizol Corp	41.71	2-1	12	586,190	NYSE
12	ACL	Alcon Inc	85.05	2-1	8	528,295	NYSE
14	NIHD	Nii Holdings Inc	56.19	2-1	4	530,695	NASDAQ
15	SEPR	Sepracor Inc	63	2-1	3	2,225,375	NASDAQ
16	GRP	Grant Prideco Inc	23.01	2-1	9	1,440,425	NYSE
17	SLB	Schlumberger Ltd	72.69	2-1	14	4,594,225	NYSE
18	SCHN	Schnitzer Steel Indust	36.72	2-1	7	775,460	NASDAQ

FIGURE 1.13 (Top) This Profiler screen is used to search out the strongest uptrending stocks; that is, the stocks with the greatest likelihood of further gains to come. (Bottom) The bottom screen shows 161 candidates of stocks in strong uptrends. By further refining the search criteria, the list of candidates can be narrowed, freeing your time to follow only the stocks that meet your criteria.

Stage 3: Distribution

Distribution is the slow process of sellers gaining control of a stock as buyers become less aggressive in their purchases. This is the third stage of a stock's cyclical movement and it represents the gradual transition to a Stage 4: Decline. During the distribution process, large holders of the stock from lower prices start to slowly move out of their positions to lock in profits. The sellers usually do not encounter much difficulty unloading their stock to the market because it is in this stage that good news is commonly associated with the stock. Unfortunately for many amateur investors, it is the "good news" that gets their attention and becomes a catalyst for them to buy. As we know, professionals anticipate good news and when it finally comes out, the professionals are only too happy to sell their stock to the eager public buyers. The public's buying can be quite strong after these news events and it allows the professionals to sell large quantities of stock that results in a stock that often gets stuck in a trading range. This process of professionals selling to amateurs is known as the stock "moving from strong hands to weak hands." As mentioned, the market is forward looking, and a basic understanding of business cycles tells you that things don't stay strong forever.

One of the easiest ways to recognize a stock is undergoing distribution comes from the moving averages. During the sideways action, the moving averages will start to flatten out as range constricts and these moving averages will also start to oscillate above and below each other (see Figure 1.14). The moving average crossovers represent indecision and that is the trend trader's clue to avoid being involved with the stock.

Once again, the Profiler simplifies finding the stocks that are undergoing distribution and may be ready for a decline. For the short seller who is searching out candidates for decline, the best results will typically be found with stocks that are in the late stages of distribution (Stage 3-3). These stocks are the most vulnerable to the pressure that allows the sellers to regain control of the trend. Stocks that are being considered for a short sale should have higher volume than you might see in an up trending stock because it can be difficult to cover your position during short-term "short squeeze" rallies. It is also dangerous to sell short the stock in Stage 3 until there is evidence of an actual downtrend confirmed by a lower low in price. Selling short early will put you at an immediate disadvantage; you will be in a position of weakness instead of entering in a strong position as the stock heads lower (see Figure 1.15).

Stage 4: Decline

Simply put, Stage 4 of a stock's lifecycle represents a bear market. Stocks that are in down trends should not be purchased for any reason, regardless

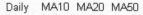

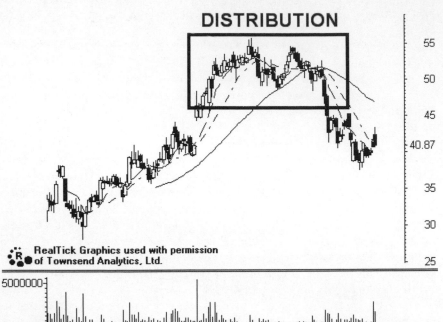

FIGURE 1.14 Moving average crossovers represent indecision and are most commonly found in Stages 1 and 3.

of how good the news may appear. If you are not comfortable selling short (see Chapter 4 for more on selling short), the best position you can have is cash as a stock makes its inevitable decline. Stage 4 is the stage that does the most damage to traders' and investors' accounts and learning to recognize these stocks and avoid their vicious declines can save the equity you have worked so hard to build in your accounts. Longer-term investors who consider buy and hold as the best strategy should pay particular attention to signs of weakness, as the bear market of 2000 to 2003 taught many participants that stocks do not "always come back."

A stock first enters Stage 4 as the lows of Stage 3 are broken. In order to assure the trend is truly lower we want to see the stock below the declining moving averages (see Figure 1.16). Further, the short-term MA should be below the intermediate term MA, which should be below the longer-term MA. Having the three moving averages confirming the direction of the stock gives us added confidence that the weakness will persist and it is not just a short-term pullback.

MarketWise Profiler ADVANCED SCREENER

| Submit | | PROFILER Home | | Trade Planner |

| Reset Defaults | | WEEKLY ADVANCED SCREENER |

STAGE 3-1 (Early Distribution) ▾

Days in Current Stage 1 to 100
Price Range 01 to 200
Average Daily Volume 500000 to 100000000
Exchanges ☑ NASDAQ ☑ NYSE/AMEX
☐ Include Only Symbols With MarketWise Ranking

56 Ticker Symbols Found with this Criteria | Symbols Only |

1 2 3

MW Rank	Ticker Symbol	Company Name	Latest Close	Stage	Days In Stage	Avg. Volume	Exchange
	ACDO	Accredo Health Inc	30.24	3-1	2	674,540	NASDAQ
	ACF	Americredit Corp	23.36	3-1	1	1,045,035	NYSE
	APCS	Alamosa Holdings Inc	12.56	3-1	9	1,145,095	NASDAQ
	APPX	Amer Pharmaceutical Ptnrs	50.8	3-1	12	690,660	NASDAQ
	ATVI	Activision Inc	21.44	3-1	2	4,112,220	NASDAQ
	BEC	Beckman Coulter Inc	68.11	3-1	2	812,115	NYSE
	BRL	Barr Laboratories Inc	46.31	3-1	12	631,040	NYSE
	C	Citigroup	47.95	3-1	1	13,213,225	NYSE
	CAM	Cooper Cameron Corp	55.12	3-1	1	1,360,390	NYSE
	CELG	Celgene Corp	27.45	3-1	1	1,273,280	NASDAQ

FIGURE 1.15 (Top) The Profiler allows the user to search stocks that are in each of the three substages of the overall primary stage, which in this case is a Stage 3 Distribution. (Bottom) The bottom scan for Stage 3-1 stocks shows results for 56 different securities. This group of stocks may be one that longer-term holders with unrecognized profits might want to sell covered calls on.

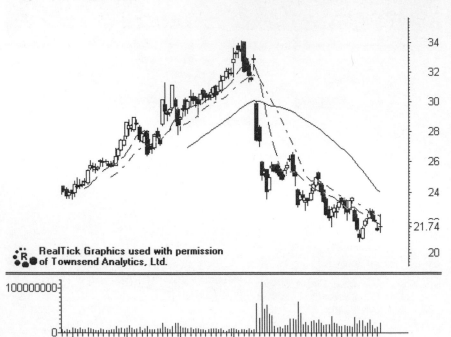

FIGURE 1.16   The typical pattern of lower highs and lower lows that define a downtrend. A downtrending stock should be considered "guilty until proven innocent." Note, the faster 10 period MA (long dashed line), leads the 20 MA (short dashed line) and the 50 MA (solid line).

There are many opportunities for aggressive traders to profit from a stock that is declining in value by participating on the short side. Short sales are a bit tricky for a couple of reasons. First you need to be sure that your clearing firm has shares to borrow. Another obstacle with short sales is that it must be done on an uptick and finding an uptick in a stock that is heading lower can be difficult. If selling short, you should anticipate that the stock may move against you for a little because you have to sell into strength as a result of the short sale rules.

The Profiler allows bearish traders to scan 6,800 securities in seconds to find those in Stage 4. Looking at the Profiler to find the best short sale candidates is easy. First we use the drop-down menu to search out stock in the strong stage of a decline (4-1) as these stocks should have the most opportunity for further decline. How long the stock has been in a Stage 4-1 is not a major factor, so we can leave the default of 1 to 100 days in place. Price range needs consideration because exchange guidelines make it difficult to

MarketWise.com
Own the knowledge.
www.MarketWise.com

MarketWise Profiler ADVANCED SCREENER

| Submit | | PROFILER Home | | Trade Planner |

| Reset Defaults | | WEEKLY ADVANCED SCREENER |

STAGE 4-1 (Strong Decline) ▼

Days in Current Stage 1 to 100
Price Range 5 to 50
Average Daily Volume 800000 to 100000000
Exchanges ☑ NASDAQ   ☐ NYSE/AMEX
☐ Include Only Symbols With MarketWise Ranking

31 Ticker Symbols Found with this Criteria   Symbols Only

				1 2				
MW Rank	Ticker Symbol	Company Name	Latest Close	Date	Stage	Days In Stage	Avg. Volume	Exchange
5	VRSN	Verisign Inc	25.37	08/04/05	4-1	2	6,491,080	NASDAQ
12	ROST	Ross Stores Inc	26.54	08/04/05	4-1	2	1,453,825	NASDAQ
13	AVID	Avid Technology Inc	40.28	08/04/05	4-1	16	1,817,595	NASDAQ
16	INSP	Infospace Incorporated	24.74	08/04/05	4-1	6	2,319,735	NASDAQ
25	PETC	Petco Animal Supplies	27.71	08/04/05	4-1	2	935,520	NASDAQ
27	ANDW	Andrew Corp	11.17	08/04/05	4-1	5	2,455,480	NASDAQ
29	NTAP	Network Appliance Inc	25.5	08/04/05	4-1	11	6,004,615	NASDAQ
38	SWFT	Swift Transportation Co	21.43	08/04/05	4-1	9	935,720	NASDAQ
41	HOTT	Hot Topic Inc	16.52	08/04/05	4-1	5	1,644,660	NASDAQ
42	MVSN	Macrovision Corp	18.17	08/04/05	4-1	3	1,096,960	NASDAQ
46	WOLF	Great Wolf Resorts	12.46	08/04/05	4-1	5	872,345	NASDAQ
58	ZBRA	Zebra Technologies Cp A	38.23	08/04/05	4-1	1	1,142,015	NASDAQ

FIGURE 1.17 (Top) Searching the strongest down trending stocks (Stage 4-1) is where you would begin looking for stocks to sell short. (Bottom) At the time the scan was run, the Profiler identified 31 candidates for potential short sales.

sell short stock under $5.00. Therefore, we type in a price range of $5 to $50. As mentioned, volume is an important factor. Because we need to be sure there is plenty of liquidity, we use a minimum volume criteria of 800,000 shares. To further hone our list, this example also shows just the stocks that are trading on the Nasdaq (see Figure 1.17).

Recognizing which stage a stock is in at any particular point in its life cycle is an invaluable tool for traders and investors alike. Because Stage 1 and Stage 3 are typically represented by lower volume and volatility they do not make for good trading candidates. The easiest way to identify if a stock is in Stage 1 or 3 is to observe the moving averages. During periods of indecision (Stage 1 and 3), the moving averages oscillate above and below price as well as cross above and below each other.

Trend following is where big money can be made when trading and investing and that is why your focus should be on stocks that are in either Stage 2 or 4. For bullish traders, the only choice should be to look for stocks that are in a solid Stage 2 uptrend. As we will learn later in this chapter, "a trend, once established, is more likely to continue that it is to reverse." Of course you do not want to blindly buy any stock that is moving higher, we discover later in this chapter how to time our entries using shorter-term time frames. Just as you can make solid returns going long Stage 2 stocks, bearish traders focus on stocks that are in established Stage 4 down trends. When a stock is heading lower, it is much more likely to continue lower than it is to turn around and head higher again.

SUPPORT AND RESISTANCE

Support and resistance levels are where you really get to see the ongoing battle between the buyers and sellers at various price levels and lets us see more clearly how prices actually move from one level to another (see Figure 1.18). The continual battle between the bulls and bears is what makes the stock market such a fascinating study of the basic laws of supply and demand. Technicians study how stocks act at levels of support and resistance so that when a trend finds renewed strength, they are sure to be on the right side from the beginning, which allows them to capture a larger portion of a move. Support and resistance levels offer the structure upon which trends are built and because of that, a solid understanding of them is imperative.

Definitions of Support and Resistance

Support levels are price levels where there is likely to be enough buying pressure (demand) to offset selling pressure (supply) and provide a tempo-

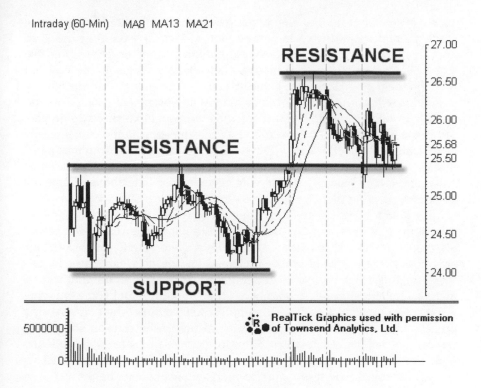

FIGURE 1.18   While consolidating in a Stage 1: Accumulation or Stage 3: Distribution, stocks trade between levels of support and resistance until the buyers or sellers gain control of the momentum and push the stock higher or lower. The moves between levels of support and resistance represent tradable opportunities.

rary halt to declines. When prices fall to a new low and then rally, it is common for buyers who missed out on the first move to place bids near the prior low in hopes of participating in the next bounce, this demand helps creates support. Another factor that helps create support at the prior low is a lack of supply. Sellers realize that the last time prices reached this low level the buyers took control of the stock, so they will often defer decisions to sell, this removes supply from the equation. Support on a daily chart is usually an area (e.g., 34 to 34.50), not a specific number (e.g., 34.20). However, on short-term time frames, support is often a specific price. This is one of the biggest advantages to timing trades on the shorter time frames. Increasing entry accuracy improves the profit potential, but more importantly, it minimizes any loss if the market does not agree with your analysis.

Resistance levels are price levels where selling pressure (supply) is likely to offset buying pressure (demand) and halt advances in the price of stocks. Resistance levels are formed because there is a large enough source of supply that the buyers cannot immediately overcome. When a stock reaches a new high and then retreats from that level it leaves many participants wishing they had sold at that high level. The next time the stock is able to rally back to the high, sellers offer stock to the point of overcoming demand, and this is the creation of resistance. Another factor that helps to establish the prior high level as a resistance area is an unwillingness by new buyers to pay up for the stock in an area where there were prior sellers. This lack of demand is also instrumental in the development of resistance. Resistance on a longer-term time frame such as a daily or weekly charts, is also defined as an area, such as 40.00 to 40.40, not a specific number; the same is true for resistance on shorter-term time frames. It is worth repeating that the benefit to traders who take the time to study shorter time frames is found in being more precise.

Think of both support and resistance as an area where buyers and sellers fought a battle. This battle often leaves a memory for both bulls (buyers) and bears (sellers). Because price levels represent where these battles were fought, participants will often return to these price levels until an ultimate victor is declared. Therefore, when looking at longer term time frames, we can expect both support and resistance to be represented by a broader area, fought out on a larger battlefield. Whereas, on short time frames, we can expect to isolate these price levels to more specific numbers. Both are valuable to know.

Now let's discuss some general rules of support and resistance that will help in not only entering trades, but in managing trades as well.

Once Broken, Support Tends to Act as Resistance

Have you ever bought a stock near a level you viewed as support, only to watch it decline in price and wish you could just get out at breakeven? This type of buyers' remorse shows up on a chart as resistance once the stock rallies back up to the prior support level, while you and others offer stock back in the attempt to break even on the trade. Obviously, one persons stock won't offer much resistance, but when the support level is an important level for the stock; many more people are involved and it becomes much harder for the stock to work through the supply being offered before it can move higher. What makes it an important level has a lot to do with how much time the stock spent at a certain price area and how much volume traded within that area. It is said that price has memory; well, that is just a function of human nature; the more participants at a prior level, the greater the memory (think resistance) will become.

Besides the people who wish to liquidate their long positions at a prior level of support, there are also short sellers waiting in the wings for the stock to rally back to that prior level. Let's use an example of a stock that had found support near $55 for a period of four months and then it suddenly breaks lower down to $48. Obviously the people who purchased at $55 are not going to be very happy and on any subsequent rally back up towards $55 would en tice a good deal of those folks who bought near $55 to offer their stock out (weak holders). Specialists and market makers are not dumb, when they see all the stock being offered they are not very likely to be aggressive bidders for the stock. The lack of demand creates a fragile environment for the stock as the bids do not support much supply, making it vulnerable to a decline. Now we need to consider the short sellers. Sharks that smell blood in the water and sense an easy opportunity to take advantage of weak holders of stock. The short sellers will be aggressive in offering out stock that they do not own, in hopes that someone will purchase it from them and they can buy it back cheaper at a later point. This added source of supply creates an even more precarious situation for the long holders; this is why stocks often fail miserably after they test support multiple times. When you see a stock that breaks down through support, get out immediately if you are long, do not wait for a bounce back up, the market is not always so accommodative! Remember that when support is broken it will not always become resistance, but it is the greatest odds that it will. With no certainties in the market we have to go with the strongest odds. (See Figure 1.19.)

Once Broken, Resistance Tends to Act as Support

For this example, let's consider a stock that has been trading in a Stage 1: Accumulation for a period of seven months. During the course of the narrow, range-bound trading in which the accumulation took place, the stock may have traded in a range of $20 to $23. Certainly there are some institutions that may have accumulated very large (millions of shares) long positions. At the same time, there are always the skeptics about a company who may have created a short position in the range. One day, the company announces earnings that are much better than what the analysts had expected and the stock immediately surges up to the $27 level on heavy volume. The institutions with the large positions are very pleased and they may even start to sell a few shares to lock in some profits. Over the course of the next week or so, the stock grudgingly drifts back down toward the $23 to $23.50 level and that is when the dynamic of prior resistance becoming support begins to unfold. The institutions realize that the stock is near prior resistance so they stop taking profits; this reduces the supply available for the stock. At the same time, the short sellers realize that this is their chance to minimize their losses and they decide to cover their positions near the level they sold short, this creates demand. Now consider the

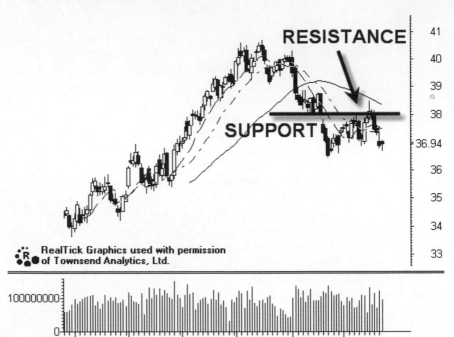

Daily MA10 MA20 MA50

RESISTANCE

SUPPORT

RealTick Graphics used with permission of Townsend Analytics, Ltd.

FIGURE 1.19 Support at the 38 level was broken and the subsequent rally could not find enough strength to push back up through that level, a classic example of support becoming resistance.

participants in cash, seeing the lack of sellers and the renewed aggressive bidders, they decide to buy stock, and this creates more demand. Without a willing source of supply combined with aggressive buyers, it is not hard to understand why the tendency for prior resistance to become support is so strong. (See Figure 1.20.)

The More Often Support or Resistance Is Tested, the More Likely That Level Is to Fail to Hold Back Price Movement

To understand this occurrence, it is once again important to consider the impact of the largest participants in the market. Suppose an institution had 1,800,000 shares of a stock that they wanted to get out of. Obviously they would not be able to sell such a large block of stock all at once; instead it may take them as long as a month to six weeks to dispose of such a large

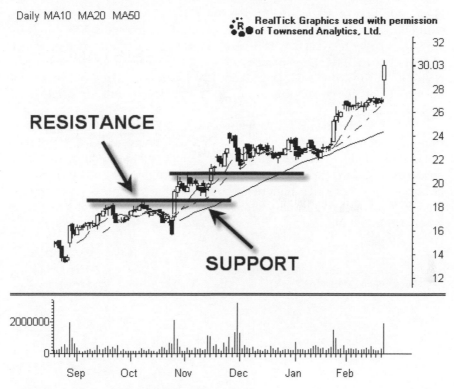

Daily MA10 MA20 MA50

RealTick Graphics used with permission of Townsend Analytics, Ltd.

RESISTANCE

SUPPORT

FIGURE 1.20 Notice how this stock found support at prior levels of resistance as it corrected the violent moves higher.

position. You have to consider how they would sell the stock. If they were to sell it aggressively on the bids their selling would create weakness that would result in a lower average price for their sales. The market impact cost of selling aggressively is why an institution would give his broker orders to "sell it between $39 and $40 and give me reports as you get fills." What he is saying is that the broker can exercise his discretion to sell between prices of 39 and 40 for as long as it takes to complete the order. The broker who receives this order sees that the stock has just rallied from $35 to $39 so he decides to start selling into the upward momentum. Over the next day or two, that broker may sell as many as 500,000 shares before the stock dips back below $39 and he stops selling. During the next three weeks, the stock trades as low as $37 and then recovers back into the $39 to $40 range where the broker once again resumes selling the 1.3 million share balance. This time, the broker is able to unload 700,000 shares between 39 and 40 before the buyers recognize there is a source of supply too big for them to overcome. This sets the stock back into a short-term correction that sees the stock trade down toward $38 before the buyers gain control and push the stock back up into the brokers sell range again. Now the broker has just 600,000 shares to sell and he is able to sell 450,000 of them before the buyers once again lose momentum and the stock corrects down toward $38.50. Days later, the stock pops back above 39 and the broker is able to sell the remaining 150,000 shares of the original 1.8 million share order.

What has happened in this institutional selling situation is that each time the stock traded into the range of 39 to 40 the primary source of supply that was holding the stock back was being depleted. Supply was being absorbed into the market until the order was finally completed. It is very common for a stock that undergoes this type of distribution to surge past the $40 level once the primary supply was bought. This type of situation is where traders should be alert for clues to go long. (See Figure 1.21.)

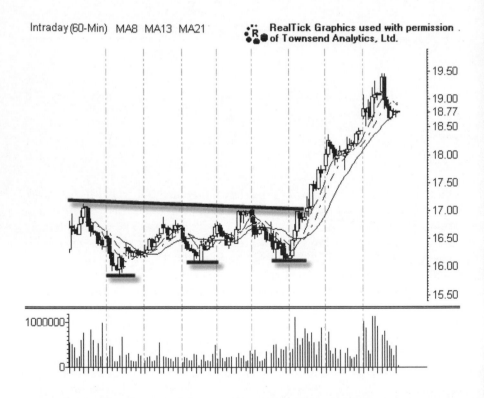

FIGURE 1.21   Resistance at the 17.00 price level was tested numerous times before the demand gradually overwhelmed the supply being offered at that level and the stock then broke out and trended higher.

The Longer the Trend Has Been Neutral (Consolidating), the More Significant the Eventual Breakout Becomes

Whether a stock is in a Stage 1: Accumulation or a Stage 3: Distribution, the longer the stock has been trading in a narrow range, the bigger a move will be once the stock begins trending. One of my favorite types of stocks to trade are the ones that have been in a longer-term accumulation and they suddenly break out past resistance on a big surge in volume (Figure 1.22). These stocks are usually not household names, at least not as they begin their moves. For long candidates, I like to use the Profiler to help me find stocks that are in a Stage 2-1 (strong markup) on a weekly time frame.

Approximately once a week, I will scan through the stocks that meet the 2-1 weekly criteria for candidates that have "woken up out of a long coma." What I watch for is at least two times the average daily volume on

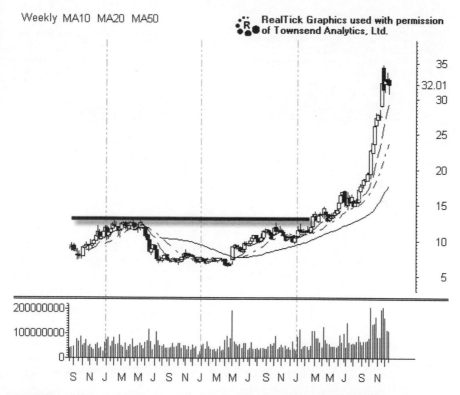

FIGURE 1.22 Example of a significant breakout after the prolonged accumulation period. When shares of this stock broke out past multiyear resistance near $14.00, the stock began an uptrend that saw gains of over 100 percent in less than six months.

FIGURE 1.23   While it is not certain that the prior support near 40 (broken) would lead to resistance that could not be overcome, buying near this level would not be as high a risk if this potential resistance level were not present.

the breakout followed by a low volume consolidation. I have found that these stocks are exceptional candidates for continued moves higher. In the case of short sales, tops usually take less time to develop than bottoms so I look for stocks that have been trading in a tight (2-3 point) range for at least 4 to 5 months, these stocks can be found by doing a search of the Stage 3-3 stocks. Once these stocks break down to new lows, they become ideal shorting candidates. One phrase you may want to remember is "the bigger the top, the bigger the drop." This simply means that the longer the stock has been consolidating in a Stage 3 pattern, the more participants will be trapped long when the stock breaks down and that can create some fearful selling over the next few months, which makes these stocks ideal for short selling opportunities. See Figures 1.23 and 1.24 for examples of resistance becoming support and support becoming resistance.

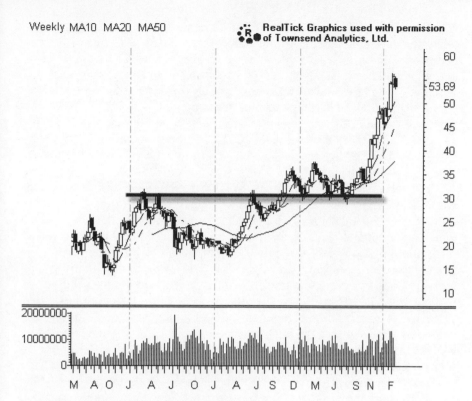

Weekly MA10 MA20 MA50   RealTick Graphics used with permission of Townsend Analytics, Ltd.

FIGURE 1.24 The multiyear resistance near 30 acted as a strong floor of support for nearly a year before this stock resumed a strong uptrend.

TRENDS

There are three things that a stock can be doing at any given time, it can go up, go down, or trade sideways. Our goal as traders is to find the high potential/low risk trades in a trending stock in an attempt to participate in the trend for as long as the market tells us to. To a lot of people that last point I made about "as long as the market tells us to" may sound confusing, so before delving into trends we cover this important topic. Technical analysis is largely about objective observation about the action of stocks, futures, or whatever you choose to trade. If you consider what we really know versus what we are told about market related events, you begin to realize that the only truth comes from price. The market is made up of millions of different participants, all with the same goal, to make money. To succeed in the market, you must view those other participants as your opponents, someone wins and someone loses. The ones who are consistent winners in the market are those who can separate the noise (analyst reports, television and radio banter, earnings reports, etc.) from the truth. The truth is represented through price. Price is the only thing that pays us in the market, which makes it the most important factor to consider in our analysis. When we "listen to the market" we are merely observing the cumulative effect of the millions of participants in order to anticipate how their future behavior will affect price movement. Once we understand human nature, we can understand market movements and be in a better position to capitalize using forward thinking analysis, rather than relying solely on what has already happened.

To succeed as traders and investors, we need to have faith in technical analysis, not blind faith, but faith in the cyclical nature of the market. This is to be backed up with disciplined implementation of a strong money management plan. If you observe market action carefully, you will begin to understand that, most of the time, the market is consolidating, either digesting gains or stabilizing after a decline. The second most likely type of market action is a continuation of the most recent trend; this is where we become interested. Finally, the least likely event is for perfect timing when the market reverses course. Since we cannot make very good money trading consolidations and because reversals are harder to time, it makes sense that trend trading is where we should focus our attentions for money-making opportunities. One of the foundations of technical analysis is that "prices move in trends" and once those trends have been established, they are more likely to continue than reverse. More likely does not mean they will always continue, but it does mean that is where our best odds for profit come from and with stops to protect us when the market does reverse, we should never get hurt too badly.

Uptrends are represented in the Stage 2: Markup cycle of a stocks life and they are defined by *a series of higher highs and higher lows* (see Figure 1.25). For swing traders, a general rule for trend determination on a daily time frame is to look at the direction of the 50-day moving average. If the 50-DMA is advancing the stock should be considered "innocent until proven guilty." Uptrending stocks will not go straight up, instead they tend to surge and then pause. It is our objective to be involved in the stock while it makes the swings higher and be out when the trend dissipates or starts to show signs of reversing. After each surge higher, the stock will experience a corrective move that allows the gains to be digested. These short-term corrections can occur one of two different ways. The will either correct by experiencing a pullback in price or they will correct by consolidating those gains through time (see Figure 1.26). When a stock experiences a quick rally, let's say from 22 to 26, there will typically be some profit taking in the stock. The profit taking will usually last anywhere from 2 to 10 days, any longer than that will lower the odds

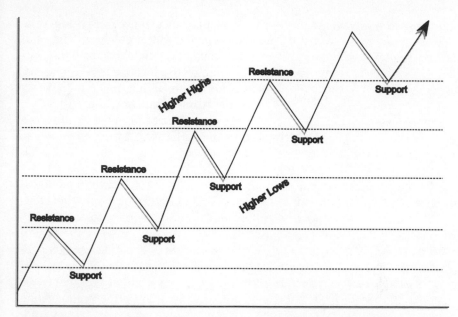

FIGURE 1.25 The diagram shows how a stock is supposed to look in an uptrend. The uptrending stock is formed as the stock makes higher highs and higher lows; it is the pullbacks that allow traders a low-risk opportunity to get long a stock whose path of least resistance is higher.

of a continued move higher. After this short-term correction, the stock may find support near $24 before continuing its ascent. The pullback in price in this case was necessary to bring the price back down to a level where supply and demand reached an equilibrium (which was found at support at $24) before buyers once again re-exerted their conviction. When a stock corrects its gains by trading in a narrow sideways range, it is said to be correcting through time. A correction through time occurs when the same stock, which rallied from 22 to 26, does not experience a price correction, instead it holds onto its gains and might find support through strong bids near 25.50. A correction through time is actually considered to be more bullish than one by price because it shows a lack of motivated sellers and more importantly, it shows there are buyers who are attempting to quietly purchase shares on the bid. While the buyers aren't aggressively purchasing from the offer, they are signaling underlying strength with their methodical purchases at the bid price. The stocks that correct through time are typically strong candidates for trend continuation once the high of the consolidation has been traded through.

A common mistake among traders is to limit their study of price action and trends to just one time frame. It is important to recognize that there are trends within trends and the longer-term trend is nothing more

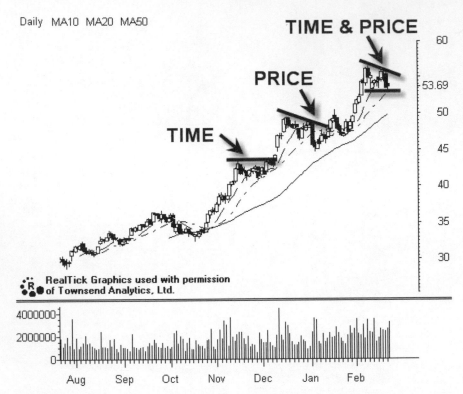

FIGURE 1.26   The corrections in a Stage 2 uptrend will occur either by correcting through time as the stock trades sideways or by pulling back price wise.

than the sum of a number of shorter-term trends. For our purposes, we will be looking at stocks that are trending on a longer-term basis and then timing our entry into those longer-term trends by recognizing opportunities on a shorter-term time frame, such as the hourly time frame in Figure 1.27. What we want to do is make sure that the short-term and longer-term trends are in alignment; this allows us to gain a statistical advantage in our trading decisions. For entering long positions, the primary trend (found on a daily time frame) should be in Stage 2 while the short-term trend (found on the 60 minute time frame) should be transitioning from a Stage 1 to Stage 2. By purchasing the stock as the short-term trend confirms the longer-term trend, we are buying the stock as momentum returns and we also have a logical place to set stops. Stops should be placed just below the low of the short-term Stage 1 that was identified on the hourly time frame.

Before we move on, it is important to point out that while it is possible to make money selling short stocks as the stock pulls back in a primary uptrend, the odds for success in this type of trade aren't very good compared

Intraday MA8 MA13 MA21

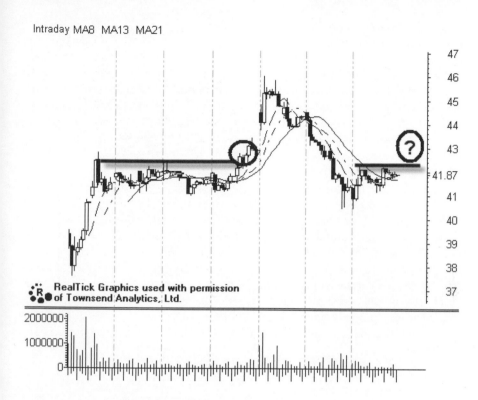

FIGURE 1.27 A shorter-term time frame like the one here with 60-minute candles over 20 days allows us to gain further clarity about a stock in a primary uptrend. This closer look at the stock allows us to time our entry into a stock just as the buyers regain control of the trend. The circled area with the question mark represents a potential buy opportunity, but only if buyers can regain control and push the stock past short-term resistance, and make a higher high.

to buying a strong stock on pullbacks. The very definition of an uptrend assures there will be greater opportunity to make money by trading in the direction of the primary trend. A series of higher highs and higher lows implies that the sum of the rallies will always be greater than the sum of the declines. It should also be noted here that news and surprises tend to follow the direction of the trend. Meaning that in an uptrend, it is more probable that news releases are likely to be positive for the stock. In trading, we want to do whatever we can to increase the likelihood of a favorable outcome and trading with the trend is the easiest first step in creating a consistent edge. The Profiler makes it easy to consistently find the stocks that are in the uptrending stage not just on the daily time frame, but also on the longer-term weekly time frame.

Downtrends are represented in the Stage 4: Decline cycle of a stocks life and they are defined by a series of *lower highs and lower lows* (see

Figure 1.28). Again, the direction of the 50-day MA is a quick reference tool to determine the overall trend of the stock and in a downtrend, as long as the 50-DMA is declining, the stock should be considered guilty until proven innocent. Just as an uptrending stock does not go straight up, a downtrending stock will not typically drop all at once (but it is a great feeling when they do and you have a short position). Stocks in downtrends will typically experience quick and sharp sell offs followed by short-term corrections of the weakness. Just as we saw with uptrending stocks, these corrections will occur either by price or through time. Let's consider a stock that drops from $45 to $40; once the sellers have been exhausted and buyers start to slowly gain control of the short-term trend, the stock will typically experience a rally that may last anywhere from 2 to 10 days. As long as the high during the corrective rally does not exceed the prior high, near 45, the stock should be monitored for opportunities to be sold short. If instead of experiencing a corrective rally, the stock begins to trade sideways in a narrow range near the lows, the stock is considered to be correcting the decline through time and that is a bearish omen for the stock. A correction through time for a stock in a downtrend shows that there is still a source of supply in the stock that prevents prices from rallying. Whether these sellers are establishing short positions or it is long liquidation is irrelevant, the value here is to

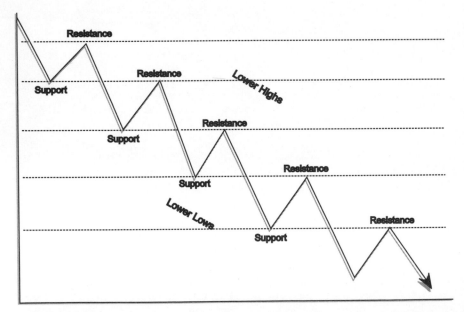

FIGURE 1.28   The downtrending stock shows a series of sell offs followed by rallies that fall short of the prior high. It is these rallies that give short sellers the opportunity to profit in a declining stock.

know that there are sellers who are preventing the stock from making any move back up. A correction through time will not typically take more than 2 to 5 days for a stock in a downtrend because there is still a healthy amount of fear in the stock and long holders will become frustrated and begin to liquidate their positions once it becomes clear the stock is unable to rally. As the stock breaks back down through the lows of the stabilization near $40 it represents an ideal time to sell the stock short. (See Figure 1.29.)

Just as we do not want to short Stage 2 stocks, there is rarely a good reason for getting long a stock that is in a Stage 4 downtrend. By its very definition, a downtrending stock assures us that there are more opportunities to profit by selling short than going long. The sum of the declines will always be greater than the sum of the rallies in a downtrend. Once a stock has been identified as being in Stage 4 (the Profiler can help save a lot of time with this task) the trader should then seek out a low risk entry price.

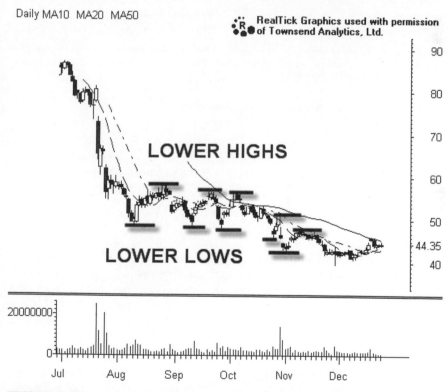

FIGURE 1.29   As a stock in a downtrend progresses lower it does so by making lower highs and lower lows, which means the sum of the short-term declines will always be greater than the sum of the short-term rallies. This is the primary reason we do not want to attempt to purchase stock for the short-term rallies when the primary trend is established lower.

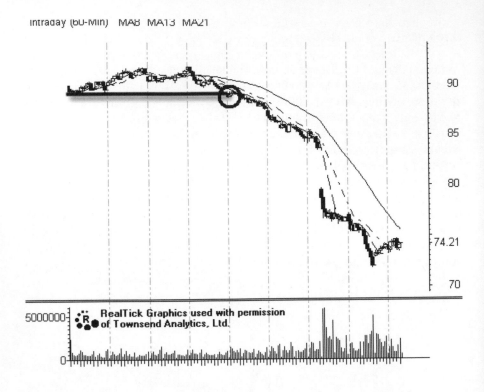

FIGURE 1.30 This 60-minute time frame allows us to recognize where the sellers regain control of the short-term trend as the stock broke below $87.00. This shorter-term time frame allows us to enter the primary downtrend just as the stock begins a new short-term decline.

This is accomplished by utilizing a short-term time frame like the 60-minute chart in Figure 1.30. The ideal time to enter a short position is as the stock transitions from a Stage 3: Distribution to Stage 4: Decline on the 60-minute time frame. Entering just as the sellers take control of the short-term trend allows us to enter when there is downward momentum that eliminates the time risk. An entry just as the stock enters Stage 4 also provides us with a clear area to set our stop (just above the high of Stage 3 on the 60-minute time frame).

Trends are a foundation of technical analysis and by utilizing them big money can be made; for this reason traders should always trade in the direction of the primary trend. It is easy to get confused by listening to analysts, journalists and even the policy of the Federal Reserve. Your best chances of success will come when you listen to the message of the market and stay focused on trends. Focusing on objective price action will put you at a tremendous advantage to those participants who choose to listen to subjective noise.

TRADING VOLUME

Volume is one of the foundational variables that we consider to be essential to have a thorough understanding of how stocks trade. Volume is the fuel for price movement. What volume really measures is the emotional intensity level of the participants in any market. How committed the buyers are or how fearful the sellers are can be inferred with an understanding of volume. All of our analysis will be focused on what we see on the chart at the present time, the forward looking part is what our analysis attempts to predict. The way that volume is displayed on the chart is shown by a separate vertical scale below price. The volume bars correspond with the candle directly above it, it measures how many shares changed hands during the specified time period in the price range represented by the candle above.

Measuring volume is relative, and it should be done by comparing the current volume to the average volume. RealTick makes it easy to

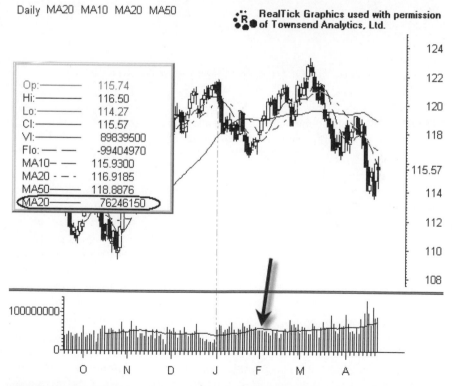

FIGURE 1.31 The moving average of volume shows the relationship between the daily volume and the average volume of the last 20 days that allows us to quickly recognize unusual trading activity that may signal we should look closer for a trading opportunity.

see an actual moving average of volume overlaid in the volume field of the chart (see Figure 1.31). I like to look at the average daily volume of the past 20 days. That is also the formula we use in the Profiler volume fields. When you initiate a search for stocks in the Advanced Screener part of the Profiler, the volume fields show a minimum of 500,000 shares to a maximum of 100 million shares per day. Of course, these numbers can be changed but I would warn you against trading stocks that trade less than 500,000 shares per day. Stocks that trade light volume (less than 500,000 shares per day) are referred to as "thin" stocks (see Figure 1.32). A thin stock is one that trades low average daily volume and this alone makes trading them quite difficult at times. It is important to understand that the volume patterns are not spread evenly throughout the day, instead, the market tends to trade the majority (as much as 60 to 70 percent) of its daily volume during the first and last hour and a half of each day. Because the liquidity in a stock is skewed so heavily toward the beginning and end of each day, it can be espe-

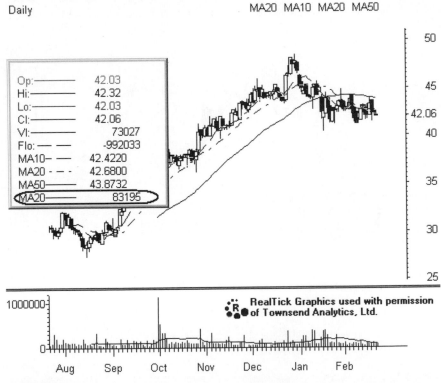

FIGURE 1.32 Only about 80,000 shares change hands each day in shares of this stock, making it a thinly traded stock. Trading thin stocks carries a set of risk factors that make them unsuitable for the majority of market participants.

cially treacherous to trade the low volume stocks during the middle of the trading day. The stocks I recommend traders (especially newer traders) stick to are the stocks that are considered "thick." A thick stock (see Figure 1.33) is one that trades a large average number of shares each day. The advantages of a thick versus thin stock are primarily one of liquidity; it will be much easier to find liquidity in a stock that trades heavy volume. Having liquidity is one of the biggest advantages stock market traders have compared to investors in other asset classes like real estate or art. Generally speaking, the more active you plan on being in the market, the higher average daily volume you should search for in your trading candidates.

Because volume is the fuel for movement we want to pay careful attention to unusually high volume events. As mentioned in the section about trends, I like to find stocks that experience large volume breakouts

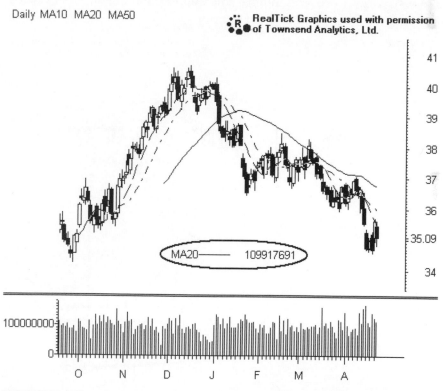

FIGURE 1.33 A "thick" stock like the one shown here trades tens or even hundreds of million shares each day. These stocks represent potential opportunities for traders of all experience level but are even better for newer traders because they assure the chance to get out of a bad (or maybe even erroneous) position quickly.

from a longer Stage 1: Accumulation. It is the big volume breakouts that seemingly take a large majority of market participants by surprise and gets the most attention, which leads to continued upside movement (see Figure 1.34). When a stock breaks past a level of resistance on large (2 to 3 times its average daily) volume it is often due to a fundamental development that the market was not anticipating. This event causes a sudden shift in perception as to the value of the company and as a result, buyers pile into the stock all at once. The initial large volume breakout should never be sold short; it is like jumping in front of a speeding locomotive and expecting it to be able to stop before running you over. Instead, aggressive traders should closely monitor intraday charts for an entry point the day after the breakout and more conservative traders should wait for either a pullback in price or a consolidation through time before entering the stock.

Large volume breakdowns are no different, they represent an immediate desire for a large amount of participants to exit a stock and when you see a stock gap down by more than 5 percent on large volume, that stock is

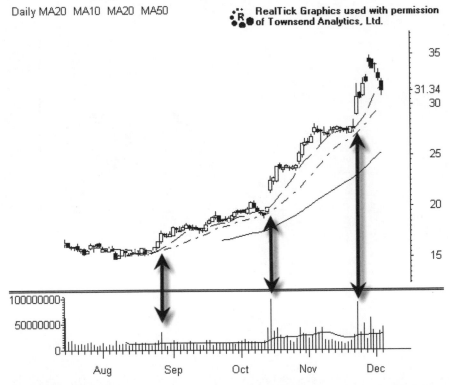

FIGURE 1.34 The high-volume spikes with large price movement signaled the beginning of short-term trends numerous times in this stock.

one that will usually continue to experience weakness over the coming months. Many traders make the mistake of purchasing the stocks that gap lower, anticipating the stock will bounce higher. The sad fact is, this is a strategy that I have seen eat through the account equity of many smart people. Whenever there is a rush or stampede out of a stock, it is usually for a very good reason. When we listen to what the market is saying, the big volume events are like the market shouting its message to us, do not ignore what the market is saying.

We pointed out the value of a moving average for volume is to determine whether the liquidity is sufficient for trading a particular stock and that is not the only instance where we will use a moving average to find a relative volume measurement. When stocks are trending, there is a very distinctive pattern that is left on the chart.

In an uptrend (see Figure 1.35), the volume should advance as the stock moves higher and diminish on the corrections (either by price or

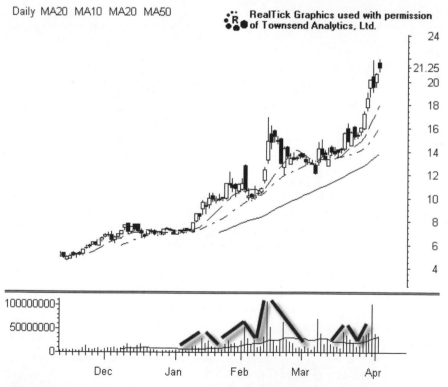

FIGURE 1.35   Notice how this stock advanced on increasing volume and then the volume diminished as the stock corrected either by price or through time. Many of the highest volume days also came toward the end of the short-term move.

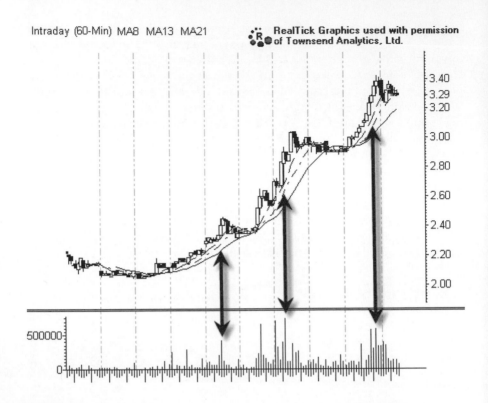

FIGURE 1.36   Big volume without further upside progress equals distribution. Traders should be alert for unusual volume after a stock has experienced a short-term move because it often signals a potential reversal could be at hand.

through time). The increasing volume as the stock advances sends a clear message that buyers are anxious to own the stock. In an uptrending stock, the largest spike in volume typically comes near the end of the move when a large source of supply is brought into the market that halts the upward movement (see Figure 1.36). The relatively light volume found in the short-term corrections also sends a clear message; the sellers are not rushing out of the stock. This message speaks to supply and demand, demand is strong and supply is low. The low volume pullbacks should be monitored closely for opportunities to buy the stock as it begins to move higher on the shorter-term time frames.

   In a downtrend, the volume will also expand in the direction of the trend and then diminish as the stock experiences its short-term rallies or corrections through time (see Figure 1.37). As the stock begins its move lower there is often a sense of denial amongst long holders who convince themselves it is okay to hold the stock because the volume is light on the sell off. This is a terrible reason to continue to hold the stock long. Volume

Daily MA20 MA10 MA20 MA50

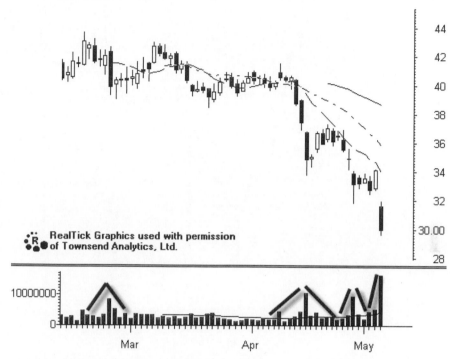

FIGURE 1.37   The volume in a downtrend increases on the short-term declines (think heavy fear) and then diminishes as the stock experiences a short-term rally within that primary decline. Also notice that many of the highest volume spikes came toward the *end* of a short-term decline.

is used for confirmation of price, not a reason to trade. After the stock has declined for one to two days, the volume typically starts to become heavier until it reaches a frenzy (see Figure 1.38). It is quite common for the largest volume to come at the end of the move when news quite often comes out and gives sellers a "reason" for the weakness. The increasingly heavy volume as the stock sells off indicates sellers are getting more aggressive while the diminishing volume of the correction tells us that buyers are not in a hurry to own the stock. This message of increased supply and decreased demand should be recognized for opportunities to sell short as the stock transitions from Stage 3 to Stage 4 on a 60-minute time frame.

Volume is a confirmation tool that allows us to gauge the likelihood of trend continuation where there is an established Stage 2 or Stage 4. Interpretation of volume in Stages 1 and 3 is more difficult for assisting us in finding good trading candidates but it does have its occasional uses. Consider a stock in a Stage 1 pattern, as the stock reaches the high end of the range, increasing volume could be a sign that a breakout could be

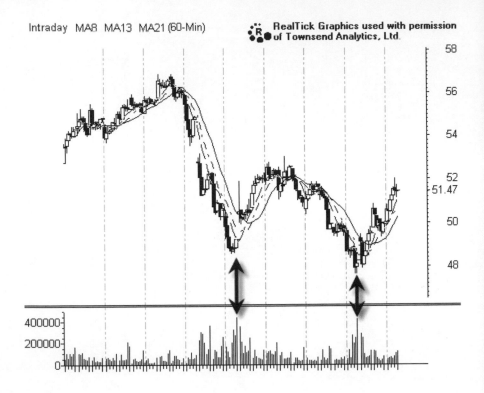

FIGURE 1.38 Heavy volume without further downside equals accumulation. It is common for short-term reversals of a downtrend to come just after the stock experiences a fearful sell off, as the source of supply becomes exhausted.

imminent, particularly if it is a Stage 1-3 (late accumulation). As far as actual tradable signals go, the only thing that would alert us to purchase a stock in Stage 1-3 is the actual breakout to Stage 2. Be sure to use volume as a confirmation tool, it is not meant to provide us with entry or exits, only price can do that.

MOVING AVERAGES

The purpose of a moving average (MA) is to smooth out price trends by calculating the average closing price over a given number of periods of time. For instance, when referring to a 10-day MA, it represents the average closing price over the past 10 days. An 8-period MA on an hourly chart would represent the average closing price over the past 8 hours. The moving averages referred to in this book and on the Profiler are simple moving

Weekly MA10 MA20 MA40

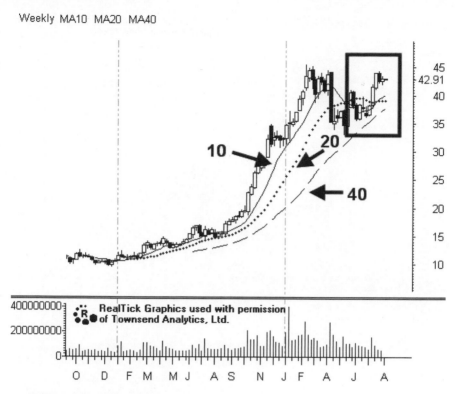

FIGURE 1.39 This weekly chart shows the 10- (solid line), 20- (dotted line), and 40- (dashed line) week moving averages laid over price.

averages. It is important to point out that besides the simple moving averages, there are exponential MAs, volume weighted MAs and a lot of other ways to complicate a simple concept. Because we use moving averages as a reference point to compare trend to, rather than as an outright trading system, it does not make much difference if you were to substitute an exponential MA with the simple MA. Too much attention has been focused on which MA is better, the simple or the exponential, and in our significant back testing, we have found no advantage to either one. We choose to use the simple MA because that is what most market participants look at and when attempting to anticipate human behavior we want to have a feel for what the majority of participants are basing their decisions on.

Moving averages are laid directly over price in the upper portion of a chart (see Figure 1.39). The moving average can be thought of as a mathematical trend line that self adjusts when new data replaces older data as the market provides us with new trade information. The way that I like to look at MAs is to have three different ones for each time frame I am

FIGURE 1.40   This daily chart shows the 10- (solid line), 20- (dotted line), and 50- (dashed line) moving averages overlaid on price.

considering in my analysis. By having three different MAs on the chart, I can quickly ascertain the short-term, intermediate-term, and longer-term trends of the time frame being studied. Starting with a long-term time frame that displays weekly information, I like to look at the 10-, 20-, and 40-period MAs as reference points for the trends of the stock (see Figure 1.39). These MAs are excellent representatives of trend for this long-term time frame and should be used for investors who wish to be involved in trends. Also note that the 10-week MA represents the average closing price for 50 days, the 20-week is the same as a 100-day MA and the 40-week MA is equal to the 200-day MA.

When analyzing price data on a daily chart, I begin with a chart that covers 150 days. On the chart in Figure 1.40, the MAs that are most widely followed are the 10-, 20-, and 50-period MAs. These three MAs offer the best views of the short, intermediate, and long-term trends.

When it comes to fine tuning entries and exits for swing trades, using intraday time frames allows us gain greater clarity of the developing

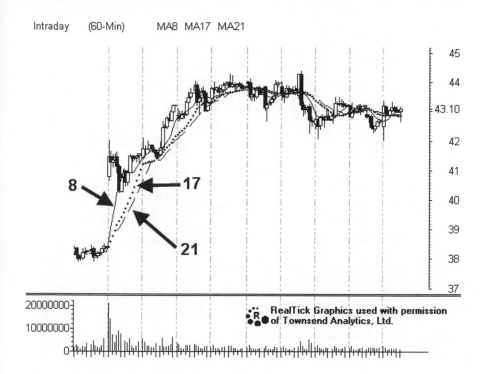

Intraday   (60-Min)   MA8 MA17 MA21

FIGURE 1.41   This hourly chart shows the 8- (solid line), 13- (dotted line), and 21- (dashed line) moving averages overlaid on price.

trends. The time frame I use to find the granularity necessary for entries and exits is the 60-minute time frame. A chart with hourly bars (see Figure 1.41) can help identify support and resistance levels that may not be visible on a daily time frame which allows us to attain entry and exit prices that might improve our executions by as much as $.20 to $.50 per share. On the hourly time frame, we have done extensive back testing of various MAs to find the ones that follow trend best and those are the 8-, 13-, and 21-period MAs. On this short-term time frame, these are the MAs that offer the best visual reference point for short, intermediate and long-term trends.

Now that we have an understanding of which MAs to use on each time frame we will explore how they can help us in our analysis. To reiterate, we do not use MAs as a trading system, they are merely an objective reference point to compare price to. In the Profiler, we have broken each of the four stages into three substages, and a large part of the stage and substage placement is determined by the MAs we have referenced.

Looking at Figure 1.42, we will now learn how the MAs can be utilized to identify which stage a stock is in. I have purposely removed all reference

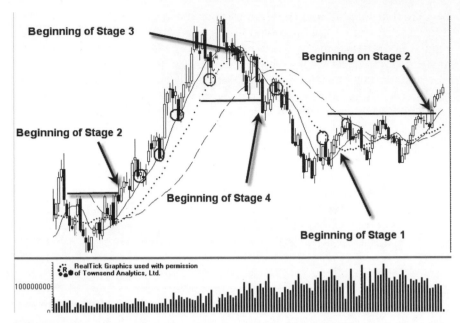

FIGURE 1.42   This chart shows the transition between stages and how moving averages can assist us in determining which stage a stock is in.

to time and price for this example because the concepts apply to any time frame. The first thing you should notice about this chart is the cyclical movement through all four stages (which are noted on the chart). Starting on the left side of the chart where it states "Beginning of Stage 2," we will examine how the MAs help us determine which primary and substage the stock is in. As the uptrend begins, you will notice that there are several circles where price meets the rising short-term MA. When the stock price is above all of the MAs with the short-term MA above the intermediate-term MA and the intermediate-term MA above the longer-term MA, the stock is considered to be in Stage 2-1 (strong uptrend).

It is quite common for the short-term MA to act as a support level for the stock. This needs to be explained further. You are probably wondering why a MA would act as support and the reason is simple, *perception.* Because MAs are viewed by so many participants as support levels, there tends to be a lot of trade activity centered near the MAs. When a stock in a primary uptrend starts to undergo some profit taking, the sellers will often cease selling as the stock reaches the short-term MA because they know there is usually support in that area, this lessens supply available near the MA. There is another group of participants that may be looking for an entry into this trending stock and recognizing a pullback to a short-term MA, they place bids at a level near the MA, and this creates demand. The lessened action of the sellers coupled with the more aggressive bids creates a situation where prices begin to find support after the short-term pullback. At this point, you may be thinking that you too should place bids near this MA. Wrong! When the stock reaches the short-term MA, we should start *acting like a buyer* but not make any actual purchases until we have studied a shorter-term time frame.

Suppose this chart is a daily time frame, when the stock pulls back to the short-term MA, we then want to put our analysis under a microscope and study the hourly time frame which should show the stock in a Stage 1. The picture on the longer-term time frame will be a solid Stage 2 uptrend but the short-term trend is now neutral. What we want to do is to watch the stock closely for further signs of strength on the hourly chart and buy just as the buyers gain control of the trend again. This allows us to be in the stock when there is momentum; we are then in the stock from a position of strength.

Moving further along the uptrend, you will notice as the trend becomes more mature, and after numerous tests of the short-term MA, the stock experiences a sharper break down to find support near the rising intermediate-term MA. This area, between the rising short-term and intermediate term trend is known as "medium markup" and is referenced in Profiler as Stage 2-2. Soon after the stock finds support at the intermediate-term MA, the pullbacks become even deeper with support found near the longer-term MA. When the stock finds support at the longer-term MA, it is considered late in the uptrend and is labeled as Stage 2-3.

The next area to note in Figure 1.42 is the area labeled "beginning of Stage 3." You will notice that the arrow points to where the short-term MA crosses down through the intermediate-term MA. When this occurs, the market is sending mixed messages to us. The message is mixed at this point because it is saying; short-term trend is lower, while the intermediate- and longer-term trends are still higher. While we can never have absolute certainty in the market, when the market is sending us mixed messages we want to stay away from the action. You have heard the phrase "when in doubt, stay out." When there is indecision (as represented by MA crossovers) on the chart following an uptrend, the stock is considered to be undergoing distribution. Stage 3 stocks are typically marked by diminishing volatility as the sellers gradually gain control of the stock. Put simply, moving average crossovers represent indecision and are a reason to stay out of the market.

As the stock breaks down below the low of Stage 3, the next point on the chart is labeled "beginning of Stage 4." In order for the stock to be in a Stage 4, there of course has to be a pattern of lower highs and lower lows. The way the Profiler algorithmically sorts the Stage 4 stocks is by using the following criteria. The short-term MA must be below the intermediate-term MA and the intermediate-term MA must be below the longer-term MA. Further, while price is below the short-term MA, the stock is considered to be in a strong downtrend (Stage 4-1). Just as the short-term MA will often act as support in an uptrend, the short-term MA will often act as resistance during the strong part of a decline. When you see a stock rallying up to the short-term MA in a primary downtrend that should be your clue to look for weakness on a shorter-term time frame, which is the best time to initiate new short positions. As the stock progresses in its downtrend you will notice that resistance is often found near the intermediate MA (Stage 4-2) and then the longer-term MA (Stage 4-3). Although the longer-term MA acted as resistance after the point labeled as the beginning of Stage 1, rallies should never be trusted while the longer-term MA is still declining. As mentioned earlier, a declining longer-term MA indicates a stock that is "guilty until proven innocent" while an ascending longer-term MA indicates a stock that is "innocent until proven guilty."

Stage 1 begins similarly to Stage 3; it is a moving average crossover that indicates indecision and the likely end to the downtrend. Remember that the end of the downtrend does not mean we should purchase the stock, as the most likely path of the stock is for reduced volatility as the buyers slowly wrestle control from the sellers. The specific beginning to Stage 3 is the crossing of the short-term MA up through the declining intermediate-term MA. Once this crossover has occurred the next short-

FIGURE 1.43 The Profiler charts visually represent not only price, volume and moving averages, but they also show the primary and substage for every stock.

term high marks the high of Stage 1, a level that will have to be eclipsed for the stock to enter Stage 2 and repeat the cycle again.

A unique and helpful tool in the Profiler is found on the price charts embedded in the application. Looking at the chart in Figure 1.43 you will notice that besides price, the chart shows the 10-, 20-, and 50-day MAs on the upper section. Just below the price area you will see an indication of which stage the stock is in. The stage analysis drawn onto the chart allows you to see exactly which primary and substage the stock is in as well as for how long. This feature allows you to speed up your learning curve for objective trend recognition that ultimately will help you find the ideas that meet *your* criteria.

Figures 1.44 and 1.45 are examples of a long setup, and Figures 1.46 and 1.47 are examples of a short setup using a daily and hourly time frame together for attaining the ideal entry price. As has been repeated, we want to find our trading ideas on a longer-term time frame. Once we have identified the powerful long-term trend, we then want to use the short-term time frame to capture precise entry points into that longer-term trend.

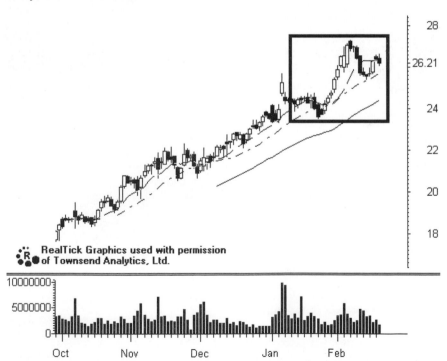

Daily MA10 MA20 MA50

RealTick Graphics used with permission of Townsend Analytics, Ltd.

FIGURE 1.44   The boxed in area of this Stage 2 stock on a daily time frame is shown in more detail in Figure 1.45. Notice how the stock found support just above the rising 20-day MA.

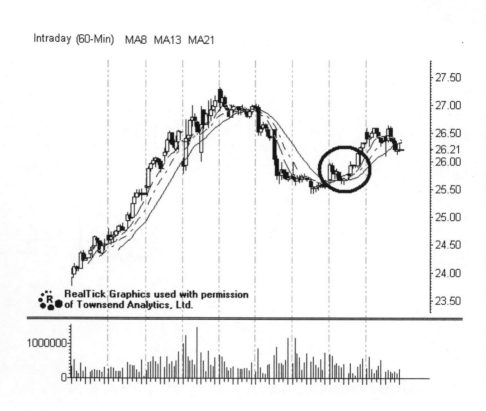

Intraday (60-Min) MA8 MA13 MA21

27.50
27.00
26.50
26.21
26.00
25.50
25.00
24.50
24.00
23.50

RealTick Graphics used with permission
of Townsend Analytics, Ltd.

1000000

0

FIGURE 1.45 This hourly chart shows the rally from 47 to 55 in greater detail. The circled areas represent the ideal entry points—that is where the buyers have regained control of the short-term trend.

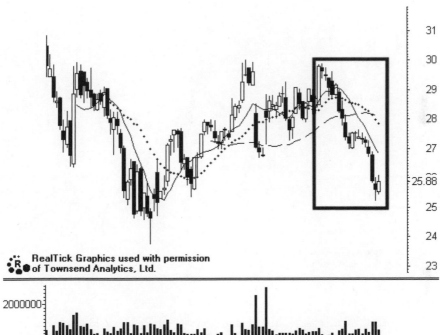

Daily   MA10 MA20 MA50

RealTick Graphics used with permission
of Townsend Analytics, Ltd.

FIGURE 1.46   Using the same concept for a short sale, we will examine the boxed in area of this daily downtrend in more detail in Figure 1.47.

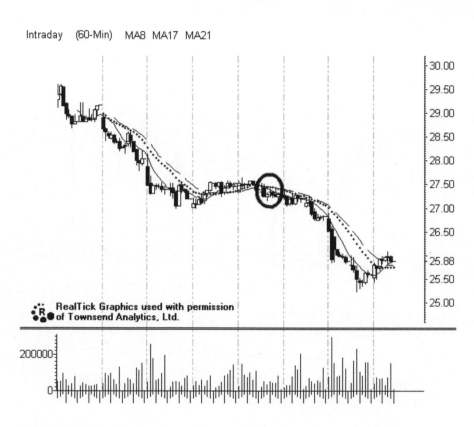

FIGURE 1.47 This hourly time frame allows us to refine our analysis so we are entering our short positions as the sellers take control of the short-term trend. The circled area shows where the ideal short sale should have been entered.

CHAPTER 2

Risk Management

The Essential Ingredient

A scientific theory states that the ability to handle risk is genetically determined—some people are born with the ability to handle high-risk situations more comfortably than others. Certainly, it appears that we all have different levels of risk tolerance. Some folks are happy parachuting out of airplanes high above the earth. Others cannot imagine attempting such a feat.

In the trading arena, many people are not willing to jump into the rapid-execution trading style known as *scalping*. These people believe that entering a trade and then suddenly experiencing a fast drawdown—even a limited one—might render them too fearful to exit the trade. Others thrive on the swift and nimble world of scalping and wouldn't dream of holding a stock position overnight, as do their slower-paced associates. (One of the benefits of trading is that a style exists to suit nearly every personality.)

This leads to one of the myths of active trading, which infers that all active traders are day traders. That is simply not true. Many active traders do a combination of intraday and swing trading. An example of a trader who moves back and forth between intraday and swing trading goes like this: A trader opens a position. If it works, he closes it out for a day-trade profit—*or* decides to carry it overnight with the peace of mind of profitability established, and protective stops set in place.

Whatever your risk tolerance, it is wise to do some inner discovery work *before* you start trading. Assessing your personal risk acceptance is definitely part of that preparation. Once you ascertain the kinds of risk, in time and money, that you are at ease with, you can develop your trading style to match your comfort level.

DISCIPLINE—THE KEY TO TRADING SUCCESS

Discipline is one of the most important characteristics a trader must exhibit. You can have a lot of technical knowledge, be talented at rapid order entry execution, and use the most sophisticated software. Yet, if you fail to integrate discipline into your trading plan and resulting actions, your chances of reaching success are slim.

Occasionally, careless investors get lucky and have successful trades, but over time, active traders are doomed without strict discipline. It manifests itself in many ways. The most obvious is reflected in the industry's often-repeated phrase, "Cut your losses short and let your winners run!"

Essentially, the trader must have the discipline to follow a system, just as systems assure that casinos play blackjack, craps, and other games of chance the same way every day—all day. In this sense, gambling and trading are similar, but this is a professional's perspective. The amateur perspective is not worth discussing, because results are dismal for amateur traders and gamblers alike. Perhaps the lesson to be learned here is to seek the advice of professionals before engaging in either endeavor.

DISCIPLINE PERSPECTIVES

One mind-set that fosters discipline is to suspend what you *believe* to be true and trade *only* what you observe. Do you passionately believe—and insist—that the Nasdaq is trading at lofty levels and should correct or retrace? Do you then sell short the market, perhaps via the QQQQ's, and refuse to cover the trade—even though the market moves higher—because you believe it should fall? Such beliefs can cause large losses in account size as well as in self-esteem. Do not defer decisions to act because of your ego. It will probably recover a lot quicker than the equity in your account.

Instead of imposing your personal opinions on the market (and on your trades), learn to trade what is. Learn to trade without emotion, except for a calm confidence born of your discipline, knowledge, and experience, and a well-thought-out plan custom-implemented for every trade.

As a trader, you must become introspective. You must ask questions of yourself and answer them honestly. Do you feel you deserve to make money quickly, or were you raised with the belief system that only those who work very hard, for a long time, deserve to make money? Did your parents convince you that "money is the root of all evil"? Is your self-esteem healthy or wavering at low levels? Do you have a strong emotional attachment to money that colors your perception of the market? Honest answers to such questions will help you identify any obstacles in your path to becoming a successful trader.

AVOID TRADING WITH SCARED MONEY

Do not consider funding your trading account with *scared money*. This can be defined as money you cannot afford to lose; if you were to lose it, your lifestyle would have to change. It includes money for paying your bills, the down payment for a new house, vacation savings, and your child's college tuition. Borrowed money is also scared money. Trading with scared money changes your perception of whatever market you are trading and all but guarantees you will incur big losses. This is because traders typically place a higher emotional value on money that they cannot afford to lose. Scared money rarely wins.

TERRA NOVA TRADE EVALUATOR

Many traders use the Trade Evaluator featured by Terra Nova Trading (www.terranovaonline.com) to help assess discipline. This tool allows traders to analyze their trading from many perspectives. It is only one of many tools active traders must utilize to evaluate their trading plan (see Figure 2.1).

YOUR GOAL: TO TRADE WITHOUT EMOTION

Trading with discipline leads to the psychological state every trader most desires (and finds most difficult to achieve): relative nonemotion.

The easiest way to trade without emotion is to establish a trading plan for each trade before actually committing your money. This includes calculating the risk-reward ratio and establishing three prices before you enter the trade (the entry, protective stop, and price target). When you have a firm, well-thought-out plan at your elbow, you will find it easier to trade without emotion. It allows you to accept losses at predetermined levels and to make profits based on the plan instead of succumbing to emotional decision making.

At MarketWise, we have incorporated into our Profiler software a concise way of determining the potential for a trade based on the action of the stock. We call it the *Trade Planner*. It allows you to "plug in" the variables that affect the outcome of the trade for any stock symbol. The

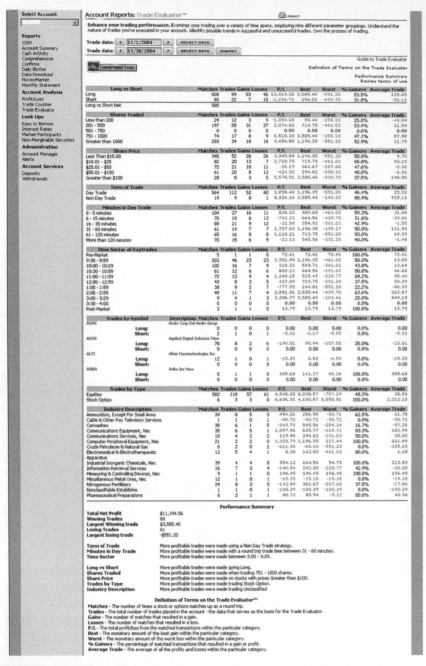

FIGURE 2.1 The Trade Evaluator is an indispensable tool that allows for objective analysis of your trading results so you can focus on what you are doing right and improve on areas where you are not achieving the results you are looking for. It is your personal statistics that does not lie or feel emotions. (Terra Nova Trade Evaluator is a trademark of Terra Nova Trading, L.L.C.)

following sections describe those factors and provide an example of the Planner in action.

PLAN YOUR TRADE AND TRADE YOUR PLAN WITH RISK-REWARD RATIOS

"If you fail to plan, you plan to fail."

Most beginning traders enter the market without a game plan. This leaves them at a great disadvantage and is probably the biggest reason they are victimized by the professionals. Coming up with a trading plan that best suits your needs and wants is no easy task. Trading your own account, either full-time or part-time, is a business. And, it needs to be treated that way.

In running a trading business, an often-overlooked fact is that more than 50 percent of your trades can go against you, yet with sound money management, you can still make profits on a consistent basis. Successful trading is not about being right all the time. There will be many times when your trades go against you, but how you handle those losing trades separates the amateurs from the professionals. Simply put, professionals cut their losers quickly at predetermined levels, whereas amateurs often compound their mistakes by averaging down in a trade.

Calculating the potential risk-reward ratio of your trade before you put hard-earned capital at risk in the market is one of the most important aspects of money management. Notice the word *potential.* No one knows for sure what will take place in a stock's immediate future, but understanding the location of support and resistance levels helps you determine a logical plan of action. This plan considers not just the potential amount of money to be made, but, perhaps more importantly, where you are going to cut a loser before it turns into a large loss.

At MarketWise, we suggest that with scalp, momentum, or day trades, you establish a risk-reward ratio of at least 1:2. That means for every dollar you put to risk, there is the potential to make two. A ratio of 1:3 is better, meaning one dollar of risk to three dollars of reward, and we recommend the 1:3 ratio for trades that are meant to be a swing trade or longer.

As you can see, the longer the time frame of your trade, the higher the reward portion of your ratio should be to compensate for the extra time your capital is at risk.

Risk-reward example: Stock XYZ presents a good setup for a swing trade. You establish the proper entry at approximately $20. Prior resistance (previous high or consolidation area) on an intraday chart of XYZ lies at $23. That price represents your initial profit target. Nearby support lies at $19.25, so you decide to place your initial protective stop just under that price, at $19.

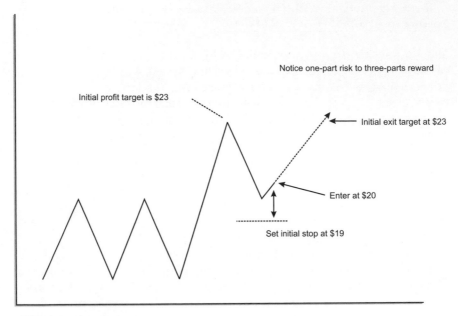

FIGURE 2.2   Stock XYZ with 1:3 risk reward ratio.

If XYZ sets up properly, you have a risk of one point (the spread between your entry price of $20 and your protective stop at $19) and a reward of three points (spread between entry at $20 and price target of $23). That equals a risk-reward ratio of 1:3. Figure 2.2 shows a diagram of how that would look in a trade progression.

Your risk-reward ratio may change soon after you enter your position. After you enter, you might adjust your initial protective stop loss a bit higher (it is unacceptable to lower it). You will fine-tune your stop later in the trade by turning it into a trailing stop. As the price nears your profit target, you can tighten the stop until it "takes you out" of the trade. We do not recommend selling just because the stock reached your price target. Your target means nothing now that the stock is moving and to obtain really large profits you must allow for your winners to run until the market dictates exiting the position. When a stock nears a prior price target, it is prudent to tighten up the stop loss because you should be less willing to allow the stock to fluctuate wildly when it reaches a level you perceived might act as resistance. This tighter stop allows you to take profits if the market dictates; otherwise, the trade will remain open as it continues to move in your favor.

SETTING STOPS—OVERVIEW

Many times, investors do not limit the losses on their positions. This can result in the stock moving up and delivering "paper" gains, only to fall back down and hand the investor an eventual loss. Traders, however, master risk management principles knowing that because the edge is small, losses are expected and dealt with quickly. Traders establish protective stops or stop-loss orders on all their trades to keep their gains and cut their losses short. Stop-loss orders are invaluable risk-management tools that can be based on the following criteria:

- Percentages of the equity in your account.
- Technical, meaning support or resistance levels designated by price or key moving averages.
- Percentage of price.
- Time.
- Fixed dollar amount.

Professional level trading systems, such as RealTick® (visit www.terranovaonline.com for a free demonstration), make setting automatically triggered stops easy and efficient. For full-time traders who have developed strong discipline, mental stop-loss points may be sufficient. No matter the methodology, a stop must exist to ensure against unexpected action that could result in a catastrophic loss.

Overall Protective Stop Guidelines

Each participant approaches the market with a set of unique circumstances (amount of capital available, market experience, individual risk, and tolerance, to name a few) that make exit decisions a personal choice. As a general rule to preserve capital, you should risk no more than 1 percent to 2 percent of your account on any trade. If you have $50,000 equity in your account, 1 percent equals $500. If you follow the 1 percent risk minimum, you would place your protective stops at a price where you would not lose more than $500 on any trade.

Using a strict percentage of account size allows traders to make objective decisions about how many shares should be traded. Imagine you were taking a position, and you placed your protective stop one point from your entry. You could logically buy 500 shares of that stock to follow your risk management. If the stock fell one point and you exited properly, you would have risked the designated 1 percent of your account, and no more.

To take this process one step further, if you were to place a stop $0.50 away from your entry, you could trade 1,000 shares and still be within your 1 percent risk parameters. Keep in mind that an absolute dollar amount is only one component of proper position sizing. You should also consider factors such as liquidity, overall market environment, your experience level, and technical conditions when determining how many shares to trade. Remember to adjust your risk percentage as your account size changes.

Having a maximum loss per day, week, and month is the best way to keep your discipline in check. If things are not going well, stops are in place to prevent you from taking a major loss. These limits can be based on a percentage of cash in your account or a set dollar amount. When first starting, we suggest a daily loss limit of no more than 1 percent of your account.

For example, a $50,000 account would risk no more than $500 over the course of a day. Assume this account lost exactly $500. The balance would now be $49,500, making the new stop loss for the day $495. This may seem like a lot or a little to some; however, using this and combining the proper risk-reward scenario to your trading can give you an advantage. Depending on your trading style, your trades can move as you anticipate only 33 percent of the time, yet you can still be profitable when you follow these money management principles.

Limiting losses, whether per trade or time period, keeps you in control of your future. Once your maximum loss has been reached, on any time frame, you must stop trading immediately. This is crucial for preservation of capital and your success.

Because discipline is one of the most important characteristics of successful traders, if you find you are ignoring your self-imposed rules, then you need to change your methods quickly. If you are unable to implement your plans in a disciplined manner, you may want to reconsider whether trading is right for you. Establishing maximum loss points and following through on that planned course of action is of the utmost importance.

Protective Stops and Trading Time Frames

Loss limits can be based on the style of trade you are taking. If you are entering an intraday trade, as previously stated, the minimum risk-reward must be at least 1:2. So, if you are willing to accept an anticipated maximum loss of $0.30, then your profit target should be at least $0.60.

In a swing trade scenario, again, the minimum risk-reward should be at least 1:3. Therefore, if you are risking one dollar (your protective stop is one point away from your entry price), your profit target should be $3 or more away from your entry.

As you approach your loss limits over any time period, decrease your trade size. For example, as you approach your loss limit for the day, trading 500 shares with a 30-cent stop, for a maximum loss of $150, decrease your share size to 300 while keeping your stop at $0.30. This lowers your maximum loss to $90.

When figuring risk-reward ratios, do not pick your stop loss based on your profit target. Your protective stop should be based on support, resistance, and key moving averages found objectively through technical analysis. The Trade Planner portion of the Profiler allows you to develop different trading scenarios to come up with a risk-reward ratio that makes sense. Looking at an example of the Planner, you can see that the screen initially has fields that you fill in to come up with a logical plan of action before you place your trade. As you can see, the first field to enter is the Ticker Symbol. When you enter a ticker symbol and click the submit button, the fields will automatically populate with useful information to help plan the trade (see Figure 2.3).

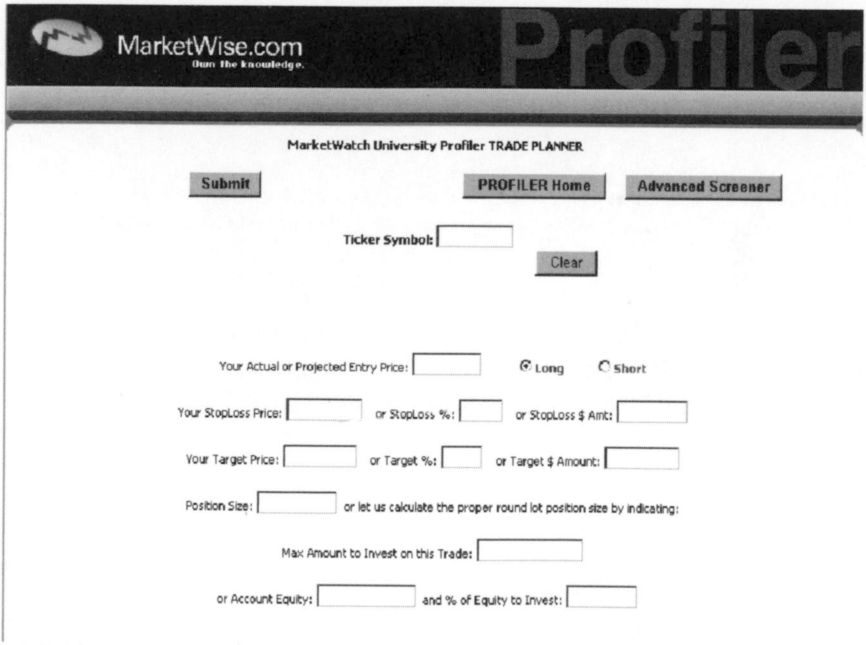

FIGURE 2.3 The Trade Planner allows you to identify the risk/reward and position size to determine if a trade is merited. This feature allows you to plan your trades before "trading the plan."

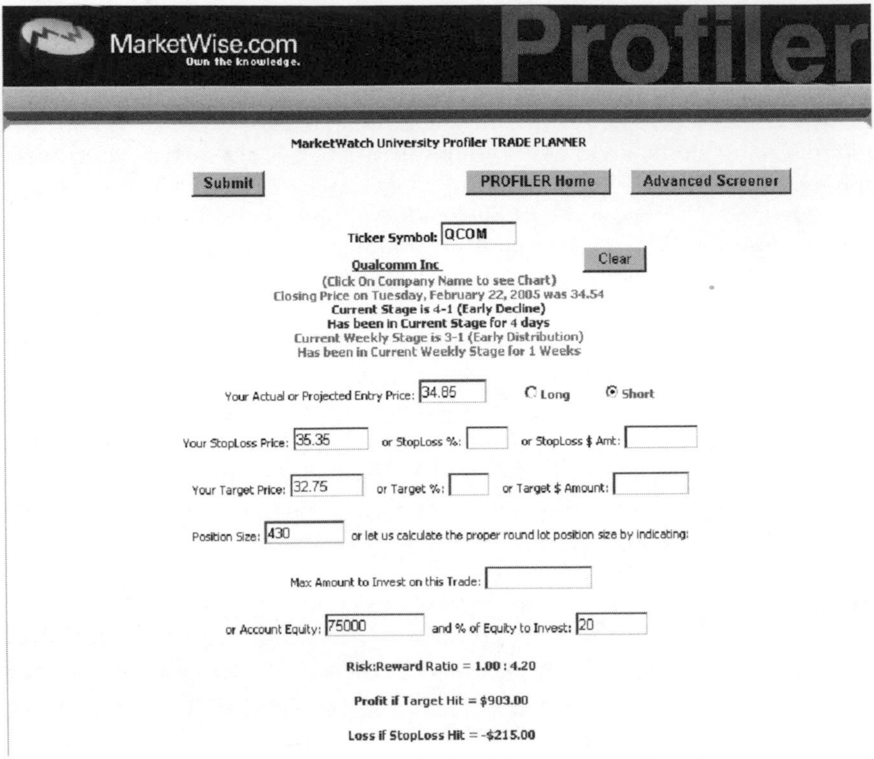

FIGURE 2.4 Once the user inputs trade details, the Trade Planner provides information that can be objectively analyzed to determine the feasibility of actually committing capital.

When we insert QCOM (see Figure 2.4), the first thing you notice is that the Planner tells you that on the daily time frame it is in Stage 4-1, a strong downtrend. Just below this is the current weekly stage, which for QCOM is Stage 3-1. Swing traders do not really need to be too concerned with the weekly time frame as those trends take months to develop; however, it is always a bonus if the weekly stage is aligned with the daily stage. In the case of QCOM, we can infer that at the time, QCOM was entering a long period of distribution, but in the short term the stock was declining. This would not make for a good purchase candidate; however, a potential short sale looks enticing. Just below the stage information, we can enter our trade setup to determine if the trade would make sense from a risk-reward standpoint. The Planner automatically calculates an entry based on the previous day's close, and it assumes a long position is desired (if looking for the short trade calculation, simply click the short button). The Planner then calculates what it would take to achieve a risk-reward ratio of at least 1:3 based on an initial stop of 1.5 percent. It then uses a target that is 5 percent away from current prices. At the bottom of the screen, the Planner calculates exactly how much money you would stand to lose or gain based on a position of 100 shares. Using the default settings is not the recommended way to utilize the Planner. It is more realistic to base trading decisions on the support and resistance levels for the stock. If we assume that we liked QCOM as a short sale candidate, the first thing we would do is enter the symbol and then click the short button. If the stock closed at 34.54, we might actually want to enter the trade on some strength so we will enter our projected entry at 34.85. The next order of business is to determine the amount of risk we are willing to consider in the position. If we determined 35.30 to be a level of potential resistance, we might want to enter our stop just above that level, say at 35.35, for a theoretical risk of $0.50 per share. Next, we will want to approximate where the stock might drop to a level of support. Looking at a chart, we might determine the potential for support to be at 32.75. If this scenario were to unfold, we would recognize a profit of $2.10 per share. By clicking Submit, the Planner tells us that the risk-reward ratio would be 1.00:3.75, meaning that for every 100 shares we were to sell short, our risk would be $60.00 and our potential reward would be $210/100 shares! That is a trade worth taking. The next question might be how many shares to sell short. We could come up with that answer a few different ways. First, we could enter a fixed dollar amount, such as $10,000, to commit to the trade. The Planner would tell us that we should sell short 272 shares, that if we were right we could make $612 on the trade, and that our risk would be $163.60. Another way to determine our position size would be to enter the amount of equity in our account, let's say $75,000, and we would commit 20 percent of our capital to the trade. In this example, the Planner tells us our position size should be 430 shares, in which case we could potentially make a profit of $903.00 for a total theoretical risk of $215.00 (see Figure 2.4).

By now, the value of the Planner should be clear; it truly is a tool that allows you to plan your trades. The next step is to have the discipline to trade according to those plans.

Percentage of Price Stops

Some swing traders use percentage stops. That is, they use a percentage of the price of the stock they are entering. A valid percentage(s) might be 2 to 3 percent of the price. If you are buying a stock for a swing trade that costs $30.00 per share, you would risk no more than 3 percent, or $0.90. (You would set your initial stop at $29.10.) Keep in mind that a percentage stop is not the ideal way of setting stops as they are somewhat random. The best stops are based on the action of the stock as seen through valid levels of support and resistance.

Time Stops

Protective stops known as *time stops* are tuned to trader discretion. They are used mostly in intraday trading; however, many traders use them in swing trading as well.

Example: You enter a scalping trade as you see a stock break out of a consolidation area on high volume. Upward momentum decreases almost immediately, though, and the stock moves sideways. Although it does not touch your protective, technical stop, time erodes and momentum subsides. Result: the stock does not act as you thought it would, so you close the position.

Were the trade a swing trade, the stock might move sideways as well, except the time frame for the time stop would be hours to days. Suppose you entered a trade one day near the close with the intent of holding it for two to five days. The next day, the stock did not move up measurably as you had anticipated. Instead, it drifted sideways in a lackluster fashion. You may decide to scale back some or all of your position before that day's market close.

There is a bottom line with time stops: If, over a designated time, the stock does not act the way you thought it would, you may want to consider exiting a portion, or all, of your position.

AVOID THIS MISTAKE

A common mistake of novice traders after taking a large loss is to succumb to the temptation to "make it all back" by initiating high-risk trades. This thinking hinges on the gambling mentality that afflicts many people in the market. If you find yourself thinking this way, do not follow through.

If you lose your discipline and allow a small loss to turn into a big loser, do not compound the problem by making emotional decisions in an attempt to recover from the original mistake. Small losses allow you to remain trading and learning, whereas larger losses can abruptly end your trading career.

REALTICK® CAN HELP

RealTick® trading software offers a trailing stop order option that is the most efficient and nonemotional means of taking profits. It automatically

Time	Order Details	Status
	▣ Order Details	
Time	Order Details	Status
9:35	Buy 500 UNTD at 16.30 on ARCA (500 traded @ 16.3000)	Executed
9:35	Bought 100 UNTD at 16.300000 with ARCA3	Completed
9:35	Bought 400 UNTD at 16.300000 with ARCA1	Completed
9:42	Sell 500 UNTD at 16.55 (Stop: 16.62) Deleted	Deleted
9:42	ARCA Order Status: Pending trigger price of 16.62	Completed
12:26	Sell 500 UNTD at Trailing Stop: .15 on ARCA 500 traded	Executed
12:26	ARCA Order Status: Pending trailing stop (trail=.15)	Completed
12:26	ARCA Order Status: New stop 17.04	Completed
12:26	ARCA Order Status: New stop 17.07	Completed
12:26	ARCA Order Status: New stop 17.09	Completed
12:26	ARCA Order Status: New stop 17.10	Completed
12:26	ARCA Order Status: New stop 17.12	Completed
12:26	ARCA Order Status: New stop 17.13	Completed
12:26	ARCA Order Status: New stop 17.14	Completed
12:26	ARCA Order Status: New stop 17.15	Completed
12:26	ARCA Order Status: New stop 17.19	Completed
12:26	ARCA Order Status: New stop 17.20	Completed
12:26	ARCA Order Status: New stop 17.22	Completed
12:26	ARCA Order Status: New stop 17.24	Completed
12:26	ARCA Order Status: New stop 17.25	Completed
12:26	ARCA Order Status: New stop 17.26	Completed
12:32	Sold 100 UNTD at 17.250000 with ARCA3 (order 0a4c-00	Completed
12:32	Sold 100 UNTD at 17.260000 with ARCA3 (order 0a4c-00	Completed
12:32	Sold 300 UNTD at 17.210000 with ARCA3 (order 0a4c-00	Completed

FIGURE 2.5   This order book shows a purchase of 500 shares of UNTD at 16.30 at 9:35 A.M. As the stock moved higher, we placed a trailing stop of $.15, which had the stop initially placed at 17.04. As the stock continued higher, the stop followed the price movement until the order was activated as the stock traded at 17.26. It is important to recognize that the position was actually sold at three different price levels, that is because the stop is a market order once it is activated.

moves the stop behind your stock as it moves, and then takes you out of the trade to the designated amount if the stock goes against you.

If you buy a stock and enter a $0.15 trailing stop on it, as long as the stock moves up your order remains open, continually adjusting higher as the stock trades upward. If the stock weakens $0.15, it will touch your trailing stop and close your position automatically. This relieves you from second-guessing your exit strategy, and it takes the emotion out of the trade. At MarketWise, we suggest tightening your trailing stops as your trade progresses, to take maximum gains with the least amount of emotion (see Figure 2.5).

RISK MANAGEMENT AND TRADING WITH THE NEWS

It is important to remain aware of world and financial news. It is common for active traders to have a television tuned to a financial network, such as

CNBC, during the trading hours. Having the television on during the trading day can be useful for keeping up with market moving events, but it is essential to avoid reacting to the news on a sudden impulse.

Imagine a fund manager praising a stock on television. As the manager talks, you put the stock up on your screen and the price begins to shoot up. You become excited by what this manager says. Watching the market respond—you buy it. Seconds later, the stock falls faster than it rose, and you have to chase it down to exit, perhaps taking a loss. Trading on that kind of news can hand you large losses. This type of trading is reactionary and based on emotion, not anticipatory and based on a solid plan. Bottom line: It is an amateurish approach to the business of trading.

You've probably heard that when reporting financial information, the media is usually wrong. Actually, the facts reported are usually correct, but as they relate to the fast-paced world of trading, the information is stale. By the time CNBC makes an announcement, most of the institutions already know about it and have already absorbed and acted on it. Individual traders are trading the day's "leftovers" that have lost their initial flavor and zest.

It is important to follow economic reports and earnings announcements. Be sure to know when these reports are due out so you are not blindsided by any unexpected volatility that may result.

Economic reports can have a dramatic impact on the market, especially if they relate to present-day economic concerns. When the United States is experiencing an economic downturn and job layoffs are a daily event, then the unemployment report—and the market's reaction to it—can be key to the market's movement that day. And the residual effect may continue for even a longer time.

Earnings announcements can affect the market, as well as individual equities. If you are holding an open position in which the company is reporting earnings that day, you may choose to lower your risk by exiting your position until those earnings have been announced. You may also choose to use options to hedge a stock position, or to make a straight directional bet.

In a bear market, even a company that announces good earnings can sell off rapidly. Why? Because high earnings expectations—possibly established by earlier guidance—can push the stock higher as institutions pile into the stock expecting good news. When the earnings are announced, the stock may sell off, operating under the "buy the rumor, sell the news" maxim.

In addition, it is prudent to remain aware of large market stocks with pending earnings announcements, especially when that stock represents a sector or industry group where any of your open positions reside. Say you own a position in software stock Oracle Corporation (ORCL). Imagine that Microsoft (MSFT), the most prominent software company in the United States, is announcing earnings after the market's close. You may want to exit some, or all, of your ORCL holdings to minimize your risk. Negative earnings from a giant like Microsoft can rock the technology sector, and even the entire Nasdaq National Market.

Similarly, if an analyst meeting on a certain large-cap company is scheduled, and you are holding a position in that company or a related one, you may want to tighten your protective stop loss to hedge against negative announcements.

You may also want to avoid biotech and pharmaceutical stocks in which the underlying company has an FDA (Federal Drug Administration) review coming up, or has pharmaceuticals that are involved in advancing trials, such as a Phase Two trial. Failure of a preparation to perform successfully can drive down a pharmaceutical firm's stock fast and furiously and other medical stocks may fall in "sympathy." Or if you short the stock, a vicious short squeeze may develop on a positive FDA result.

One of the most important events to watch for is "Fed day," or the day on which the Federal Open Market Committee (FOMC) meets to decide interest rates. The period just before and after the announcement, which usually takes place about 2:15 P.M. EST, is usually volatile. The remainder of that afternoon can also be erratic, which results in a rocky trading environment. This type of trading is risky and is best left to the large institutions.

Finally, options expiration days fall on the third Friday of each month and result in whippy, choppy price action. Four times a year, in January, March, June, and September, options expiration days are referred to as "Triple Witching Days." On these days, futures contracts expire, as well as stock and index options. These days (and the days leading up to them) are particularly unpredictable, and many traders avoid the markets completely.

If you insist on "playing the news," play the reaction to it, rather than the news itself. If you knowingly take positions ahead of an important, news-driven event, make sure you are protected against the potential for catastrophic losses that may occur if the event does not unfold as you expected. Failure to protect yourself, either with smaller shares size or with an options hedge, makes you a gambler. While you may have a few winners, in the long term very few people survive in this difficult business by making bets.

RISK MANAGEMENT AND SHARE SIZE

If you are relatively new to trading and still unsure of your skills, you will probably want to trade with a limited number of shares. You can decrease your risk and learn how to trade just as well with 300 shares as with 1,000 shares.

Another way to determine share size is to have a fixed share size for every trade based on your comfort level or a percentage of your portfolio. We recommend no more than 20 percent of your account size in any one trade except when attempting a scalping trade. Then you may end up using most of your capital, since this is an extremely short-term trade that you can exit quickly, if need be. If you have a cash account with $50,000 in it, you should commit no more than $10,000 in any one position. If the stock price is around $20, then your share size should be no more than 500. Either strategy for share size selection works just fine, but make sure you are consistent with all trades. This makes it easier to compare trades over an extended period.

Share size can also vary for the following reasons:

- Price volatility (reduce share size in volatile, risky stocks).
- Market environment (in choppy markets, you may want to "get small," or reduce share size to reduce risk).
- Time-of-day (e.g., taking on a large share size for a day trade during midday doldrums can be dangerous to your wealth).
- Seasonality (e.g., tech stocks usually correct from April through October, and an old market adage states, "Leave in May and stay away").
- Price liquidity (Liquidity = Volume. If you are trading a stock with average daily volume of less than 500,000 shares a day, you may want to reduce your lot size; a thinly traded stock is many times harder to exit at the desired price than a stock that trades high volume.)

SUMMARY

You can see how important it is to learn how to manage risk when taking trades, whether short term or long term. You are 100 percent responsible for managing the risk in each trade you make.

Start by assessing your personal strengths and weaknesses as they pertain to trading. Then develop a sturdy discipline through which you filter all of your trading choices. Next, study risk-reward scenarios by paper trading (planning and executing imaginary trades on real charts, in real time). Remember to establish three prices before you enter each trade: the entry, initial protective stop, and profit target.

As you progress, study stop-loss points and determine the maximum losses you will take relative to your account size and your personal risk tolerance. Finally, take note of how the news, including economic reports, earnings, options expiration days, and FOMC meeting days affect the markets and stock performance.

As you move forward, you will feel much more confident in your trading skills and you will have made large advances on your journey to trading success.

CHAPTER 3

Basic Chart Formations

In Chapter 1, we discussed the key elements of technical analysis. But there are other factors that you should be aware of and take into consideration in your analysis. These are the basic chart formations that traders learn when they first study the stock market. Classic chart formations often signal directional changes in price trends or that the trend is expected to continue or stall. Being able to recognize these signals is important because they are so well known that they often become self-filling prophecies. There is always the risk of trading against one of these common formations when the majority of traders recognize the pattern and are responding to it. In this chapter, we describe the most common chart patterns.

Proper trading in any market means consistently stacking the odds in your favor. One of the most important ways to stack the odds in your favor is to trade with the trend. A trend is one of the foundations on which technical analysis is built and it should be considered the core in developing a trader's directional bias. In this chapter, we discuss how to identify trends, the proper way to trade within a trend, how to measure their strength, and how you can use trends for position entry decisions.

Entering a trade at the proper time offers you the greatest probability of increasing your profits and allows you to formulate intelligent levels for placing stop-loss orders as protection against unexpected price moves. A trend is defined by a series of peaks and troughs moving in one direction. The direction of these peaks and troughs (highs and lows) determines the

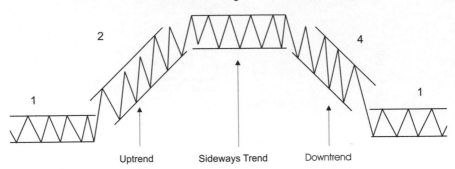

FIGURE 3.1 The three trends.

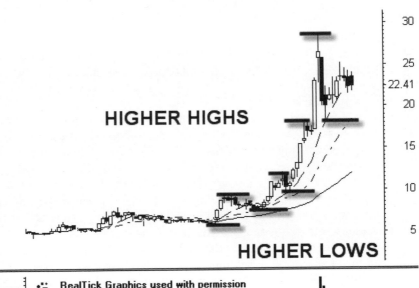

Daily MA10 MA20 MA50

HIGHER HIGHS

HIGHER LOWS

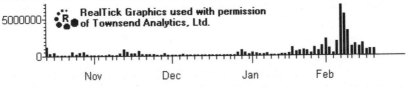

FIGURE 3.2 An uptrend, which is found in the stage 2 markup phase of a stocks cycle, is defined by a series of higher highs and higher lows. In an uptrend, the pullbacks offer traders low risk opportunities to get long a stock whose path of least resistance is higher.

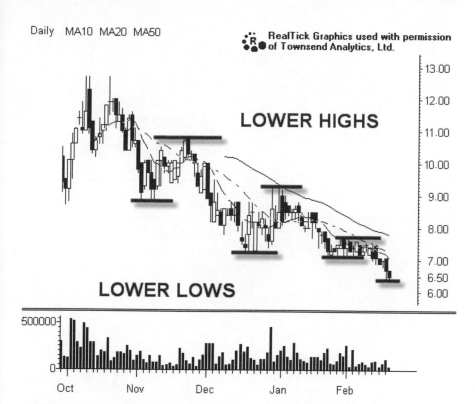

Daily MA10 MA20 MA50

RealTick Graphics used with permission of Townsend Analytics, Ltd.

LOWER HIGHS

LOWER LOWS

FIGURE 3.3 A downtrend, which is found in the stage 4 decline phase of a stocks cycle, is defined by a series of lower highs and lowers lows. In a downtrend, rallies offer traders low risk opportunities to get short a stock whose path of least resistance is lower.

direction of the overall trend. Lets revisit our stages from Chapter 1 to begin to identify trends (see Figure 3.1).

Figure 3.2 breaks down the Stage 2 uptrend to show more detail of how an uptrend forms and continues. Figure 3.3 breaks down the Stage 4 downtrend to show the details of how a downtrend forms and continues. Figure 3.4 shows the characteristics of a sideways trend in detail. Note the indecision shown by the crossing of the moving averages.

Trading with the trend is ideal as the odds are continuously on your side. In measuring the strength of a trend, there are several things to consider. First, if the distance between the higher highs (in an uptrend) is increasing, this suggests the trend is becoming stronger. If the distance between the higher highs is decreasing, odds are the trend is becoming weaker and that the trend may soon change. Second, volume is to a trend

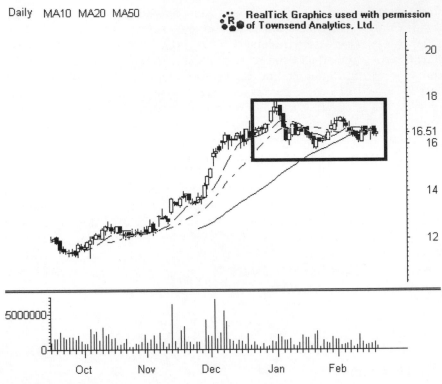

FIGURE 3.4   A sideways trend, which is found in stage 1 Accumulation phase and stage 3 Distribution phase of a stock cycle, is defined by relatively equal highs and equal lows. In a sideways trend, rallies to prior highs offer traders the low risk opportunity to sell or get short and declines to prior lows offer traders the low risk opportunity to buy or get long. While money can be made within what some call a channel, I choose to avoid these sideways trends.

is as fuel is to an automobile. An uptrend needs more buyers to sustain itself. A healthy uptrend has steady growth in volume as the trend moves higher. Also, pullbacks in an uptrend should be accompanied by low volume suggesting a lack of aggressive sellers.

To identify trends, look at the daily, weekly, and sometimes, monthly chart. To take a position in a stock or futures contract with the trend, first identify the trend on the larger time frame and then look to the smaller time frames for a low-risk entry.

TIME FRAMES

Deciding which time frame you should focus on depends on your objectives, which are largely dictated by personality traits. Some people prefer to be long-term investors and should therefore focus on weekly and daily charts and be less concerned about the day-to-day action on the intraday charts. More aggressive traders, who consider two to three days as long term, have an obvious need to emphasize intraday charts, studying 60-minute or even 10-minute bar charts. You do not need to learn new concepts for various time frames. A chart is a chart, and once you are comfortable analyzing the concepts and relationships between price, moving averages, volume, and other studies on a daily chart, looking at shorter periods is an easy transition. A short-term chart puts our analysis under a microscope where we can pick up on the minitrends and see how they fit into the bigger picture.

So what time frame is best to start with? Whether you plan on investing or actively trading, the best place to start is the daily chart. By getting a sense of the bigger picture, you are sure not to miss out on the larger and stronger trends of a stock. Many traders who focus only on short time frames tend to lose sight of the forest through the trees and take profits much too early by not observing that a powerful trend may be setting up on the daily chart. The following sections describe four valuable time frames and explain who should use which one and at what time. One of the most difficult questions—which moving averages to apply on any time frame—is also addressed.

Weekly Charts

Most software packages allow you to look at a substantial amount of data. The time available varies among data providers; however, most allow you to look at data that go back for approximately three years. Three years is a perfect time span because rarely will an event that occurred longer than three years ago affect the trading environment today. Investors in particular benefit from these charts, which show where a stock has been in a time frame that they want to consider using (one to two years).

Although weekly charts have limited applicability for short-term traders, using one makes sense when a stock is at a new high for the year and trading history at these higher prices cannot be seen by looking exclusively at recent data. Except for traders with the shortest time horizons, it is valuable to look at weekly charts to have some perspective on how the stock has traded at these levels.

Because weekly charts are most useful to longer-term investors, mutual funds, large pension funds, insurance companies, and other big money investors use them a lot. The most common moving averages for these investors to key off of are the 50-day, 100-day, and 200-day moving averages. To get this data on a weekly chart, we need to set our moving average periods for 10 weeks ($\times$ 5 days = 50 days), 20 weeks ($\times$ 5 days = 100 days), and

40 weeks ($\times$ 5 days = 200 days). It is important to remember that the moving average settings (MAs) on most charting packages are set for the number of periods being studied, not days. These MAs represent the short-, intermediate-, and long-term trends on this time frame. The MAs are a large part of the logic behind the Profiler in calculating which stage a stock is in. In the Advanced section of the Profiler (which allows you to customize screens on weekly charts) the 50, 100 and 200 day MAs are instrumental for stage placement.

Daily Charts

The daily chart is, by far, the most popular period for analyzing price. The daily charts available on most programs usually allow the viewer to look at a minimum of 1 year's worth of trading history. RealTick® has a standard default for 200 days, but with the proper settings, you can view as much as 1,000 days' worth of data. Using the analogy of a microscope, a daily chart is like a weekly chart magnified at 5×. It is easier to see trends developing and areas of unusual volume on the daily time frame than on the weekly chart. Investors will find the daily chart to be extremely useful in identifying entry and exit points for their investment decisions. To a trader, the daily chart is most useful in being able to identify candidates that may become good vehicles to trade; it is where traders create their shopping list, usually called a *watch* list.

Although big investors tend to key off the 50-, 100-, and 200-day moving averages, it is helpful to have a 10- and 20-day moving average overlaid on the chart that measures daily data. The 10- and 20-day MAs are especially valuable to swing traders. These periods follow the price action much more closely and allow the trader to see the short-term trends changing more clearly and define the strength or weakness of a trend at a quick glance. If you are an investor, you should not ignore these shorter moving averages, as they are particularly helpful in timing purchases accurately. More precise entries reduce your risk of having a position move against you immediately after purchase. On the daily time frame, we usually recommend displaying just the 10-, 20-, and 50-period MAs and we use these three averages as a representation of the short-, intermediate-, and long-term trends, much the same as we used the 10-, 20-, and 40-period MAs on the weekly time frame.

Intraday Charts

Intraday charts are where the trader lives and makes his or her money. Once again though, investors, or anyone who is trying to get an edge in timing purchases and sales of stocks, should not ignore them. The technology today allows us to look at the price action on any time frame; we explore two intraday time frames in this chapter. The periods we are studying use data on 60-minute bars and 10-minute bars. Intraday data can be plotted on just about any time frame; we chose these two time periods because each offers a different perspective and both include the data that most market participants look for.

Sixty-Minute Charts

The trends for price and volume on this time frame are easy to spot without getting overanalytical, as sometimes happens with shorter time frames. Although investors have different objectives than the traders who make their livings in this kind of time frame, looking at a 60-minute chart can provide valuable data, particularly if the user is attempting to purchase stocks that have already begun to move in an identifiable trend where the risks may be greater. For traders, this is the next step in identifying a good trade opportunity after studying the daily charts. To put it into perspective, the hourly chart is like a weekly chart magnified 35× or the daily chart at 7×.

For a short-term trader who has identified a trend on a daily chart and wants to keep it in perspective on an hourly chart with moving averages, the question once again is which ones? After extensive testing of various moving averages over the past 10 years, we have found the 8-, 13-, and 21-period MAs are most effective for easy identification of the short-, intermediate-, and long-term trends on the hourly time frame.

Ten-Minute Charts

At this point, we are looking at data on a weekly chart magnified at 210× and the daily information at 42×. By now it should be getting easier to see how stocks really trade—they move around a lot! The movement you will be able to observe on a chart with this time frame is great for making trades that last anywhere from 30 minutes to 3 to 4 hours or for better entry and exit points for swing trades. This action has little appeal for a long-term investor, but most investors find it fascinating to contemplate.

When intraday charts were first becoming popular for analyzing stocks, few people had access to them, and they usually left the same moving averages (the 20-, 50-, and 100-periods) on their programs in looking at a 10-minute chart that they had on their daily charts. Advances in computer technology have made this information available to almost anyone who has a basic computer. These moving averages are still the most commonly used on a 10-minute time frame and generate the best timing signals. Because these time frames are 10-minute periods, a 20-period MA is a moving average of 200 minutes of trading history, a 50-period MA represents 500 minutes of trades, a 100-period MA represents 1,000 minutes of trade data.

INTERPRETING CHART PATTERNS

Chart patterns are created as the result of supply-and-demand dynamics in the markets. Whether the pattern is a continuation or a reversal setup, you must be careful in trading it and more importantly, must interpret it properly. If you interpret chart patterns as many others do, you can potentially run into a major problem. Keep in mind how we make money trading. When we buy (get long), we need others to buy after us at higher prices if we are to make money in the trade. If we enter a position with everyone else, based on a pattern that everyone else trades the same way, who will buy from us? The goal is to enter before others, at the right time. We must have an edge. This is the low-risk, high-odds entry.

Another way of explaining the warning here is to imagine a frozen pond with many people standing on it. Do you want to remain with everyone else on this sheet of ice? Of course not; you want to stand away from them, by yourself, because that is where you will be safe. Others may find comfort in numbers while taking on more risk as they stand in the same place on the ice, which is likely to break with all the weight. Trading with the crowd may feel better mentally, but it is likely to harm the growth of your account.

The following chart patterns have stood the test of time, but by no means do they represent a definitive study of chart formations. The examples used are a diverse mix of Western bar charts and candlestick charts.

REVERSAL PATTERNS

Head and Shoulders Chart Formation

When found in an uptrend, the head and shoulders reversal pattern is one of the best known and most reliable of all the major reversal patterns (see Figure 3.5). Here is how it works as a topping pattern: Eventually, in an uptrend, the series of ascending peaks and troughs begins to lose momentum; the price action at this point begins to slow; and the forces of supply and demand are generally in balance. Sellers enter the market at the highs (left shoulder) and the buyers return at the lows (beginning neckline). Buyers eventually push through the previous highs that formed the left shoulder to new highs (head). The chartist might notice that volume on the break through the previous highs that formed the left shoulder to the new high (head) was stronger than the previous rally; this is ideal and is to be expected. However, the new highs (head) immediately reverse and the downside is tested again (neckline). Tentative buying emerges and the market

Daily MA10 MA20 MA50

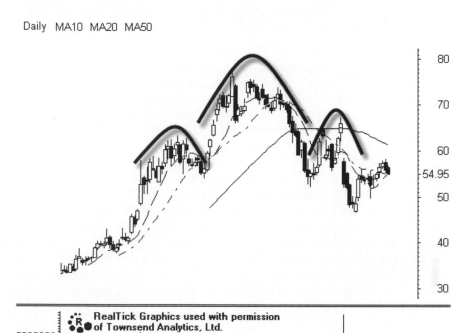

FIGURE 3.5   The head and shoulders top resembles the profile of a person when viewed head on. The first rally represents the left shoulder, the second rally represents the head, and the final rally represents the left shoulder.

rallies one last time. At this point, the peak of this rally (right shoulder) should be made on very light volume. Sellers enter the market and the downside is tested again. The trend line (neckline) for this pattern is drawn by connecting the lows of the pattern. At this point, more selling comes in and the buyers exit. The pattern is complete when prices break below the neckline, which is when this classic pattern calls for an entry (short in this case). Look for volume to be strong on the break of the neckline. What is ironic is that one of the most powerful patterns is the failed head and shoulders breakout. Simply put, a failed pattern refers to times when many participants are expecting a breakdown and get short when a sudden and unexpected source of demand comes in to trap those short sellers as new buyers force prices higher. The higher prices motivate short sellers to repurchase the shares, which adds further upside pressure. The point where a topping head and shoulders pattern becomes visible is typically in Stage 3-3 or Stage 4-1, which the Profiler makes easy to find. A scan of Stages 1-3 and 2-1 would be best for finding an inverted head and shoulders—a bullish pattern.

Long Base and Saucer Formations

Long base and saucer formations are reliable, easy-to-recognize patterns that usually precede a big move and give participants plenty of time to see them setting up. These patterns are most common on a stock that had been a big winner in the past, got beat up very badly, and has taken up to one to two years for the bullish and bearish forces to reach equilibrium. These patterns are what make the accumulation phase of a stock not only identifiable but actionable. Both these patterns can go on for a long time, and it makes no sense to tie your money up in one of these stagnant issues. It is, however, important to be able to recognize when the accumulation period may be close to completion because the gains that follow can be large if traded properly. Although these bottoming patterns are usually associated with daily charts, they can also be seen on intraday time frames and their interpretation is the same. The best time frame for a short-term/momentum trader to study this formation is on the hourly chart.

While a stock is building a long base, it will trade sideways (in a range between support and resistance) for an indefinite time. Only the most aggressive traders will want to attempt to trade the range, as the stock can be unpredictable during these times and the ranges are narrow. Significant money can be made as the stock breaks out of the range, as it often signals the start of a new uptrend for the issue. By being alert, investors can catch the breakout and by using trailing stop-loss orders, capture big moves. If you are an aggressive trader, once a stock breaks out of one of these formations, it will give you many opportunities to move in and out of the stock as a new trend gets underway. The basing pattern will be recognized in Stage 1-3 or 2-1 after the stock has broken into an uptrend.

Volume   During the sideways, basing action, volume is of little significance until the stock actually breaks out above the resistance level (see Figure 3.6). There are, however, clues that you should anticipate such a move. Unusual volume, as the stock approaches longer-term moving averages or as it gets to the top of its consolidation range, becomes one of the best signs that resolution of the range may be coming. Anticipating a breakout is gratifying to the ego, but it rarely gives you a big advantage over those who get in after the breakout has already occurred. When a stock breaks out, expect to see large volume if the stock is going to have any meaningful follow-through.

As a minimum you want to see at least two times the daily average on a breakout to have any faith in the coming move. The larger the volume, the

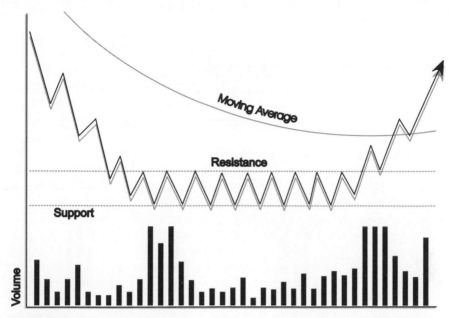

FIGURE 3.6 Long basing patterns can take years to develop and they only become of interest once the stock can break out of the range that had contained it for so long.

more likely the stock will follow through to the upside in a meaningful way over the weeks and months to come. As traders, we want to enter immediately on the breakout if we are aware that it is occurring. If you weren't alert to the initial breakout as it occurred, you usually get a second chance to buy, as the stock pulls back to its new level of support. At this point, you can gauge a stock's strength by the volume it trades as it pulls back. As with any pullback in a strong stock, expect the stock to come in grudgingly; that is, it finds very little selling pressure, and strong bidders are taking in the stock as it consolidates its gains. The strongest stocks will not pullback to support but rather build a "launching pad" where they go sideways for two to five days, then continue to move in the direction of the breakout.

Time Frame   As the name implies, a base may be made over a long period of time, in some cases, years. Let others do the dirty work of buying in the basing area and instead attempt to participate in the easier money following a breakout. Traders can find similar patterns on intraday charts, the only difference being the shortened time frame for the pattern to take shape.

Targets   Price targets are difficult to measure, but you can expect significant moves once a stock breaks out of any bottoming pattern. Many of

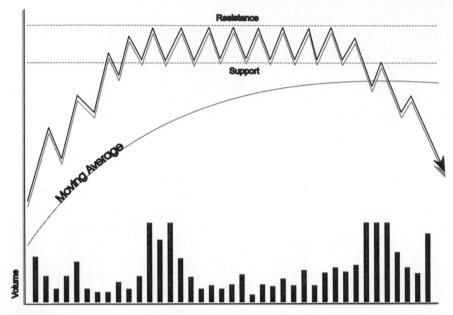

FIGURE 3.7 Tops typically take less time to develop so the basing top will be less common than the bottom, but when stocks break down from these formations, they often experience large selloffs.

the biggest moves in a stock's history have occurred after it breaks out of a long base.

A long base top is a lot less common than a stock that has put in a bottom. When a basing top has been completed by breaking down through support, it usually precedes a big turndown and is a safe candidate for short selling. Remember, the bigger the top, the bigger the drop (see Figure 3.7).

Saucer Bottoms and Tops

A saucer bottom or top is similar to a long base and has similar implications for the moves that will follow the completion of such a pattern. These patterns, like all the patterns we study, can be seen on all time frames, the one difference being the time they take to fully develop. One of the main differences between a long base and a saucer is it that it takes a lot less time for a saucer to develop. Like a basing formation, a saucer occurs after a stock has been heavily marked up or down and needs time to digest the gains or losses before heading in the opposite direction again. The main characteristic of a saucer pattern is the easy-to-recognize saucerlike shape it takes on.

Volume   The volume in a saucer has more distinguishable characteristics than when it is in a basing formation. The volume itself also takes on a saucer shape with heavier volume near the beginning and end of the shape. Another volume trait unique to the saucer is the common occurrence of a spike in volume near the middle of the formation. The most important volume trend is on completion of the pattern. Like the long base, a big surge in trading volume should occur as the stock clears resistance and enters a new trend.

Targets   Price targets here are also difficult to quantify, but a significant move can usually be expected on completion of the saucer. The volume surges near the midpoint of the saucer help us approximate when the stock may eventually break out of the pattern. If the surge in volume comes after six to eight weeks of recovery, we can expect the completion of this pattern in another six to eight weeks. By having an approximate time frame for the resolution of the pattern, we can position ourselves to anticipate what others will be doing. Call options often will be cheap during this time and are a fun and lucrative way to participate in what the crowd will be doing.

Cup and Handle Formation

The cup and handle formation is a slight variation of the saucer pattern (see Figure 3.8). William O'Neil, of the *Investors Business Daily*, often mentions this formation in his books and newspapers, which has helped make this pattern popular over the past decade. As the name implies, this formation got its name based on its resemblance to a coffee cup turned sideways where you can see the handle. These formations are usually referred to on the daily chart, where they typically take three to six months to form, although they can also be found on intraday time frames as well.

Although talked about a lot less than the traditional cup and handle, the *inverted cup and handle* is a valid pattern that often leads to continued downside once support is broken. It sets up just the opposite as the regular cup and handle.

Saucer Tops are less common, but can be very rewarding patterns to recognize as they show the new trend developing at an early stage (see Figure 3.9).

Bull and Bear Traps

When trading the breakout of any pattern, it is important to continually monitor the stock to determine whether it is performing the way we anticipate. Never forget that technical analysis is an art, not a science. If a stock

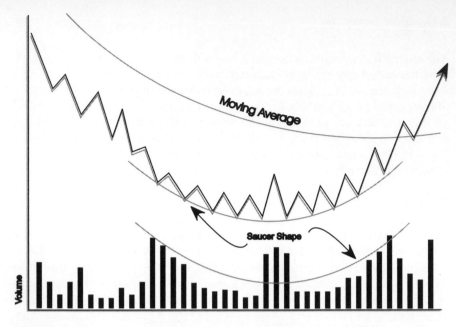

FIGURE 3.8 The saucer bottom derives its name from the rounded shape that develops.

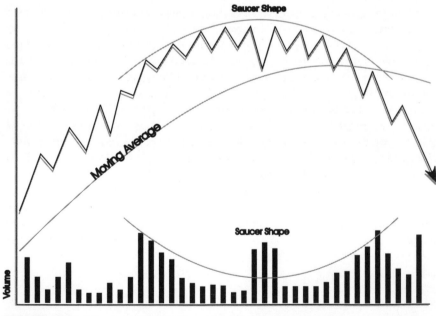

FIGURE 3.9 The saucer top is found in the stage 3 distribution area and it typically leads to lower prices.

isn't acting as expected, it is best to get out at a sensible, predetermined level instead of relying on hope. When in doubt, get out!

Occasionally, a stock will breakout to the upside, fall back into support, and then continue to decline to new lows. This action, which leaves all the new holders of stock with losses in their account, is known as a *bull trap*. When stocks break out to new highs it encourages many players to either add to existing positions or initiate new positions in a stock. This action of renewed strength also encourages short sellers to buy back their stock before they suffer large losses. What happens next is that this strength brings into play a large supply of stock that was not anticipated to be for sale at these levels. This new supply most likely comes from a large institutional holder that has been waiting for strength to sell out of any remaining position it may still be holding after the stock has made a big upward move. The new supply pushes prices back into the base and then down through the support level that was previously holding it up. Many times, the follow-through to the downside is quick and severe as stops are hit, short sellers become more aggressive, and those long the stock sell out before their profits evaporate. Those who did not have an exit strategy in place will quickly be left with losses that may become substantial. Having a plan in place for handling the risk will prevent these losses from becoming large and preserve trading capital for other ideas.

A bear trap is the reverse of a bull trap. A *bear trap* occurs when a stock breaks down through a support level, looks like it is going lower, then suddenly reverses back up through the previous resistance and continues higher. All the people who were looking to profit from further downside action by selling short are now "trapped" and begin to suffer losses as the stock moves higher. The completion of a bear trap can often lead to a big upward move due to the number of buyers competing to buy stock. At this point, the buyers who overcame the selling and forced the stock higher will become more aggressive. Another group of buyers—traders— will see a big surge in volume and be attracted to the potential for quick profits, which helps deplete any supply quicker.

A third group will enter a stock in this situation; they are the market professionals who specialize in "squeezing shorts." These savvy players will monitor the short interest in a stock and once they see that the short sellers are in trouble, they will enter the market and buy as much stock as they can to produce losses for the short sellers. Once the shorts have a position moving against them, they become overrun by fear and start to buy back their shares quickly to limit their losses. A final factor that helps the stock move up quickly is that the "weak holders" of stock were most likely shaken out of their positions as it first broke down and that element of supply has been taken out of the equation. The stock market is not a nice place and others are trying to take money away from those who are less informed or slower to act.

These traps can be vicious in the way they eventually play out if you are on the wrong side of them. Aggressive traders should be on the lookout for these setups because the profits that follow can be large and quick. Bull and bear traps can be found on a fairly regular basis on daily charts, and they occur with regular frequency on intraday charts. The reason that bull and bear traps occur more on these charts is that it is easier for market makers and specialists to manipulate stocks on a short-term basis. Many short-term players let their emotions get in the way of what the long-term trend may be. The ability to recognize these opportunities will allow you to make rational choices in your trading decisions.

These patterns, or false patterns, are important to recognize and will remind you to listen to what the market is telling you. If you get caught in a trap, you must act immediately by taking your loss before it turns into a disaster. If you are really aggressive, you may want to turn around and go the other way (if you were long on a false breakout, sell the long stock and then sell short additional stock).

CONTINUATION PATTERNS

Because trending stocks are where substantial money can be made in stocks, you need to be able to recognize patterns in trending stocks that favor the odds of a trend continuing. Investors can benefit from interpreting these formations by having a way to judge whether the action in their positions is healthy or indicates a potential problem. Swing and day traders stand to benefit the most from these patterns because they identify low risk areas to enter a strongly trending stock.

Even the strongest trends do not continue uninterrupted; they run into profit taking and periods where they simply must consolidate after a big price move. Continuation patterns are short- to intermediate-term formations that usually resolve themselves in the direction of the original trend.

Rectangle (Box)

This easily recognized pattern represents a pause in the trend during which prices move sideways between two parallel horizontal lines. These lines represent levels of support and resistance for the stock. The action inside a rectangle is sometimes referred to as a *basing period* (see Figure 3.10).

Time Frame   This can range from a couple of weeks to as long as three to six months on daily charts, or two to five days in intraday time frames.

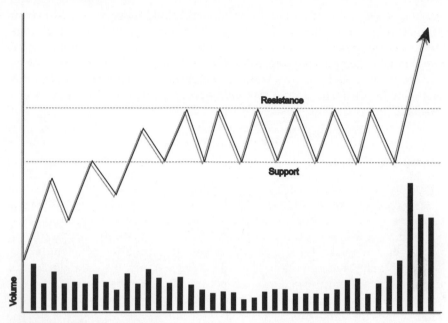

FIGURE 3.10 The rectangle formation is a stage 2 continuation pattern.

The hourly chart is the best time frame to study one of these consolidations on an intraday basis.

Volume Near completion of the pattern, volume will tend to pick up as a large seller or buyer may be "taken out." Once the pattern is completed, we want to see volume expand in the direction of the resolution of the pattern. It is also important to study the volume patterns as the rectangle develops. Look for increased volume on the days that the stock trades higher and lower volume as it pulls back to the support area of the pattern.

Moving Averages It is common for a rectangle to resume its move in the original direction after touching briefly on the 20- or 50-day MAs. Because the bullish rectangle occurs after a significant correction through time, this pattern is most likely to be found in Stage 2-3. For the bearish rectangle, this pattern will typically be found with a Profiler search of Stage 4-3 or late in the downtrend.

Price Objective A minimum price objective would be the point difference between the lower end of the rectangle and the point that the stock breaks out of the pattern. Adding this figure to the number that the stock actually breaks out from gives us an approximate price target.

Having a price target in mind in advance helps keep us disciplined enough to avoid the temptation of taking a quick profit when larger returns can be expected. Before entering the trade, we want to make sure there is a reasonable risk-reward ratio based on where we think the stock can trade up to and the level where it makes sense to place a stop. In this case, the best area to place a top will be just below the support level that forms the pattern.

Flags and Pennants

Flags and pennants are two of the most reliable continuation patterns there are. It is possible to make a living trading these patterns exclusively. These setups usually take no longer than two to three weeks to form providing swing and short-term traders a terrific opportunity for short-term profits. It is common for flags and pennants to form after a violent breakout of a Stage 1 Accumulation. The bullish flag is typically found during the early stages of an uptrend, while a bearish flag is most likely to be observed in a downtrending stock. In the Profiler, you are most likely to find bullish flags and pennants by searching out Stage 2-1 and Stage 2-2 stocks. The bearish flags and pennants are most likely to be found in Stages 4-1 and 4-2.

The formation of a flag or pennant is quite similar. The main characteristic they share is a surge in volume that results in a large directional price movement. For a bullish formation, the stock will rise quickly while a bearish formation sees the stock experience a sudden drop in price. After the initial surge in volume and the price movement, the stock will typically experience a low volume consolidation of the original move. For bullish flags (see Figure 3.11), the stocks consolidation will typically be marked by a series of lower highs and lower lows that can be seen on the individual candles. This slight downward move in the pattern resembles a flag blowing in the wind with the sharp move higher providing the "flag pole." For a bearish flag (see Figure 3.12), the stock will have a slight upward bias as the stock recovers from the quick sell off, making a short-term series of higher highs and higher lows. The proper time to enter a trade based on a flag is once the original direction becomes apparent again. For bull flags, that means to go long as the short-term downtrend is broken. For bear flags, traders should consider selling short once the bottom of the rising channel that forms the flag is broken.

Pennants are like flags in many ways. The formation of pennants occurs with a large and sudden directional movement that is followed by a short-term correction of the move. The corrective action that forms a pennant tends to have a much narrower range with the correction occurring

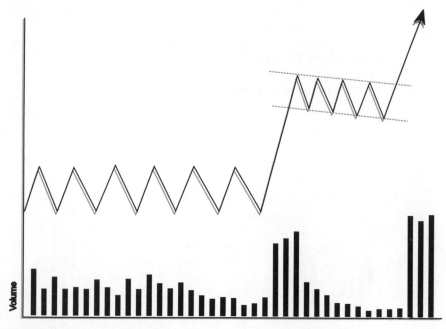

FIGURE 3.11   A bullish flag has a slight downward angle to it.

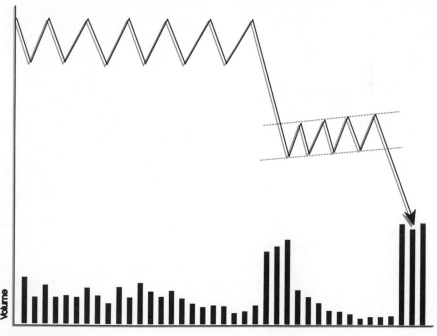

FIGURE 3.12   A bearish flag formation has a slight upward slope.

FIGURE 3.13   A bullish pennant has a low volume consolidation.

more through time than price. Bullish pennants (see Figure 3.13) are characterized by a sudden and sharp move higher that is followed by a narrowing range as the stock makes higher lows and lower highs. As the volatility is wrung from the stock, the formation resembles the shape of a pennant. Once the stock breaks past the upper descending trend line, the pattern is considered to be complete and that is when purchases should be made. Bearish pennants (see Figure 3.14) begin with a sharp move lower that is followed by a correction marked by lower highs and higher lows. The completion of a bearish pennant occurs when the stock breaks down through the lower ascending trend line, it is when this occurs that traders should consider selling short.

The following characteristics are shared by flags and pennants:

- Both formations are preceded by an almost vertical move up or down, which is the flagpole.
- The flagpole is characterized by heavier than usual volume (usually at least two times the average daily volume).
- The trend will consolidate for a period of 3 to 10 days as it digests he violent move; this consolidation forms the shape of the flag or pennant.
- The consolidation will often "bounce off" one of the short-term moving averages, with the 10-day being most common.

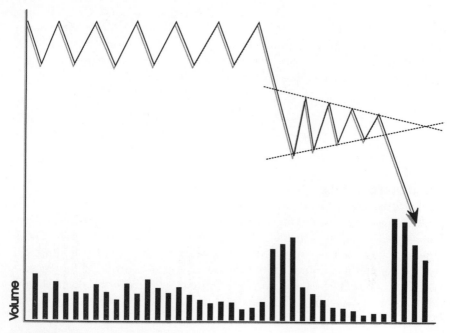

FIGURE 3.14   A bearish pennant.

- Both patterns typically take less time to develop in a downtrend.
- The patterns are considered to be complete once they resume in the original direction of the flagpole.

Targets for bullish formations are determined by taking the difference between the point of the original breakout and the top of the formation and *adding* that figure to where the bullish trend resumes on completion of the pattern.

Taking the difference of the point where the stock originally broke down and the bottom of the pattern and then *subtracting* that number from where the bearish trend resumes on completion of the pattern determines the targets for bearish formations. If the consolidation period extends beyond three to four weeks, the chances of continuing in the original direction are diminished.

Triangles

Triangles are continuation patterns that are formed most commonly in Stage 2 and Stage 4 stocks. The patterns are formed by drawing two trend lines along a price range that gets narrower over time. Because this pattern is always distinguished by two valid trend lines, we need a minimum of four reversal points for a true pattern to emerge (a valid trend line must be drawn by connecting a minimum of two points). While four reversal points are the minimum, it is more typical to see six reversal points before the pattern is resolved. The three types of triangles are:

1. Symmetrical.
2. Ascending.
3. Descending.

Symmetrical Triangle   The formation of a symmetrical triangle occurs as two trend lines converge to the apex of the pattern. The upper trend line slopes lower along a series of lower highs, while the lower trend line slopes higher as a result of higher lows. Whether the overall trend is higher or lower, it is estimated that after the pattern is completed, the stock resumes its original direction nearly three-fourths of the time. A symmetrical triangle can be found on daily as well as intraday charts and is not classified as being a bullish or bearish formation. A symmetrical tri-

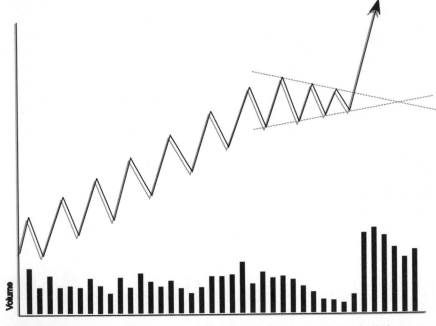

FIGURE 3.15   In a stage 2 uptrend, the symmetrical triangle is a bullish continuation pattern.

angle most often precedes a move in the direction of its most recent trend. Although the chances for a resumption of trend are likely, sometimes triangles do not act as expected and you must be prepared to take quick action, if necessary, to correct a trade that was entered on the assumption of a trend continuation.

Because a symmetrical triangle can be found in both uptrends (see Figure 3.15) and downtrends (see Figure 3.16), it is considered a Stage 2 or Stage 4 pattern. For the bullish symmetrical triangle, formation typically occurs near the middle of the uptrend. It is a pattern that will be found most often in Stage 2-2 in the Profiler. The bearish symmetrical triangle is just the opposite; it is typically found in Stage 4-2, which is approximately halfway through the downtrend.

Time Frame   The time frame usually resolves itself in six weeks to six months. A general rule is that it should break out somewhere between one-half to two-thirds of the horizontal width of the triangle. Knowing this gives us an approximate time when it is likely that others will become motivated to buy.

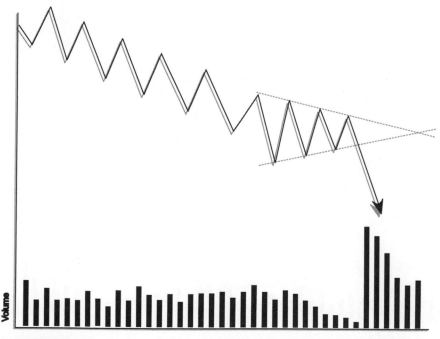

FIGURE 3.16   Symmetrical triangles typically resolve themselves in the direction of the original trend.

Volume   As with other consolidation patterns, volume should dry up while consolidating and pick up again on completion of the pattern. We also want to watch the volume trends as the stock consolidates between the boundaries of the triangle for clues to the strength of the stock and the intensity of the buyers and sellers.

Price Objective   A minimum price objective can be determined by measuring the maximum height of pattern and adding that figure (or subtracting if trend is down) to the point where the breakout (or breakdown) occurs.

Ascending Triangle   The ascending triangle is formed by a horizontal trend line which acts as reisistance and a lower ascending trend line. The upper resistance level forces prices lower as the supply is too difficult for the market to immediately overcome. These sell-offs become weaker and weaker as they progress, creating the upsloping line. This ascending line represents an increased demand on each pullback, where the buyers become more impatient to own the stock. When the demand finally overcomes the supply at the resistance level, the stock breaks out above it, completing the pattern. Because the ascending triangle is a bullish pattern, it will be found in Stage 2 stocks. An ascending triangle (see Figure 3.17)

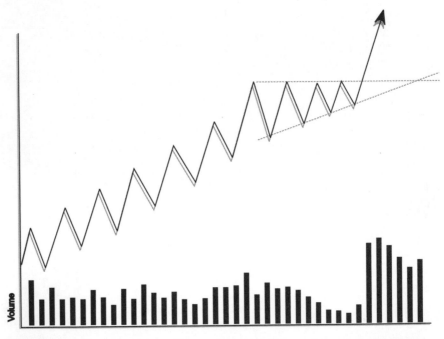

FIGURE 3.17   Ascending triangles are considered complete when the stock breaks above the upper resistance level.

typically occurs after the trend has been intact for a few months, so searching for these patterns is most likely to yield results in a Stage 2-2 or 2-3 search in the Profiler.

Time Frame As with the symmetrical triangle, the ascending triangle breakout usually occurs somewhere between one-half to three-fourths of the width of the pattern. The pattern becomes suspect if it does not develop by the time it has reached the ¾ point of the triangle. Another characteristic that makes for a stronger move out of the triangle is the amount of time it takes to return to the highs. A stronger stock will take less time to return to its highs between pullbacks, making the eventual breakout more likely to be a strong one.

Volume As with other consolidation patterns, we want bigger volume on rally days and lighter volume on pullbacks. Each time the stock rallies up to resistance, it should do so on heavier volume, as the buyers become more aggressive in their attempt to move prices higher.

Price Targets To derive a price target for an ascending triangle, you use the same method as for symmetrical triangles.

Descending Triangle This bearish continuation pattern is graphically represented by an upper declining trend line and a lower horizontal level of support (see Figure 3.18). The declining trend line which gives the pattern its shape indicates sellers are getting more aggressive as the supply overwhelmes demand at successively lower prices. The horizontal level of support will continue to hold prices up until the buyers dry up and supply pushes the stock through the support level. This action completes the pattern and it is where to enter short positions. Searching for these patterns will yield the best results by searching through Stage 4-2 and 4-3 stocks.

Time Frame Resolution of this pattern should occur at a point that is one-half to three-fourths the width of the pattern.

Volume Each successively lower rally up to the descending line will generally occur on less volume than the previous high. As the sellers overwhelm the buyers and the price breaks through the support, there is a large pickup in volume.

Measuring Finding a price target is the same as with the symmetrical and ascending triangles.

Here are a few things to remember about triangles:

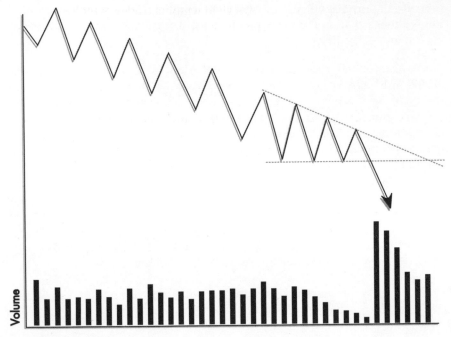

FIGURE 3.18   Descending triangles are considered complete when the stock breaks down through support.

- The odds strongly favor resumption of the trend once the pattern has been completed.
- The order of reliability for continuing the preceding trend is ascending, symmetrical, and then descending.
- Because triangles have a high reliability ratio, they can be used effectively for entering a trade when you anticipate a move.

As mentioned, when it comes to classic setups or patterns, you must be very cautious because entering and exiting with the crowd (who know these patterns as well) is not always the most profitable way to trade. These patterns invite the amateur pattern trader to the trade, and when these participants enter the mix, mass psychology takes over (fear and greed), we want to be in the trade long before the crowd enters. It is essential to have a plan that takes advantage of mass psychology in the markets. At MarketWise, we keep things simple and pride ourselves on taking the low risk/high potential reward entry before others. To consistently make money in the market, we use an anticipatory approach and can objectively recognize the technical events that may motivate the reactionary crowd into a trade where we are already positioned. Of course, even an anticipatory approach will not always yield winning trades, which is why it is imperative to map out our risk and plan for it with stops.

SUMMARY

The price trend signals associated with many common chart formations have a funny way of coming true. Is it that there is some type of natural law, a mathematical reason, or just that all the lemmings in the market respond the same way whenever one is revealed? Always keep in mind that none of them are anywhere near 100 percent reliable. Practice looking for the most prevalent formations to hone your skills and always protect your positions with stops.

CHAPTER 4

Going Short

Trading Like a Bear

Traders and investors sell a stock short when they expect its price to decline. Short sellers initially borrow shares to sell in the market from a broker. They make a profit when shares that the short sellers purchase at a lower price replace the borrowed shares. An analogy would be a car dealer who gets a call from a customer willing to pay $50,000 for a vintage Ferrari. The dealer might not have the car in stock, but could nonetheless promise delivery of it and ask the customer for payment up front. The dealer would now, in a manner of speaking, be "short" a vintage Ferrari. If he can procure the car—perhaps from another dealer—for less than the $50,000 his customer has paid him he earns a profit once he delivers the car to the customer.

Similarly, short sellers of stocks sell something they do not own, in hopes of replacing—or "covering"—it at a lower price. The short sale could be covered just minutes after the initial sale, hours after, or even weeks, months, or years after. But regardless of the time frame, short sellers always have the same goal: to close out the short position at a profit by covering the borrowed stock at a lower price. A patient seller who is bearish on XYZ stock's long-term prospects might short a hundred shares of it at $52 per share and cover the position two years later for $13 a share. That would represent a profit of $39 per share, or $3,900 for the hundred-share lot less transaction costs. It is up to the seller when to cover a short position, but if the stock pays a dividend, it goes to the owner of the stock, at the expense of the short seller who has to pay the cash out.

113

Also note that if XYZ's price rises, the short seller will have a paper loss, and if it is significant, he will have to put more money into his trading account to meet a margin call, just as if he had bought the stock on margin and the price dropped below a certain level. If the strategy works, the trader's profit is the difference in price the shares sold for and what the short seller paid to replace them less the transaction cost (commissions and fees). Remember, when you are short a stock, you buy it back to close (cover) the position.

Let's say a trader opens a short position in XYZ stock at $49 and days later buys it back for $44.00:

- *Opening trade:* Sold 100 shares short at $49.00
- *Closing trade:* Bought back 100 shares at $44.00
- *Gross profit:* $5.00 × 100 = $500.00
- *Net profit:* $500 − $30.50 (commissions and fees) = $469.50

A warning: You can be "bought in" (your position can be closed out by your broker or dealer) at any time if the broker is notified that he must return the borrowed shares to the owner. This is a risk mainly in thinly traded stocks and hot new issues, and for this reason initial public offerings (IPOs) cannot be shorted for 30 days. We must always be prepared for anything in the market, say that a hot new issue rises from $85 to $300 in three months, and then stalls. You short the stock at $280, but weeks later it continues to rise, to $310. You decide to hold your position, but while you are waiting for the price to fall, the owner of your borrowed shares decides the stock has peaked and sells the shares. Your broker discovers there are few more shares available in the market to borrow, so you will be forced to cover for a loss of $30 per share so that your broker can deliver the shares to the new owner. While this is an extreme example, it happens from time to time. It is a greater risk to the long-term trader than to the active electronic trader who covers positions intraday or within a few days.

Psychologically speaking, the general investing public finds selling short to be an unnatural way to engage the market. But traders who cannot accept selling short limit themselves to a mere fraction of the opportunities provided by a stock market constantly in motion up and down. The fact that stock prices have generally risen over time skews most traders and investors toward strategies favoring long positions. But keep in mind that there are always opportunities on both sides of the market.

Even when the tide is rising, there will be waves and ripples created by a market constantly pulling back to "digest" rallies. Indeed, in both bull and bear markets, there are daily opportunities to go short when stocks hit resistance levels. To the extent you learn to get comfortable selling short, you can increase your trading opportunities dramatically (and, we must add, your opportunities to lose money as well).

FINDING SHORTING OPPORTUNITIES

As the old saying goes, it takes longer to climb a tree than to hit the ground if you fall from it. The same holds true for stocks: They tend to fall much faster than they rise. For this reason, when you are looking for opportunities to get short you should consider stocks that have been up sharply and are toward the end of their distributon (Stage 3-3) or just beginning to decline (Stage 4-1). Stocks that have risen sharply and then undergo distribution and start to decline rank among our favorite short plays. Let's look at some of the things to consider when trying to spot promising shorts. First, a caution is in order: Do not attempt to force short trades when there are no good opportunities. Simply because you have a new tool at your disposal does not mean that everything you see is a nail waiting to be hammered.

The following strategic indicators are described in detail:

- Price/earnings ratio imbalance.
- Gap openings, generally following good news.
- The "loaded spring."
- Resistance failures, where stocks fail to make higher highs.
- Day-trading tape resistance.
- The short squeeze (a long play).

Price/Earnings Ratio Imbalance

Two yardsticks that fundamentalists use frequently are earnings per share (EPS) and the price/earnings ratio (P/E). EPS is considered the best tool for measuring a stock's overall returns. Earnings per share will either be distributed as dividends or retained to finance a company's growth. Calculating EPS is simple. For example, if, over a given period, XYZ Corporation earns $2 million, and has five million outstanding shares, the EPS would be $2,000,000 divided by 5,000,000, or 40 cents.

The P/E ratio is just as easy to determine. If XYZ stock trades for $100, then the shares would be priced at 250 times the 40 cents earned per share. Thus, the P/E ratio would be expressed as 250:1. In the lingo of investors, the stock would be trading at a "multiple" of 250.

This would be an extremely high ratio and a strong indication that XYZ stock is overpriced, although many growth stocks sport even higher multiples. What it implies is that investors think XYZ's future earnings will be much higher than current earnings. To take this a bit further, if the company earns 50 cents per share next year and the average multiple for it and similar companies is still 250, then the stock should be valued at $125 for the next year (EPS × P/E = 0.50 × 250 = $125). When no dividend is paid, the benefit to the shareholder comes in the form of market appreciation. This is one of the most important valuation techniques used by fundamentalists and other market players. Most mutual fund managers use this tool to help make investment decisions about growth companies. Accordingly, it behooves traders to closely monitor the stock whose price is rising faster than the earnings needed to support the rise, based on a given PE.

Question: If XYZ Corporation shares are selling for $100 and the company fails by $.02/share to reach its earnings target in a particular quarter, what might the impact be on the price of its shares?

Doing the Arithmetic   First, annualize the 2-cent (quarterly) shortfall, making it 8 cents per year. That translates to a $400,000 earnings shortfall over a 12-month period (8 cents × 5 million shares), implying earnings of 32 cents per share. If we multiply that by a 250 P/E (250 × 0.32), we find that the stock should sell for $80, or $20 per share less than its current $100.

If investors react even more negatively to the earnings report, causing the stock to fall by $30 instead of $20, this would reduce the implied P/E multiple to 218.75 or $70 × 0.32. If the stock should fall just $10/share, the P/E will rise to 281.24, or 90 × 0.32.

As P/E ratios continue to rise, the steeper the rise, the greater the likelihood that a company's shares will fall hard on negative news or a change in sentiment. Therefore, we like to short companies with a strong P/E ratio, especially when it is high relative to others in a given industry or to the index of which it is a part. If the stock has already begun to show signs of weakness and shows up as a Stage 4 stock on the Profiler, it makes this type of short even more tempting. A word of caution to those who are selling short ahead of earnings reports: Because it is difficult to predict earnings and even more difficult to predict the market's reaction to an earnings report, the risks are extremely high for this type of trade. One way to mitigate some of the risk that an earnings report brings about is to consider buying puts on the stock instead of attempting an outright short sale.

Gap Openings

Now let's look for a shorting opportunity from a technical analytic perspective. News can create shorting opportunities when investors react too strongly to seemingly favorable developments. When news is released in the market, we think of the stocks most immediately affected as *charged*. Such stocks become heated, reflected by a spike in volume and a quick run-up in price. Instead of joining the stampede, as a prudent trader, you should patiently wait for fading exuberance to set up an ideal shorting opportunity. By watching the ticker tape, you will see volume fall as the stock becomes too richly priced and enthusiasm begins to taper off. Remember, when stocks gap higher, market makers and specialists must provide liquidity. To protect themselves, they will often open a stock high enough to ensure that it will drop back quickly to reasonable levels, allowing them to profitably cover shares they shorted into the opening.

The price at which supply and demand are in true equilibrium does not occur on gap openings, when stocks rise or fall to some arbitrary level, but after the effects of the news have quieted. Stocks can certainly continue higher after a gap-up opening, but as a rule, when a stock opens significantly above its normal trading range, this will represent a good shorting opportunity, particularly when the stock is already in a Stage 4 decline (see Figure 4.1).

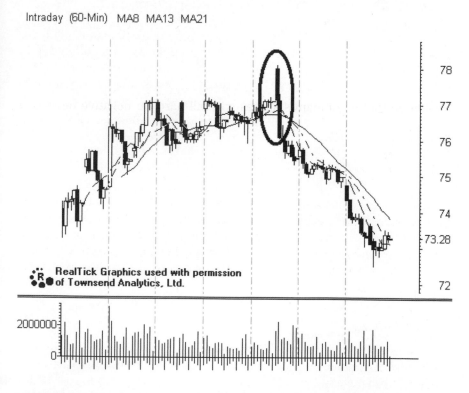

FIGURE 4.1 Stocks that gap open after experiencing a few days of strength are prime candidates for failure, particularly if the stock is in a longer-term downtrend.

The Loaded Spring

Figure 4.1 shows how a stock that goes too far too fast can become a ripe short. To deconstruct the action shown in this chart, it will be helpful to picture a spring that compresses as the stock surges to some short-term peak, then decompresses quickly as the stock falls back. The opposite holds true for the stock as it plummets to some low, then rebounds. In the first instance, a sharp rally, we should infer that the market makers are stepping up their selling at each higher price. As the stock rises, buyers will tend to become less enthused, resulting in a drop in volume. Then the rally will stall, with the spring fully compressed, causing sellers to become more aggressive as they seek to sell shares before the drop quickens. This inaugurates the spring's decompression phase. As it occurs, the spring will begin to compress again, ensuring that yet another bounce occurs from some low. The market makers, who shorted stock on the way up and near the high, return to cover their shorts by buying at or below the bid on the way down. This type of short sale goes against the primary trend and makes the strategy one that should be attempted only by the most disciplined traders who have a strong appetite for risk.

Watching the Level II (a visual display of all the participants bidding or offering stock and the depth of their liquidity) ticker, we can often see the dominant or "ax" market maker(s) sell stock at ever-increasing prices. As a particular market maker or group of them sell stock on the way up, they often reveal a shorting opportunity. The market makers in this case are selling into strength, eager to unload shares into the hands of buyers anxiously lifting offers. This continues as market makers sell at higher and higher prices. As the ax market maker sits on the offer and sells, and then moves to a "higher, best-offer" price, the stock is on the rise and the market makers could well be selling short.

Our Strategy   Be ready to sell short as the buying momentum begins to subside. You will need an uptick to get short. Under this scenario, we generally offer stock short at the ask price (this is known as a passive order, as opposed to an aggressive order where we sell to the uptick bid). That way, if our offer gets taken, we are creating the uptick that gives us a legal short sale. The downside is that we cannot expect to sell the exact top of a given rally. But be prepared to take some heat! The stock will generally go against you before it goes with you because to short stock on the offer, buyers must be willing to pay up for it, thus indicating a bullish bias. Once the market makers are no longer willing to sell at a higher best price, the stock will roll over and fall. The idea is to enter the short at a point where the stock will fall lower, putting you in a position to cover the short profitably. *The heat represents the risk of a trade going against you; this is* *common when shorting stock, and you need to be aware of it. In fact, you should expect it.* You must know where you are wrong and be prepared to cover if the stock continues to rise above your mental stop (the price at which you are prepared to acknowledge that you were wrong).

What to Look For

- Ax market makers, exchanges and electronic communications networks (ECNs) sit on the offer and remain there for several executions.
- The market makers and other participants hide their selling intentions by showing just a small portion of their actual order through the reserve feature. Just as you would not expect an opponent at poker to announce he has Kings, you would not expect a market participant to show his true buying and selling intentions on the Level II screen. In this case, participants often stay at the offer and sell several thousands of shares.
- Once they leave the offer, the ax market makers move to a "higher, low-offer price" and continue selling stock at this higher price. For example, the market maker may have sold 5,000 shares of XYZ at 23.25 and realized there was still demand for the stock; he raises his offer to 23.27 where he may sell a few thousand more shares before he once again raises his offer to a level where his price represents the lowest price available. The astute trader can use the Level II screen to recognize that this participant is a large seller of stock.
- As eager buyers see prices rise and rush in to lift the offer (pay the offer price), the ax market makers continue to sell more stock (short) to them.
- The lesson here is to shadow the market makers, not the eager (emotional) buyers.

How to Enter the Trade

- Your goal is to initiate the short at a point where the stock is likely to fall below your entry point, allowing you to cover the position profitably. At this point, you should ask yourself: *Is my downside bias greater than my upside bias?* If the answer is no, then do not take the trade. By concentrating on stocks that show up as Stage 4 on the Profiler, we should automatically have a bearish bias. It is important to remember that, except for scalp trades, you should always trade in the direction of the prevailing trend on a daily time frame because that is where your highest probability trades will come from. The Level II screen is a tool of execution and last minute fine tuning of your timing, it is not a reliable idea generator. The traders who attempt to trade based solely on the information in Level II run a tremendous risk of over trading based on the confusion that market makers attempt to create with games played out in the Level II screen.

- If stock is being sold by market makers at "higher, best-offer prices" and the buying volume is growing, this reflects strong upside momentum and is therefore *not* a good time to get short. It is best to wait for the velocity to slow down before entering a short sale.
- Prepare to sell short just as the volume starts to subside. You will enter your order to sell short just before the buying strength evaporates to be sure of getting an up tick bid, which is required for entry.
- When the ax market makers stop raising the offer price and either remain at the current offer or downtick to a lower offer, that is your cue that the rally has likely peaked. Once the market makers are no longer willing to sell at higher, best-offer prices, the stock will typically roll over and experience a quick fall. This will decompress the spring, pushing the stock lower and open the door to a profitable trade.

In the preceding scenario, the good news is that by selling into strength, you had an uptick to get short on- to sell on the offer, that is. The bad news is that you probably will not be good enough, or lucky enough, to sell the exact top so be prepared to take some heat. If you are unfamiliar with the Level II screen, additional training is available via online courses at www. Marketwise.com.

Risk Elasticity   To repeat: The stock will almost always go against you before it starts to decline and your short starts to move into a profitable position. Be prepared for that. If you are not, you will continually lose by covering the trade too soon. Shorts generally go against you before they go with you, but as the cliché goes, it is easier to slide down a hill than to climb one. When the stock finally rolls over, it will tend to fall faster than it rose.

Be careful not to sell short too soon, such as when volume is strong to the buying side. Remember, stock tends to follow the trend. As noted, if the market makers are selling stock while buying volume is strong, upside momentum is at work and therefore not a good time to get short. But as the volume begins to subside, you should be preparing to sell short in the moments before supply overwhelms demand, causing the stock to fall.

If you are wrong, the stock will stall or consolidate and flatten out, then rally anew with another high-volume run-up. If this happens, admit your mistake and bail out immediately. If you are right, however, the stall will occur with accompanying lower volume and a reversal will follow. The stock will then fall on its own weight with increasing volume and fear. *The risk of being wrong is called speculation and is what this profession is all about.* Figure 4.2 illustrates the theory of risk elasticity.

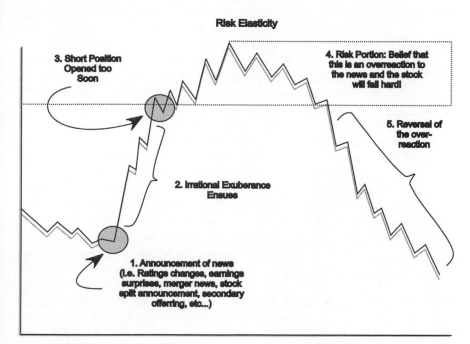

FIGURE 4.2 Risk elasticity does not mean taking uncalculated risk; it simply means that, because of the uptick rule, most shorts will go against you before going with you. Accordingly, you must set your risk stops prior to getting in the trade. Risk elasticity applies to Level II trading, news stories, and many other scenarios, but the concept is the same, know in advance where you are wrong!

Exchange Rules Governing Short Selling Rule number one is that orders to sell a listed security short on an exchange may be executed only on a *plus tick* or *zero-plus tick*. A plus tick (uptick) is a price higher than the last reported price. A zero-plus tick occurs when the last trade for the security was made at the same price as the trade before and *that* trade was higher than the one that preceded it. The plus tick or minus tick carry over from the previous day.

Nasdaq Short Sale Rules Nasdaq's short sale rule prohibits member firms from entering short sales in Nasdaq National Market (NNM) securities at or below the current inside bid (instead of an actual sale or tick taking place) whenever that bid is lower than the previous inside bid. An opening bid is a *down bid* if it is lower than the previous day's closing bid, or the same as the previous day's closing bid if that closing bid was a down bid.

Sell-Order Tickets   *Sell orders must be identified.* The Securities and Exchange Commission (SEC) requires that all sell orders be identified as either long or short. No sale can be marked "long" unless the security to be delivered is in the account of the customer or is owned by the customer and will be delivered to the broker by the settlement date. If securities owned by the customer are not to be delivered to complete the sale, the customer is going *short-against-the-box.*

Short Scalping   If you were attempting to day trade or *scalp* shorts, ideally you would sell stock on the offer and cover on the bid. This contrasts with scalping long, where one buys on the bid and sells on the offer. In practice, neither is easy, and your broker might make more in commissions than you do in profits. The strategy of shorting is suited to a longer time frame than scalping, unless the momentum is high. If momentum is high, the risk factors also go up, therefore scalping is a very difficult game! For many new traders, attempting to scalp stocks from the short side of the market is not a good idea.

Computerized Trading Platforms Track the Rules   When stock is shorted, electronic trading systems can do some of the housekeeping and compliance for the trader. For one, the system will ascertain whether there is stock to borrow when you click a box to sell short. The system will also check for uptick compliance, since you cannot sell short when a stock is falling. This uptick rule is in place to prevent stocks from being pounded to zero by short sellers. The question then is, why are market makers and specialists allowed to short stock without an uptick? The exchanges would say it is because the professionals provide liquidity to the market. They buy stock when supply exceeds demand and others won't buy, and they sell stock when demand exceeds supply and others won't sell. Therefore, they provide a service to the market and are not held to the same rules. I suppose I agree with this as long as the rules are not abused (as they sometimes are).

Day-Trading "Tape Resistance"

You can spot resistance levels on the tape, or time-and-sales window, by monitoring a stock's ups and downs and noting how it acts at each price level. If a stock butts up against a given price several times without getting past it, this indicates a psychological resistance level—and possibly a good shorting opportunity. The tape tells the tale in real time. For example, if shares of XYZ Corporation were trading $78.37 bid, $78.45 ask, but with a range between $78.00 bid, $78.81 ask over an hour, you might infer that XYZ is a good short at $78.81, where tape resistance is evident, and a good buy at $78.00, where tape support is evident. An important caveat is that, once you are in a trade, never deviate from the time frame of your entry strategy. In this example, the positions are day trades. But what might appear to be good support and resistance levels within a one-hour time horizon might be completely outside the support and resistance levels for a three-day pattern. To repeat: Never mix a day trade with a swing trade.

The Short Squeeze (Be Cautious)

When there is a downtrend, inexperienced traders will tend to get aboard late by joining the short sellers. Traders who are new to the short side of the market will often fall victim to this deadly mistake. Market makers often know when the short sellers are in the market, or at least have a good feel for it, since many customers of the firms for which the market makers work are sending in short orders. As a downtrend continues, market makers will often bid the stock to cover their shorts on Level II. An indicator of this would be a consistent number of market makers joining the bid or going "high bid," as well as trades going off at the offer price. *When market makers pay the offer price for a stock and you see Level II offers rolling counterclockwise (meaning that the number of participants offering stock is decreasing while the number of participants bidding for stock is increasing), this indicates that a short squeeze is in motion.*

As they continue to bid the stock, demand begins to overwhelm supply and prices start to rise, squeezing out short positions. Market makers will continue to bid the stock higher to squeeze out shorts until their maximum threshold of pain is achieved. At this point, market makers who were short earlier are now squeezing the amateurs. The amateurs are covering their belated shorts, and the market makers are only too happy to oblige by taking the other side. Quite often, just as the amateurs are covering their shorts (buying back shares), market makers (who covered earlier) are once again selling them shares (short), causing the stock to fall again, putting the pros back "in the money." Understanding this common tactic of market makers will help you detect their maneuvering early, allowing you to join them, and to fade the amateurs (see Figure 4.3).

Executing the Short Sale   Competence at executing orders is critical to success in trading. Following are suggestions for both passive and aggressive short sellers.

Passive Short Seller   In general, short sellers must be aware of more side issues than long buyers. First and foremost, you must determine if there is stock available for shorting. You can access the short list from most computerized systems or view the web site of the firm you trade with. Also, you must anticipate a stock's fall and lead the trade by selling into minor strength (not to be confused with trend). Many short sellers will see a stock trade against them for a period before the trade goes their way, however, a short position can move with you with lightning speed.

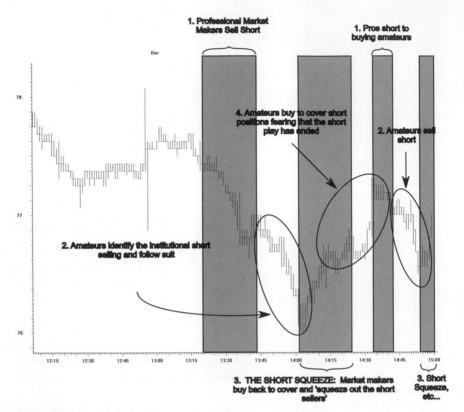

FIGURE 4.3 The sort squeeze in action, a play-by-play from David Nassar: "I know this was a classic short squeeze because I traded it. I watched the market makers on my Level II screen like a hawk. I won't tell you I sold the top and bought the bottom, but I made a nice profit by seeing the trend develop and noticing that the stock started to strengthen around $76.25, where the squeeze began."

Methods of Entry

1. Place a limit order by selecting the Archipelago (ARCA) exchange at or above the offer with short sale box marked.
2. Let the market come to you and take your offer.

Aggressive Short Seller With the short sale box marked, you can attempt to sell short at the market and the system will try to fill the trade on an uptick. There is a true skill to being able to get short in a falling market, and it takes practice to get proficient. Many times you will not want to flood the system with market orders you do not feel have much chance of getting filled. Instead, you need to pick an offer price where you see a bounce coming.

Methods of Entry

1. Place ARCA limit order at the bid, selling short with short sale box marked.
2. Be prepared to cancel and change limit order to lower bid if market moves lower.

What Stocks Can You Short?   The brokerage firm that you work with must have the stock in its inventory or be able to borrow it for you to sell it short. Reputable firms keep a list indicating which stocks are available for shorting each trading day. The short list should be posted on the firms' web sites and built into your computerized trading software.

Borrowed stock comes from margin accounts. When you open a margin account, you agree to have the stock you bought on margin available to be borrowed or hypothecated. Because you bought stock on margin, the firm you trade with lent you capital to make the purchase (up to 4:1 margin); therefore, they require you to sign a hypothecation agreement. This agreement allows the firm to lend the securities (up to a certain percentage) to other firms that they have relationships with, so that those firms can send shortable shares to their customers. The short seller must also have a margin account to short stock.

Because the concept of shorting begins with margin, we should review what margin is and how it works. While this information won't make you any money, it will help you understand how your account is handled, and this is important.

MARGIN ACCOUNTS

Shorting stock begins with the concept of margin because you must have a margin account to short. Margin implies the ability to borrow money from a brokerage firm, based on certain criteria. The regulators have established these criteria based on NASD, NYSE, and SEC rules, as well as house rules set by brokerage firms that can be even more stringent.

The term *margin* refers to the minimum amount of cash or marginable securities a customer is required to deposit on the purchase or sale of additional securities. The rules governing margin are as follows, though subject to change without notice.

The Federal Reserve Board's Regulation T

The Securities Exchange Act of 1934 grants the Federal Reserve Board (FRB) authority to regulate credit extended in the purchase of securities. The FRB established Regulation (Reg.) T, which sets forth the equity or margin required in a purchase of securities in a margin account. Regulation T stipulates which securities may be purchased on margin based on rules by which all member firms must abide. A cautionary note: If a firm permits higher margin or credit than that established by regulation, *stay away!* These firms are breaking the rules, and therefore you should not entrust your business to them.

Opening a Margin Account

The customer is allowed to place orders for investments and asked to deposit only a percentage of the cost, currently 50 percent. The account holder must pay interest on the unpaid balance at the broker's call rate, or the margin interest rate set by the firm. The securities purchased are held in what is known as *street name*. This allows the firm that lent you the money or stock, to lend the securities to other firms with customers who might want to borrow your stock for a short. By holding the stock in street name, they can do that. If it were held in your name and owned without margin, then they could not lend it for shorting.

When investors decide to deploy their money, the broker calculates the amount that needs to be deposited, or the margin requirement, needed for the purchase. The margin account also serves as a potential source of cash. If you have fully paid-for securities in the account and need cash, the firm can lend money against those securities (or margin them) up to the current margin limits set by the FRB.

The margin agreement contains the following:

- *Credit agreement:* Discloses the terms under which credit is extended.
- *Hypothecation agreement:* Gives the firm permission to pledge (hypothecate) securities held on the margin.
- *Loan consent agreement:* Gives the firm permission to lend the customer's securities held in a margin account to other broker/dealers.

By borrowing a portion of the purchase price, investors can *leverage* their capital. For example, compare the return on investment for a customer who purchases 1,000 shares of XYZ stock at $16 per share in a cash account to the investor who has bought those shares on margin (assumes 2 : 1 margin, but rules allow up to 4 : 1):

- *Cash customer:* If the price of 1,000 shares of XYZ, purchased for $16,000 ($16 per share), increases to $24 per share, the customer's equity in a cash account will be $24,000, representing a 50 percent return ($24,000 less the initial outlay of $16,000 equals $8,000 and $8,000 divided by $16,000 is 50 percent).

- *Margin customer:* If the purchase is made in a margin account, the customer's equity will be $16,000 ($24,000 less the loan of $8,000 on the initial purchase price that is still owed to the firm), representing a return of 100 percent on the initial cash outlay of $8,000, less interest paid to the broker/dealer for the $8,000 loan. Conversely, if the market turns down, a customer with a margin account would experience a magnified loss.

The current required minimum deposit is 50 percent of the overnight marginal securities, aka 2:1 margin. This means that for every $100,000 worth of securities purchased, the customer must deposit $50,000, and the broker/dealer advances the other $50,000 as a loan against the securities. (Note: Day traders need to put up just 25 percent, effectively giving them 4:1 margin, but there is a minimum account size of $25,000 for "pattern day traders." Also, house rules override federal securities rules.)

Marginable Securities include:

- Listed stocks on an exchange, such as the NYSE.
- Stocks listed as eligible for trading in the Nasdaq National Market.
- Certain OTC securities designated by the FRB.

Rules Pertaining to Forced Liquidations

- If a margin customer does not meet a Reg. T call by the third business day and no extension has been applied for, the broker/dealer must liquidate enough securities in the account to satisfy the account in full.
- The firm must *freeze the account for 90 days.*
- No credit may be extended to the customer during that period.
- For amounts less than $1,000, the broker/dealer can choose to take no action.
- If payment is received for the "buy side" within three business days from the trade date, the account is unfrozen.

Calculating Initial Requirements

An active margin account is characterized by the following:

Current market value (CMV)

Debt (DR) = The loan from the broker firm on which interest is charged

Equity (EQ) = The difference between the market value and the loan balance

Example 1: Buy $64,000 Worth of ABC Stock

A customer opens a margin account and purchases 1,000 shares of ABC at $64 per share:

$$CMV - DR = EQ$$

$$\$64,000 - \$32,000 = \$32,000$$

Reg. T initial margin call: $32,000 (50 percent of the cost of the stock).

The equity in an account represents that portion of the securities fully owned by the customer.

Excess Equity

Excess equity (EE) is the amount by which the customer's equity exceeds the Reg. T requirement; it generates buying power.

- A customer can use the excess equity to buy more securities or withdraw the excess equity in cash.
- To determine buying power, multiply the dollar amount of excess equity by 2.

$$EQ - Reg. \ T \ (50 \ percent) = EE$$

$$EE \times 2 = Buying \ power$$

As the market value of a stock goes up, equity in the account increases. The debit balance stays the same until cash is either deposited to or withdrawn from the account.

The customer purchased 1,000 shares of ABC. If the stock appreciates from $64 to $72 per share:

- The CMV of the account rises from $64,000 to $72,000;
- debt remains $32,000;
- equity increases from $32,000 to $40,000;
- the increase in CMV increases equity dollar for dollar, and
- the Reg. T requirement is 50 percent of the CMV (which is now $72,000), or $36,000.

$$
\begin{array}{ll}
\$72,000 & CMV \\
-32,000 & DR \\
\hline
\$40,000 & EQ \\
-36,000 & Reg. \ T \ (50 \ percent) \\
\hline
\$4,000 & EE \\
\end{array}
$$

Using Excess Equity to Purchase Stock   The customer now has excess equity of $4,000, which can be used to purchase $8,000 of stock. (Because the current Reg. T requirement is 50 percent, $4,000 meets the initial deposit requirement for an $8,000 purchase.)

Calculating Maintenance Requirements

NASD and NYSE Requirements

- *$2,000 minimum deposit:* Overriding all initial margin requirements is the NASD/NYSE margin rule requiring that each new margin account be opened subject to a minimum deposit of $2,000. An investor must meet the larger of either the 50 percent Reg. T requirement or the NASD/NYSE requirement of $2,000.

Minimum Maintenance Requirements

The NASD/NYSE maintenance requirement for long common stock is 25 percent of the CMV. Therefore, if your account falls below this level, you receive a call to bring the account back up to minimum maintenance.

Maintenance Calls

- A maintenance call is sent to a customer whose account falls below the minimum required equity level of 25 percent for long and 30 percent for short positions.
- If the equity in the account falls below $2,000 due to a change in market value, no maintenance call will be issued.
- The NASD/NYSE requirement prevents a brokerage firm from lending money to a customer or permitting withdrawals of cash or securities by a customer whose account equity is $2,000 or less.

Change in Market Value

If an account drops below the required minimum maintenance level, the firm will *mark to the market* (calculate the difference between the maintenance margin and the current equity in the account), and the client will receive a maintenance call. The following is an example of the change in status of an account in which the market value of 100 shares of stock initially purchased at $60 falls to $36.

Example 2: Stock Is at $60 per Share

$6,000	(100 percent)	CMV
−3,000	(50 percent)	DR
$3,000	(50 percent)	EQ
$1,500	(25 percent)	NASD/NYSE requirement

Stock Drops to $36 per Share

$3,600	(100 percent)	CMV
−3,000	(50 percent)	DR
$600	(16.7 percent)	EQ
$900	(25 percent)	NASD/NYSE requirement

Because the equity in the account is less than the required minimum maintenance, the customer will receive a maintenance call.

To calculate minimum maintenance, multiply the current market value by 25 percent. A maintenance call must be met by depositing cash, depositing any security acceptable to the firm, or liquidating securities in the account promptly to bring the minimum equity back up to 25 percent.

Short Sales and Margin Requirements

You must also learn a separate set of rules for short selling to help you maintain your account, a responsibility that will always precede trading strategies.

- The Reg. T initial margin deposit requirement on short sales is 50 percent of the sale proceeds.
- Reg. T uses the phrase "150 percent of the current market value of the security" to indicate that the full amount (100 percent) of the sale proceeds *plus* an additional 50 percent initial margin on the position must be deposited in the account.
- The deposit is expected promptly but is required within three business days.
- Reg. T initial margin on short sales can be met either with cash or through the deposit of marginable securities with a loan value equal to the amount of the call.

Example 3: A customer sells short 100 shares of Ajax Corporation for $60.

To calculate the margin deposit requirement, use the following:

$6,000	Proceeds	(100 percent)
+3,000	Reg. T	(50 percent)
$9,000	CR	(150 percent)

NASD/NYSE Minimum Deposit on Short Sales

When establishing a short margin account, a customer must always deposit a minimum of $2,000. Even if only $100 worth of stock is sold short, the client must still deposit at least $2,000.

Margin Maintenance Calls on Short Sales

NASD/NYSE margin maintenance requirements on short positions (30 percent) are higher than on long positions (25 percent), and house maintenance requirements on short positions might be even higher.

When a short sale position moves adversely, under minimum requirement rules, there must be enough credit in the account to cover 100 percent of the now-higher current market value, and 30 percent of the current market value must also be on deposit as margin. This is the equation for determining a customer's equity in a short position:

$$CR - SMV \text{ (short market value)} = EQ$$

Example 4: Customer sells 1,000 shares short.

Assume that a customer sells short 1,000 shares of stock at $64 for proceeds of $64,000, which are credited to the margin account. The customer then deposits the 50 percent Reg. T initial margin requirement of $32,000 for a total of $96,000, which equals 150 percent of the market value:

$64,000	(100 percent)
+32,000	(50 percent)
$96,000	CR (150 percent)
−64,000	SMV
$32,000	EQ

Shorting-against-the-Box

Selling short-against-the-box is the same as a regular short sale except that the customer already owns securities identical to the securities being borrowed to sell short. (Note: You may need your broker's permission to put on this type of position.)

- *Tax benefits:* Customers borrow a stock they already own to sell short-against-the-box primarily for tax deferral.
- *Closing out:* A short-against-the-box transaction is closed out when the customer instructs the broker/dealer to release the box stock and pair off the long and short positions. A customer can close a short-against-the-box position in either of two ways: by delivering the long position to the lender or by buying stock to deliver to the lender.

SUMMARY

Short selling gives you more opportunities to trade. To become proficient at short selling, you must execute trades. The emotions involved with shorting should mellow quickly, and once they have, you will be indifferent about whether you are going long or short. Active traders see the market with an open mind and have no preconceived opinions. Read and react, don't try to predict!

CHAPTER 5

Other Trading Vehicles

Using E-Mini Contracts, Options, and Exchange-Traded Funds for Additional Leverage

This chapter provides an introduction to futures trading, with special emphasis on the electronic markets that in recent years have helped to level the playing field between day traders and institutional professionals. Not long ago, it was almost impossible for the retail customer to compete. While the professionals had direct access to exchange bids and offers, the little guys always lagged a crucial step or two behind, dependent on their broker for timely quotes and executions. And while the upstairs traders could execute with just a few keystrokes, the little guys had to phone their broker and dictate a string of instructions that literally tongue-tied the order itself. For this wonderful opportunity to become some institutional shark's lunch, the customer paid round-turn commissions of $100 or more. In a game where split seconds often separate winners from losers, and where hefty transaction fees steadily erode hard-earned profits, the amateur's disadvantage was all but insurmountable.

All this has changed dramatically in just the past few years as electronic communication networks, or ECNs, have evolved. The ECNs go by such names as Archipelago (now an exchange and traded publicly under the symbol AX) and Instinet, and they now blanket the earth. Exchange-based trading of stocks, commodities, and options has gone "virtual," and the markets are accessible to anyone in the world who possesses some basic computer equipment, a trading software platform, and a sound Internet connection. Nowadays, day traders can access the same real-time bids and offers as the pros and can buy or sell stocks, futures, and options instantaneously with a few keystrokes like the most sophisticated arbitrageur. Commissions have come down dramatically as well, allowing the retail customer to focus on trading tactics without being distracted by their attendant costs.

This electronic revolution in trading, permitting 24-hour access to markets around the world, has fueled explosive growth in the securities business. Activity in futures markets in particular has mushroomed and, in just the past decade, contract volume has soared, greatly exceeding the dollar value of all common stocks traded in the United States.

All this has come in response to the trader's dream of finding the perfect vehicle. If such a thing existed, it might have the following characteristics:

- Has excellent liquidity.
- Has narrow spreads.
- Shortable on downticks.
- Trades day and night.
- Provides single-source liquidity.
- Requires a relatively small amount of capital.
- Offers substantial leverage as well as tax benefits.

Well, it turns out there is such a vehicle: the E-mini S&P 500 contract. This contract is the most active among a growing list of electronically traded futures.

WHAT IS AN E-MINI S&P 500 CONTRACT?

While your focus may initially be on trading equities, you will undoubtedly always have an eye on what "the market" is doing. Most traders and investors have an opinion of what "the market" will do at anytime and for individuals, there is a very effective way to trade the market. First we should define which market we are looking at and the leading market index is the S&P 500. The S&P 500 is a widely diversified group of stocks that can be traded very efficiently by way of the S&P 500 E-mini futures contract.

The term "E-mini" applies not just to the S&P 500, but to contracts that have been created for electronic trading. The contracts are known as "mini" because the value of the contract is a fraction of the pit traded contracts. The S&P E-mini is one-fifth the value of the pit traded contract, meaning that for each point the S&P 500 makes, the E-mini value will change by $50/contract. The minimum movement for the E-mini is a .25 point increment, which would be $12.50 per contract.

E-MINI SYMBOLS

The equity index futures contracts are on a quarterly basis, with contracts expiring, as noted, in March, June, September, and December. These months are standardized by the exchanges and have not changed since the contracts' inception.

CME

March	H
June	M
September	U
December	Z

For example, an E-mini contract expiring in June 2007 would be found on RealTick® by typing in the following: /ESM7. (Note: The /ES root remains constant while the last number changes yearly.) Let's take a quick look at the specifications (specs) for the ES contract as promulgated by the CME:

Specification of the ES Contract

- *Ticker symbol:* ES.
- *Contract size:* $50 times the S&P 500 stock index.
- *Price limits:* 5 percent, 10 percent, 15 percent, and 20 percent.
- *Tick size:* .25 index points = $12.50 per contract.
- *Contract months:* March, June, September, December.
- *Trading hours (Central Standard Time [CST]):* 5:00 P.M. on Sunday until Monday at 3:15 P.M. Closed M-T from 3:15 to 3:30 P.M. and from 4:30 to 5:00 P.M. Open remaining hours until Friday at 3:15 P.M.
- *Terra Nova (www.terranovaonline.com) trading hours:* Consistent with Chicago Mercantile Exchange trading hours. Note: Different brokers may modify access. The E-minis are closed daily from 3:15 P.M. to 3:30 P.M. CST.
- *Last trading day:* Up to 3:15 P.M. CST on the third Thursday of the contract month.
- *Final settlement date:* The third Friday of the contract month.
- *Position limits:* Determined in conjunction with existing S&P 500.
- *Position limits:* Please check www.cme.com.
- *Rollover:* Expiration of one futures contract takes place at 8:30 A.M. on the third Friday of the expiration month; typically the rollover into the next contract occurs the Thursday prior to expiration. Unlike equities or some other futures, there is no delivery on these contracts, only

cash settlement. The rollover period prior to expiration phases out the expiring month, transitioning to the new lead, "front or nearby," month, which is normally the most liquid. The new contract will officially become lead on the Thursday before the week of expiration. Example: March futures are set to expire on Friday, March 21; however, volume starts to roll to the June contract on Thursday, March 13. From a trading perspective, what you need to know is that you should begin trading the June contract on or soon after March 13 for that is where the liquidity will be.

INITIAL AND MAINTENANCE MARGIN REQUIREMENTS

As a rule, the CME and Chicago Board of Trade (CBOT) set the minimum performance bond needed to initiate a trade in an E-mini contract; however, each brokerage house can increase (but not decrease) the amount needed to trade a particular futures contract. As of this writing, the initial margin for the E-mini S&P contract is $3,938 per contract, while the maintenance margin rests at $3,150. Day traders are able to cut these rates in half (as long as the position is not held overnight), and Terra Nova adheres to the margin directives of the CME. This is significant leverage, since, with the E-mini S&P at 1247, the investment value-trading instrument becomes $62,350 (1247 × $50). For those interested in the E-mini Nasdaq-100 issue, the multiplier is $20, allowing a trader to leverage $32,540 (1627 × $20) with a current performance bond listed at $2,250 (initial margin). The Dow mini-contract (YM) has an initial margin of roughly $2,500, leveraging an underlying investment value of $53,000 (Dow 10,600 × $5 multiplier = $53,000).

Caution: The margin on any futures contract can change without warning. If it increases while you are in a trade, you may be required to add more money to your margin account. This is called a margin call.

TREATMENT OF SETTLEMENT

Every futures account is marked-to-market, allowing a trader's account to be either debited or credited at the end of each business day. Equities, on the other hand, settle on the transaction date plus three days (T+3). This forces futures traders to deal with losses almost immediately, possibly triggering a margin call—a demand from your brokerage firm to you, the trader, to supply the necessary cash to hold the position. If you do not meet a margin call, your brokerage firm has the right, as stated in the account papers you sign when opening the account, to sell out your positions to meet the margin call, which could result in a loss to your account. Given the wide margin between a trader's cash deposit and minimum maintenance, a disciplined approach is critical.

THE E-MINI CONTRACT VERSUS THE PIT-TRADED CONTRACT

What about using the pit-traded S&P contract instead of the E-mini? Exchange members trade in an octagon-shaped pit on the floor of the CME. Their membership in the exchange, which can be bought or leased, allows them to capture the edge implied by the spread between bids and offers. With the multitudes of games played between members in the pits, it is no surprise that average daily volume is closer to 55,000 in the full-size contract, almost one-tenth the volume seen within the E-mini contract (ES).

As mentioned, the ES is one-fifth the size of the pit-traded contract (SP); therefore, traders have the option to buy or sell five E-mini contracts and close the position with a single offsetting contract in the main futures pit. The opposite is true as well. Another factor that lures traders to the E-mini is the contract's lower initial and maintenance margins.

The SP (full-size futures contract) has an initial margin of $19,688 or approximately five times that of the E-mini (please check with www.cme.com for possible changes), as well as a maintenance margin of $15,750. The multiple is $250 (from 1246 to 1247, a one-dollar change represents $250), and the minimum tick size is 0.10 or $25. The full-size contract is traded either in the pit or on Globex, while the E-mini is solely electronic. We recommend that you stick with the E-minis and the 5:1 ratio, since that will help facilitate scaling in and out of positions.

PRICE AND PERCENTAGE LIMITS

The CME establishes daily price limits on a quarterly basis. The trader should check periodically on the CME's web site the limits for both the SP and ES. The limits vary, depending on the volatility of the underlying contract. If the SP contract is lower by 5 percent during a particular session, trading can occur at or above this limit offer for 10 minutes or until 3:30 P.M., whichever occurs first. Trading will then halt for 2 minutes if the primary futures contract is still limit offer at the end of the 10 minutes or at 3:30 P.M. Trading will then resume with the 10 percent limit in effect.

If the 10 percent limit is reached prior to 2:30 P.M., trading can occur at or above this limit. If the primary future is limit offer and the New York Stock Exchange (NYSE) has declared a trading halt (due to a 10 percent decline in the Dow Jones Industrial Average [DJIA]), trading will completely halt. Resumption will take place with the 15 percent limit in effect when 50 percent (capitalization weights) of the underlying S&P 500 stocks reopen. After 2:30 P.M., trading can occur at or above this limit for 10 minutes. Trading will then halt for 2 minutes if the primary futures contract is limit offer at the end of 10 minutes. Trading will resume with the 15 percent-point limit in effect.

As far as GLOBEX is concerned, the 5 percent upside price limit will be removed at 9:28 A.M. This only applies to the upside price limit and does not affect the downside price limit. GLOBEX trading will be delayed until 7:00 P.M. if an NYSE trading halt is in effect at 4:00 P.M. or if the primary big S&P 500 futures is locked limit at 4:15 P.M. All these limits might sound confusing, and these limits are not met very often; nevertheless, a trader should be aware of the aforementioned possible scenarios.

SINGLE-SOURCE LIQUIDITY

Further helping the success of the E-mini contract is single-source liquidity through the CME. By definition, this means there are no market makers or specialists—only price, size, and depth of the market. Each trade sent via GLOBEX is directly routed to the CME, and it is easily matched without having to line up with a particular ECN. During the day, an average inside bid/ask can experience size up to several hundred contracts. If the bid is at 100 contracts, this would translate into a notional amount of $6,235,000 ($50 × 1247 × 100).

When trading E-minis, all market participants have equal access. This means single-source liquidity will not discriminate between an entry-level trader going up against a multibillion-dollar hedge fund. A first-in, first-out (FIFO) matching algorithm is used by the CME's Globex electronic trading system. Whoever is in first will have priority, effectively creating a level playing field.

E-Mini S&P 500 Contract (IESZ7), Level II Speculative Trading Example of E-Mini S&P 500

- *Performance bond:* Approximately $3,938.
- *Settlement of ES contract:* 1247.
- *Gain in position:* $0.00.
- *Value of account:* $5,000.

- Position closed the following session at 1257.
- Gain in position is 10 points × $50 = $500 per contract.
- Variation margin (change in account): $500 credit.
- Value of margin account: $5,500 minus commissions.

This is a 10 percent gain with a relatively small amount of capital tied up.

E-MINI STANDARD & POOR'S 500 AS A HEDGE

When hedging a portfolio with E-mini futures, an investor *long* $125,000 in a basket of stocks could *sell two* E-mini contracts (with ES at 1272, this would be just over $125,000 in underlying value) to hedge a potential downturn. Of course, an investor's portfolio should be a good representation of the S&P 500 Index. When would a hedge make sense? Most likely if a trader had a short-term bearish outlook, thus offsetting a potential decline in one's portfolio. A trader could also implement a hedge for risk management purposes, sacrificing upside reward for protection in case the market turns lower.

Hedge Example
- The S&P Index falls 10 percent to 1116.
- An investor's portfolio falls 10.5 percent.
- S&P futures falls 10 percent to 1122.30.
- Initial value of portfolio: $125,000.
- Value of portfolio after decline: $106,250.
- Profit/Loss on portfolio ($18,750).
- Initial price on S&P futures contract 1247.
- Price after decline 1122.30.
- Difference 124.7 points.
- Gain on short hedge $6,235 (124.70 times 50).
- Multiply by number of contracts (2) $12,470.

Unhedged Scenario
- Loss on portfolio ($18,750).
- Gain from futures hedge N/A.
- Total profit/loss ($18,750).

Hedged Scenario
- Loss on portfolio ($18,750).
- Gain from futures hedge $12,470.
- Total profit/loss ($6,280).

TAX ADVANTAGES WITH THE E-MINI

If the E-mini contract is chosen, traders automatically get favorable tax benefits. Futures *in general* are taxed at 60 percent long-term rates (20 percent) and 40 percent short-term rates (ordinary income rate assumed at 39.6 percent). Form 6781 from the IRS is used and the amount is then carried forward onto Schedule D. An example follows:

Suppose Trader A makes $10,000 trading the Spiders (SPY), while Trader B is able to make $10,000 trading the E-mini. What would be the tax advantage to Trader B?

Trader A: $10,000 in gains × .396 = $3,960

Trader B: $6,000 × 0.20 = $1,200

$4,000 × .396 = $1,584

Total = $2.784

A savings of $1,176, compared with Trader A.

THE E-MINI NASDAQ 100

Another popular futures trading instrument is the E-mini Nasdaq contract, or NQ. This contract mimics the NDX Index, or Nasdaq-100 contract, and can be compared with the Exchange Traded Fund contract, the QQQQs, as well (covered later in this chapter). As shown here, the NQ contract has a multiplier of $20 versus $50 for the ES contract, whereas the tick size is $10 per 0.50 index points per contract:

NQ Contract Specifications

- *Ticker symbol:* NQ.
- *Contract size:* $20 times E-mini Nasdaq-100 futures price, or one-fifth pit-traded contract (ND).
- *Price limits:* 5 percent, 10 percent, 15 percent, and 20 percent.
- *Minimum price fluctuation (tick size):* .50 index points = $10 per contract.
- *Contract months:* March, June, September, and December.
- *Regular trading hours (CST):* 5:30 P.M. (Chicago Time) on Sunday until Monday at 3:15 P.M. Closed Monday through Thursday from 3:15 to 3:45 P.M., and from 10:00 P.M. until 11:00 P.M.
- *Terra Nova trading hours:* 6:30 A.M. to 7:00 P.M. CST Monday through Thursday, and 6:30 A.M. to 3:15 P.M. CST on Fridays. Note: The E-minis are closed daily from 3:15 P.M. to 3:45 P.M. CST.

- *Last trading day:* Trading can occur up to 3:15 P.M. (Chicago Time) of the Thursday prior to expiration Friday.
- *Final settlement date:* The third Friday of the contract month.
- *Position limits:* Position limits work in conjunction with existing Nasdaq-100 position limits. Please check www.cme.com for the current levels.

CHICAGO BOARD OF TRADE MINI-DOW FUTURES USE $5 MULTIPLIER

This mini-size contract trades with a $5 multiplier of the Dow Jones Industrial Average, which is a price-weighted index of 30 of the largest, most liquid U.S. stocks. The pit-traded contract is standardized at $10 instead of $5, and has a prefix ticker symbol of DJ. The $5 multiplier has a prefix of YM. The YM contract has an average daily volume of 80,000, with open interest of 80,000. This compares with open interest in the ES and NQ of 1,000,000 and 350,000, respectively. Since the inception of the electronic Dow Futures $5 multiplier on April 4, 2002, liquidity continues to build and is showing promise for day traders. Nevertheless, until liquidity increases, traders should generally avoid trading the YM contract. The ticker symbol on RealTick® follows the CBOT symbology, which is as follows:

CBOT Ticker Calendar Month Symbols

January	F
February	G
March	H
April	J
May	K
June	M
July	N
August	Q
September	U
October	V
November	X
December	Z

Specifications of YM Contract

- *Ticker symbol:* YM.
- *Contract size:* $5.00 times the DJIA.
- *Minimum price fluctuation (tick size):* 1 index point = $5 per contract.
- *Contract months:* March, June, September, and December.

- *Regular trading hours (CST):* 5:30 P.M. on Sunday until Monday at 3:15 P.M. Closed Monday through Thursday from 3:15 to 3:45 P.M., and from 10:00 P.M. until 11:00 P.M..
- *Terra Nova trading hours (CST):* 6:30 A.M. to 7:00 P.M. Monday through Thursday, and 6:30 A.M. to 3:15 P.M. on Fridays. Note: The E-minis are closed daily from 3:15 P.M. to 3:45 P.M..
- *Last trading day:* Trading in expiring contracts closes at 4:15 on the last trading session.
- *Final settlement date:* The third Friday of the contract month.
- *Position limits:* 50,000 contracts in all contract months (combined limit for DJIA futures and options and mini-sized DowSM futures: $2).

WHO REGULATES FUTURES TRADING?

The Commodity Futures Trading Commission (CFTC) regulates all commodities and futures accounts, working closely with Congress, the National Futures Association, and the futures industry to maintain a flexible structure tailored to the specific products and participants in a given market. The CFTC worked with the Securities and Exchange Commission (SEC) to repeal an 18-year ban on trading single-stock futures and provide legal certainty for the over-the-counter derivatives market.

Because futures (CFTC) and stocks (SEC) are regulated by different bodies, a trader must open a separate account for each fund to be used for futures and must segregate equities trading. The formation of separate accounts should work to the advantage of futures traders, since a disciplined approach will in most cases be very different from that of the equities trader, who may bring to the task a day trader's mentality.

PROGRAM TRADING AND FAIR VALUE

According to the NYSE roughly 55 percent of the weekly volume on the NYSE in a recent year was generated by program trading related to the index futures and options contracts. With the futures industry witnessing 800 percent growth in electronic contracts over the past five years, some 750,000 futures accounts, 27 million stock accounts, and 5 million option accounts could be affected when program trading takes place. Program trading derives from a calculation of *fair value*.

If you have ever tuned to the financial news shows during the day, you have probably heard this term. Its derivation is somewhat complicated, but it is used by traders mainly for two purposes: (1) to predict whether the stock market will open higher or lower on a given day, or (2) to determine exactly when institutional buy and sell programs will be activated. Thus, an abrupt movement in market prices could result in a profit or loss for anyone in the market at that time. Therefore, it is to your advantage to be aware of fair value.

The simplest way to think of *fair value* is that it is the cash value of the S&P Index, plus the interest you would pay your broker to buy all the stocks in it, minus the dividends paid on those stocks. Strictly speaking, the little guy would not use fair value in the manner just described, since buying or selling all the stocks listed in the S&P 500 Index would be logistically impossible as well as prohibitively expensive. But institutional arbitragers can manage the expense because (1) they possess the technological means to execute trades simultaneously in each of the S&P Index's 500 stocks; and (2) they can arbitrage those shares profitably against S&P 500 futures contracts. In practice, institutional trading desks do this kind of thing all day long, and that is why it is essential for the professional arbitrageur to know, at any given moment, whether buying the S&P 500 futures is a better deal, theoretically, than buying a basket of 500 S&P stocks for cash.

The *fair value premium* needed to answer this question is simply the theoretical futures price minus the cash index price, as described previously. Once fair value has been reckoned, it is a simple matter to determine whether the S&P 500 futures are overvalued or undervalued relative to the cash S&P 500 Index. If the futures are overvalued, traders sell S&P 500 futures contracts while buying an equivalent dollar amount of all the S&P 500 stocks. Alternatively, if the futures are undervalued relative to the basket of stocks, then they buy futures contracts and sell the basket comprised of S&P 500 stocks.

Let's say the futures are fairly valued on a given day when trading exactly 10 points above the cash index. This means the two would be theoretically in line if the cash S&P 500 Index were trading at 1237.00 when the futures were at 1247.00. However, if demand for the futures increased momentarily, pushing them up to 1250.00 with no corresponding increase in the cash index, the two would be out of line relative to fair value. This in turn would create an arbitrage opportunity enticing to anyone able to sell the futures while simultaneously buying the 500 stocks for cash. If this were attempted all at once by several large players, the effect would be to quickly "arb" the cash and futures back into line, so that they would again be separated by a 10-point spread.

TABLE 5.1 Fair Value Indicator

If S&P Fair Value Is:	If S&P Futures Are:	Market Open Indication
−5	+15	+20 or Dow + 200 points
+5	+10	+5 or Dow + 50 points
−5	−20	−15 or Dow − 150 points
+5	−20	−25 or Dow − 250 points

PREDICTING THE OPENING

As mentioned, it is possible to predict how the stock market will open each morning by using the fair value indicator. Table 5.1 shows how this is done. Looking at the top row of the table, you see that fair value for that day has been calculated at −5. This means the futures should theoretically be selling at a 5-point discount to the cash index when fairly valued. But in early morning trading, before the Dow Industrial stocks had opened, the futures are actually priced +15 above the cash S&P 500 index. This 20-point differential is typically interpolated to mean that the Dow will open up 200 points that morning. Try working through the other rows. When you have grown comfortable with the calculation, try it with real numbers when the market opens. You will not have to calculate fair value yourself, since it is available on CNBC and in numerous places on the World Wide Web. If you want to do so, however, you can use the following instructions, with the correct calculations taken from the CMEs web site.

HOW TO CALCULATE FAIR VALUE

Fair value is the theoretical assumption of where a futures contract should be priced given such things as the current index level, index dividends, days to expiration, and interest rates. The actual futures price will not necessarily trade at the theoretical price, as short-term supply and demand will cause price to fluctuate around fair value. Price discrepancies above or below fair value should cause arbitrageurs to return the market closer to its fair value.

The following formula is used to calculate fair value for stock index futures:

$$\text{Fair Value} = \text{Cash}\left[1 + r\left(\frac{x}{365}\right)\right] - \text{Dividends}$$

If you would like to delve even more deeply into the fair value mathematical concept, a Web search on those two words will turn up voluminous information.

WHAT ABOUT EXCHANGE-TRADED FUNDS?

By definition, an exchange-traded fund (ETF) is a basket of stocks that reflects an index; however, it is *not* a mutual fund. An ETF will give traders instant exposure to a diversified portfolio of stocks, as well as allow them to short on a downtick, receive a dividend, and buy on margin. Annual expenses exist but are lower than those, even, of a no-load mutual fund. A few examples are Standard & Poor's Depository Receipt Trust Series I (SPY), Nasdaq 100 (QQQQ), and Diamonds (DIA).

When comparing the SPY contract to the ES contract, the capital needed to trade two ES contracts is roughly $8,000 ($125,000 in underlying security). On the other hand, buying a thousand shares of the SPY ($124 \times 1,000 = \$124,000$, approximating the underlying value of the two ES contracts) will require margin of either $62,350 (Regulation T, applied if kept overnight) or $31,175 if 4:1 margin is achieved ($25,000 minimum in a trading account, as well as being classified as a "pattern day trader"). One S&P 500 E-mini contract is equivalent to 500 shares of SPYs. That means the recent average daily futures volumes of 700,000 contracts is equivalent to a daily volume of 350 million shares of SPYs. SPY average daily volume is only a fraction of this amount (closer to 45 million shares changing hands).

Breaking down the Spiders, one SPY contract is equivalent to one-tenth the value of the S&P 500 Index, trading off the American Stock Exchange (AMEX). In fact, most ETFs trade on the AMEX. The minimum price increment, or tick, is $0.01 for the SPY, compared with $12.50 for the E-mini. When trading the SPYs, the trading platform involves specialists and different ECNs, whereas the E-mini is only on GLOBEX and, as noted, is single-source liquidity. Comparing transaction costs from bid/offer reveals roughly 7 to 10 basis points for the Spiders, while only 2 to 4 basis points for the E-mini. An ordinary broker can be used for trading the Spiders; however, when buying or selling the SPY contract, there is an annual management fee that equates to roughly 18 basis points (0.18 percent). Additionally, a quarterly dividend is paid one month after the ex-dividend date for the ETF contract, kept in a non-interest-bearing account.

Studies have shown that the management fee and dividend have kept the index from either keeping up with or possibly outperforming the ES contract. Compared to cash required to open a trading account, the initial investment for an SPY contract is $25,000 if one plans to day trade, whereas an E-mini futures account opens with as little as $10,000. Other differences involve favorable tax benefits when trading the ES contract, noted earlier.

THE QQQQs

The Nasdaq-100 Index Tracking Stock, or QQQQs, is an ETF representing ownership in a unit investment trust established to accumulate and hold a portfolio of the equity securities that comprise the Nasdaq-100 Index. (Note: The QQQQ's initial market value approximates $\frac{1}{40}$ of the value of the underlying Nasdaq-100 Index.)

Comparing the NQ futures contract to the QQQQs highlights differences akin to those between the ES and the SPY. The trading platform for the QQQQs involves both a specialist and ECN, while the NQ contract is available only on the GLOBEX platform (hence the letter "E"). With respect to the QQQQs, there are small transaction costs of 7 to 18 basis points per year, a small dividend, and annual expenses of roughly 18 basis points. Moreover, the QQQQs do not trade as often as the electronic contract. An investor can buy options on the QQQQs, as well as the NQ futures.

E-MINI IS HARD TO BEAT

The E-mini, especially the ES contract, is made to order for day traders. Although a futures trader needs to open a separate account, the offsetting advantages more than compensate for the inconvenience. They include great liquidity, low margins, high volatility, single source liquidity, preferential tax treatment, and expanded trading hours. The ES contract can be used to effectively hedge a portfolio, and its fixed relationship to the SPY, with one ES contract equal to 500 shares of SPY, is appealing to institutional traders. Similarly appealing is the NQ contract, which is equal to roughly 800 shares of QQQQs. Relative to ETFs, the E-minis are not weighed down by either annual expenses or dividends. Those who trade the E-minis are obliged to respect their high leverage, since this implies commensurately high risk.

PUT AND CALL OPTIONS

We need to discuss one more popular trading vehicle to round out the chapter: options. There are two types of option contracts—call options and put options. Options resemble insurance contracts in some ways. Both have a stated life span, a premium value, and an exercise or payout contingent on certain conditions being met. In this chapter, we highlight the many similarities and differences between options and insurance contracts.

A BRIEF HISTORY

Options developed as a way to manage certain types of risk, not as a vehicle for speculation. They were created by merchants who wanted to ensure there would be a market for their goods at a specific time and price. One such merchant was the ancient Greek philosopher Thales. As a student of astrology and general businessman, Thales predicted a great olive harvest in the spring while it was still winter. With little activity during this time of year in the olive market, Thales negotiated the price he would pay for olive presses in the spring. The great harvest came. Thales collected on his predetermined price, and then rented these presses out to other farmers at the going rate.

The best known historical account of the options contract was the tulip craze in seventeenth-century Holland. Tulip traders and farmers actively traded the right to buy and sell the bulbs at a predetermined price in the future to hedge against a poor tulip bulb harvest. A secondary market began to develop that was traded, not by farmers, but by speculators. Prices were volatile as the market exploded; members of the public began using their savings to speculate. The Dutch economy collapsed in part because speculators did not honor the obligations in the contracts. The government tried to force people to honor the terms but many never did, throwing options contracts into bad repute throughout Europe.

About 50 years later (in 1711) in England, the public began to buy and sell options on the South Sea Company. Fascinated by the explosion in the company's share prices because of the trading monopoly it had secured from the government, investors quickly drove up South Sea's stock price 10-fold. When the firm's directors began selling stock at these high levels, significantly depressing the price, speculators were unable or unwilling to deliver on their obligations. Option trading was subsequently declared illegal.

Option trading slowly made its way to the United States after the creation of the NYSE in 1790. In the late 1800s, puts and calls could be traded in the over-the-counter market. Known as "the grandfather of options," Russell Sage, a railroad speculator and businessman, developed a system of *conversions* and *reverse conversions*. It uses the combination of a call, a put, and a stock to create liquidity in the options market, a system that is still used today. Despite these positive steps to encourage options as a legitimate trading vehicle, the 1900s took a toll on the reputation of options. Bucket shops, option pools, and other shady setups lent to the unscrupulous view of the option trader. After the 1929 Crash, the SEC was formed and the regulation of options trading began.

Herbert Filer, the put/call dealer and author of *Understanding Put and Call Options*, testified before Congress during this time, with the objective of shedding positive light on the option industry. Congress approached this hearing with the distinct intention of striking out options trading. They cited their concern that the vast majority of option contracts expired worthless, 87 percent to be exact. Congress assumed that all trading was done on a speculative basis but Filer replied, "No sir. If you insured your house against fire and it didn't burn down you would not say that you had thrown away your insurance premium." The SEC ultimately concluded that not all option trading is manipulative and that properly used, options are a valuable investment tool. The Investment Securities Act of 1934, which created the SEC, gave the SEC the power to regulate options.

PUTS AND CALLS AND STANDARDIZED OPTIONS

The first and most important element of an option contract is the underlying security—the asset on whose value the option is constructed, including but not limited to stocks, bonds, indexes, commodities, futures, or interest rates. Standardized contracts trade on the option exchanges, and their uniformity allows traders to quickly enter and exit positions without having to negotiate every characteristic of the contract. There is a very small market for some options that are individually structured for a particular investment situation. These products are designed by structured products trading desks at different brokerage firms, and are priced and traded over the counter. Their uniqueness makes them illiquid and difficult to access, so we will limit this discussion to standardized contracts.

An option contract can theoretically be constructed on top of any underlying asset. The most widely traded options are equity and index options based on stocks and stock indexes. All options derive their existence from an underlying security and are therefore considered derivatives. Futures, swaps, forwards, and warrants are other types of derivative products.

SHARES PER OPTION

Options that trade in the United States were standardized in the 1970s and are backed by the good faith and credit of the Options Clearing Corporation (OCC). Option contracts represent 100 shares unless they have been specially adjusted due to a stock split or corporate merger. Be aware of adjusted option contracts, for if what they represent is not perfectly understood, they can be hazardous to your trading health. Most adjusted contracts represent a different share amount than the widely accepted 100. For stocks that have undergone 3-for-2 stock splits,150 is a common number. Companies that have listed options, which get acquired, may have to adjust their contracts to reflect the merger. So instead of a contract representing 100 shares of XYZ, it may be altered to represent 80 shares of ABC, plus $3 per contract. These adjustments can and will affect the price of a contract, and many individuals have suffered heavy losses because they neglected to try to fully understand something that sounded too good to be true. A caveat: If a contract looks like free money, have your broker confirm with the exchange what, specifically, it represents. The CBOE web site is also a good resource to confirm the specifications of a particular contract.

PRICING

The factors that affect the price of the option are:

- Price of the underlying stock.
- Striking price of the option.
- Time remaining until expiration of the option.
- Volatility of the underlying stock.
- The current risk-free interest rate.
- Dividend rate of the underlying stock.

The price of an option reflects the value per share of the underlying stock, plus time premium. Because contracts are standardized at 100 shares, the formula to calculate their value is easy: Multiply the price of the option times the number of round lots of stock represented, times 100 shares. (Note: One hundred is called the multiplier, and it is important to remember for index options.) If a contract is quoted $2.50 bid and $2.75 ask, a trader would receive $250 ($2.50 × 1 × 100) for selling it, or would pay $250 ($2.50 × 1 × 100) if buying it. If 10 contracts were traded, a seller would receive $2,500 ($2.50 × 10 × 100) and a buyer would pay $2,750 ($2.75 × 10 × 100). Even if the contract were to represent 150 shares in our 3-for-2 stock split example, the premium would still represent the cost of each share in the contract.

Option contracts all expire in a uniform and consistent manner: the Saturday following the third Friday of the month they represent. However, they will stop trading on different days based on the exercise style: American or European. American options stop trading on the third Friday of the month and can be exercised at any time during the life of the contract. European options stop trading on the Thursday before the third Friday of the month.

All equity options are American, whereas many index options are European. For example, the OEX or S&P 100 are American, but the SPX and S&P 500 are European. There are other differences between the two expiration styles, but we will not discuss them all here, since our focus is American-style options.

Prior to the expiration of American-style options, if you own an option contract and would like to exercise it to buy or sell shares, you must instruct your broker to do so. At expiration, the option will either be in-the-money (ITM) or out-of-the-money (OTM).

If it is OTM, the contract will expire worthless and literally disappear from your trading account before the market reopens. If it expires ITM and you are short contracts, you will most likely be assigned the stock. If you are long contracts and they expire ITM by at least a certain fractional amount, the contracts will automatically be exercised on your behalf by the OCC. To remove any confusion or potential problems, you should explicitly inform your broker you would like to exercise options instead of leaving the decision up to the broker. Confirm the details with the broker so that there are no mistakes. Monday morning is the effective day or trade date of the exercised position in the account, so if the net position is long or short, Monday will be your first chance to trade the shares after expiration.

While equity options require that stock be used to settle the terms of an exercised contract, index options settle in cash. Using the 100 multiplier, if the underlying index is, say, 105, traders exercising a 100-strike call will receive the 5-point difference times 100, times the number of contracts. It would be impossible to deliver full and fractional shares of the S&P 500 or other similar indexes, and for this reason cash settlement is used.

SYMBOLOGY

Option symbols are unique and are constantly changing. Each option has a root symbol that represents the underlying security. This root symbol can have one, two, or three characters, but no more. The last two letters in an option symbol always represent the month first, then the strike price second. A through L represent the months for calls while M through X are used for the months with puts. Most option strikes are given in 5-point increments starting with the letter A for 05, B for 10, C for 15, and so on. Option chains on software trading platforms or the Internet are the best way to determine an option symbol. However, many option traders have kept themselves out of trouble because they have learned the basics of the symbology. For example, you give an order to buy DELL puts to open and your broker reads back the symbol DLQAJ. You're able to catch his error because you know that the letter A is for calls, not puts.

SETTLEMENT

The settlement period for options is T+1 (trade date + 1 day) meaning the option trade settles the next business day. Stock trades, on the other hand, have a T+3 settlement period that requires paying for the trades by the third business day after the trade is executed. For most of us, that means the funds have to be in the account before a trade is placed. Most brokerage firms will not allow an options trade unless the account already has the required capital at the time of the trade.

IN-THE-MONEY OR OUT-OF-THE-MONEY

The reference to an option as being in-the-money, at-the-money, or out-of-the-money communicates that the stock price is above, below, or at the strike price of a particular call or put contract. The money reference is not a statement about the profitability of the particular option. In fact a trader cannot make any assumptions about the profitability of an option based on its mark-to-the-market value. Call strikes below the stock's price are ITM, strikes at the stock's price are at-the-money, and call strikes above the stock's price are OTM. Put strikes that are above the stock's price are ITM, strikes at the stock's price are at-the-money and strike prices below the stock's price are OTM. Options have *intrinsic value* to the amount they are ITM. An OTM option has no intrinsic value, only time value depending on time to expiration and the volatility of the underlying entity.

RIGHTS VERSUS OBLIGATIONS

Option trades can be entered in four basic ways:

1. Buy to open.
2. Sell to open.
3. Buy to close.
4. Sell to close.

This discussion includes the opening and closing designations, but ultimately you will either be long or short the contracts in your account; it is the initial trade that opens the position. Buying to open gives you the *right* to *exercise* the terms of the contract, normally done when it is favorable to do so. If you have bought calls to open, you have the *right* to buy stock at the strike price of your option contract. If you buy puts to open you have the *right* to sell stock at the strike price of your contract.

Traders who sell to open have the *obligation* to abide by the terms of the contract and must either buy or sell shares at the price that is being *assigned* to them. Traders who sell calls to open have the obligation to sell stock at the stated strike price of the agreed-on contract. If any of the parties do not live up to their end of the agreement, the OCC will initially cover the defaulting side of the trade. It will then pass all responsibility to the brokerage firm to settle the difference. These situations are why clearing firms require brokerage firms to make initial clearing deposits in the millions and millions of dollars.

OPENING AND CLOSING TRANSACTIONS

One of the concepts to know in advance of actual trading is how option trades are either opening or closing. Opening a trade establishes the option position in the trader's account while closing a trade removes the position from the account. Whether a trade is opening or closing is an indication that must be made at the time the trade is placed. The following are the possible order entry combinations: buying calls to open, selling calls to open, buying calls to close, selling calls to close, buying puts to open, selling puts to open, buying puts to close, and selling puts to close.

OPEN INTEREST

When an option trade is entered through an electronic platform or directly with a broker, the order must indicate whether it is opening or closing. This indication does not affect the order's ability to get traded, but it does affect open interest. Open interest is the number of positions open across all exchanges in one particular contract. For example, the first time a series is rolled out, all contracts in that series have zero open interest, and nobody has traded the newly issued series, much less established a position. If a contract has zero open interest and one trader enters an order to buy to open at $3 and another trader sells to open at $3, this trade creates an open interest of one contract. If these two traders agree to close out their positions before the end of the day, open interest would be back to zero. The open interest number is calculated on a net basis at the end of the day, that is, all opening versus all closing trades. If the trade examined in the previous example was done many times in one day, volume may end up being heavy but the open interest may hardly change.

The OCC is responsible for clearing all option trades at the end of the day and confirming that each buy order is matched with a sell order at the right time, at the right price, for the right contract, and the right amount. During this clearing process, open interest is determined as each trade is matched and cleared. Before the market opens the next day, the OCC reports the newly calculated open interest from the previous day to all the exchanges, brokerage houses, and quote-vending firms that have contracted to receive the information.

Open interest is a measure of activity and liquidity, and it is no coincidence that the front month, at-the-money contract typically has the highest open interest. Institutional and active traders use these contracts in different styles and strategies, but the majority of volume for at-the-money contracts comes from the creation of institutional synthetic positions and delta hedging (both of which are discussed later in this chapter). This additional open interest provides liquidity when needed. For example, if a particular option has an open interest of 20 and one trader wants to open a 100-contract position, the trade may eventually get done but the price will be negotiable as liquidity is found at a higher or lower price. This trader will eventually represent 83 percent of the option's market, and when it comes time to close the position, liquidity will again become an issue.

Like a stock, illiquid options have larger spreads; there just are not as many players jockeying for the inside position. If a large trader wants to buy an illiquid stock, the price can increase substantially as she tries to pry stock away from sellers at higher and higher prices. In the options market, market makers have additional liquidity tools at their disposal. The options market maker can use a combination of stocks and options to provide liquidity for the customer through the use of synthetic positions.

OPENING ROTATION

The world does not stand still when the U.S. equity markets close; indeed, events continue to take place and prices change even after we go to bed. American stocks listed on foreign markets and futures trades that take place throughout the night on the GLOBEX allow trading day and night around the world. Trading in Europe and Asia can significantly affect the perceptions and attitudes of U.S. markets. News events can cause price vacuums or gaps when markets open for trading in the United States.

Options are derivatives and derive their price from the underlying security, but the security must first be priced before the option can be. Each option exchange must re-price each contract every day before trading begins. This event is called opening rotation. Each market maker will consider the opening price of the stock, any changes in historical and implied volatility, and how the remaining time until expiration affects the price of each option. Any orders entered before the open that the market maker is aware of may also impact the opening option price. Market makers traditionally went through each option in a predetermined fashion, calling out to the crowd of traders assembled around their posts on the exchange floor. Members of the crowd would call back prices they were willing to quote and hence the opening price was established. The advent of computers has moved option exchanges almost entirely to electronic systems, allowing for opening rotation to be completed at the click of a button. It still takes some time, though, so option quotes typically don't display on quote systems for 1 to 10 minutes after the stock has opened. If traders want their orders to be considered in the opening rotation sequence of events, orders must be received before the market opens.

OPTION POSITIONS

A trader has three different positions available: long stock, short stock, or no stock (i.e., cash). Ownership conveys certain privileges and rewards. Investors often buy stock not just for the potential price appreciation, but also for the dividend or voting rights. The mechanics behind hostile takeovers involve one entity purchasing the majority of issued shares. Wealthy investors use dividends to increase their income. It is a conservative approach when compared with that of a trader.

Long Stock

Long stock is the street's way of saying that you own the stock; it is the American way. People are born bulls, and that is what stockbrokers preach—to the benefit or detriment of their clients. But the vast majority of stock owners do so for the potential price appreciation.

Short Stock

Short stock is a little more complicated than simply being the opposite of long stock. Traders who "go short" are trying to accomplish the same thing as a long-stock trader: buy low and sell high. But short traders do so by reversing the order of events. Instead of buying low and then selling high, short traders attempt to sell high and then buy low to close the position. The trader virtually borrows the shares from someone else's account to sell on the open market, and when it is time to replace those shares, the trader repurchases them in the open market and returns them back in the account. Not every stock can be borrowed for shorting, however, and the stock must first be marginable. It also has to be above $5 and trade executions must be done on upticks. These additional requirements and restrictions are why traders who believe a stock is headed lower will use options to take a bearish position instead of shorting stock.

Long Call

Buying calls to open gives the call purchaser the right to buy stock at the stated strike price up until the expiration of the contract. If a trader buys one of the XYZ October 40 calls, owning this contract gives him the right to buy, or "call away" XYZ stock at $40 any time before the October expiration. For several reasons, this is a popular strategy for traders with a bullish opinion. First, long calls are easy to understand. And second, buying calls is a cheap way for traders to bet that a stock will go up.

Short Call

Selling calls to open obligates the seller (writer) to sell stock at the stated strike price any time until expiration. If a trader sells one of the XYZ October 40 calls, she is obligated to sell (deliver) stock at $40. (If this happens, she is said to have been *called out* of the stock.) Short calls are most often used when a trader already has stock in the account; selling a call against this stock is referred to as writing a *covered call*. If the short call writer is called out, the request is covered by the stock that already exists in the account. If there is none, the net effect will be to create a short position in the account.

Long Put

Buying puts to open gives the purchaser the right to sell stock at the stated strike price up until the contract expires. Put buyers are doing just the opposite of long call buyers. Long puts traders are betting that the stock will go down. If a trader buys an XYZ October 40 put, he has the right to "put" the stock to another trader at $40 any time before the October expiration. He would hope to sell the stock at a stated price, at a higher level than is being offered in the open market. Going long puts is a cheap way to capitalize on a falling stock price without actually shorting it. The strategy is also widely used as an insurance policy on long stock a trader may own. As the stock price decreases, the put price increases. It works the same way as an insurance policy on an asset.

Short Put

Selling puts to open obligates the writer to buy stock at the stated strike price any time before expiration. It is the opposite of buying puts to open and therefore obligates the put seller to "get put the stock" at the strike price. If traders were to sell puts to open on XYZ at $40, they would have to buy the stock at $40 any time before expiration. Short put writes are often done to "get paid to place a limit order." If a stock is trading at $50 and traders are thinking about placing limit orders to buy at $40, instead of just waiting for the stock price to drop, they could sell puts and collect the premium while waiting for the stock to go south.

CONVERSIONS, REVERSALS, AND SYNTHETICS

The conversion/reversal relationship is fundamental to all aspects of options trading. Floor professionals use conversions and reversals to create risk-free profits as an alterative to buying Treasury bills. Closely akin to conversions and reversals is the *synthetic*, which allows one to effectively own stock, a put, or a call without actually buying a stock, a put, or a call. Combinations of stocks and calls can be used to create synthetic puts, just as stock/put combos can create synthetic calls. For example, being long one October 50 XYZ put and short one October 50 XYZ call has the same effect as being short 100 shares of stock. Conversely, being long an October 50 XYZ put and long 100 shares of XYZ is the same as being long one October 50 call.

Using the example of being long one October 50 XYZ put and short one October 50 XYZ call to synthetically create 100 shares of short stock, this is how to calculate the actual prices. With the stock trading at $50, we open the following position:

Long 1 October 50 put for 1.50.
Short 1 October 50 call for 1.50.

Now suppose the stock falls to $46. If you had simply shorted 100 shares of stock at $50, you would have made a $400 profit before commission and fees. Would you have achieved the same results with options? Let's calculate it out. The put that you bought for $1.50 ($150) would be worth $400, for a net profit of $250; and the $150 you had received for the short call would be yours to keep, since the option expired worthlessly OTM. So, $250 + $150 = $400. Thus, being long an October $50 put and short an October $50 call is the financial equivalent of simply being short 100 shares of stock.

Continuing our example, suppose you had bought 100 shares for $50 against this option position. The three-sided position is called a *conversion*, and, with the options side exactly offset by the stock, there would be no risk in holding it. If, against the options at the above prices, you could have bought the stock for less than $50, you would have locked in a risk-free profit.

This three-sided conversion relationship will remain fixed no matter what the stock does. The reverse conversion, or *reversal*, is just the opposite: You would short the October 50 put, then hedge the sale by shorting 100 shares of XYZ and buying an October 50 call. Here is a conversion with some actual prices. Assume this position is put on in mid-September:

- Buy 1 October XYZ 50 put @ 1.50.
- Buy 100 shares XYZ @ $50.00.
- Sell short 1 October 50 call @ 1.75.

Now let's work out the math relationships on the day the options expire. If the stock is trading for $50 at the final bell, you will have neither lost nor gained anything on it, except the transaction costs. The call you bought for 1½ will be worthless, giving you a loss of $150, but it will be more than offset by the $175 you make on the short October 50 call. Overall, then, the position will yield a net gain of $25.

But suppose the stock was trading at $54 at the time the October options expire. That would give you a $400 gain on the stock, a $150 loss on the put (you bought it for $150 and it went out worthless), and a $225 loss on the call (you shorted it for $175, but it would be worth $400 at expiration with the stock trading $54). Thus, $400 − ($150 + $225) = $25. In fact, no matter where the stock is trading on the day the October options expire, you will have a net gain of $25. In the parlance of traders, you "locked in" the $25 gain when you put on the position. This also means that the position was essentially risk free, since no loss was possible—only a $25 profit, no matter what happened to the stock.

There is one more crucial point to consider: In putting on this position, you would be tying up $5,000 of your capital to buy the stock. Why go through all the trouble to do this risk-free trade if you could simply have put the money, equally risk free, into T-bills? The answer to this question is fundamental to the valuation of stock options.

Suppose you actually had taken the $5,000 and put it into a 30-day T-bill yielding 4 percent. That 4 percent is an annualized number, and your actual yield over 30 days—$\frac{1}{12}$ of a year—would be 0.04 divided by 12 × $5,000, or $16.66. So in this instance, the trader/investor would do better by putting the $5,000 into risk-free conversions than into T-bills. Even factoring in a $4 commission that the exchange member/floor trader would pay for putting on the conversion, the trader would still net a $21 profit. But just a little change in the price of the options could diminish the appeal of the conversion relative to T-bills. If the puts had been offered, not for $175 but for $170, the conversion would have yielded $4 less in risk-free profits, making it no better or worse, after adding in $4 for commissions, than simply buying a T-bill. So why go to all the bother of putting on a three-sided stock/options position? Why, indeed? Most traders in fact would not bother; they would simply park the money in T-bills.

But if all the price relationships were as first given, and a broker came into the trading pit to buy 5,000 of the October 50 puts that might push the puts up to, say, $1.90 ($190). You can understand why a market maker would be eager to sell 500 of this put, assuming she could still buy stock for $50 a share, and sell October 50 calls for $1.50. The 15 additional cents realized on the conversion would lock in a risk-free profit of 0.40 ($40), versus the $25 of the original example.

In practice, the instant the bid for 500 puts materialized, the market makers would quickly buy all the stock offered at $50, and whack the $1.50 bid on the October 50 calls. The effect would be to push the stock price up and the call price down, so that the conversion would once again yield about the same risk-free yield over 30 days as the 4 percent T-bill.

This example highlights an important aspect of determining option prices with reference to the risk-free return on Treasury paper. Also, if T-bill rates were to rise, it would affect put and call prices by pushing them higher because these puts and calls, when used in conversions and reversals, are in effect risk-free surrogates for T-bills.

While discussing conversions and reversals, we need to mention another aspect of option pricing: volatility. Volatility is one of the "Greeks" discussed later in this chapter. Basically, it is a measure of risk premium in the options that is determined by the volatility of the underlying stock. If XYZ's price movement turned erratic for a week or two, the put and call options would pick up volatility (premium). The reason is simple: The seller of an option incurs certain risks on exercise, and these risks are compensated by the premium the seller receives for the option. So if a stock jumps around, it stands to reason that the puts and calls will sell for higher prices than those offered on a stock that trades over a $2 range for weeks or months. In the preceding example, if rumors arose that the company was going to report spectacular earnings the next week, what do you think would happen to the October 50 calls? Very probably, they would start to rise in the way that call options do when rumors of this sort get around. But now we could also predict that the put prices would rise along with the stock; if they did not, and the calls rose with no corresponding change in the price of the stock or the puts, it would allow market makers to do the conversion (short October 50 calls, buy October 50 puts, buy stock) for prices that would give them risk-free profits far in excess of what they could earn from T-bills.

We should also work through one example of a reverse conversion, or reversal, to better understand the concept. Using the first example, the reversal would involve buying an October 50 call, shorting an October 50 put, and shorting 100 shares of stock. Suppose the prices were fairly close to those given in the earlier example:

- Short 1 October 50 put @ 1.50.
- Short 100 shares XYZ @ $50.
- Buy 1 October 50 call @ 1.60.

With the stock trading for $50 at expiration, the person holding this reversal would make $1.50 on the short put, lose $160 on the long call, and break even on the stock, for a net loss (without commissions) of $10 per reversal. Why would anyone want to put this position on when it would guarantee a $10 loss? The answer, again, is related to the risk-free return on Treasury bills.

In this instance, the floor trader has shorted $5,000 worth of stock, so he has $5,000 of someone else's money in his account. If he were to take that money and park it in a $30-day T-bill, we already know that it would generate a return of $16.66. So although the trader would lose $10 on the reversal, he would have that $5,000 from someone else to deploy in T-bills that would return $16 over the 30-day holding period. If you could lock in $6.66 of profit every time you did the reversal for a guaranteed profit, would you do it?

In fact, institutional players would do it thousands of times if they could. But that would push the price of the call up just enough, or the put price down enough, so that there would no longer be so much of an edge in the reversal. It is likely that the calls would get pushed down 2 to 3 cents and the puts up by the same amount to bring the reversal/conversion "back in line." Relative to parking the money in T-bills, putting on such positions would present no great advantage.

While conversions and reversals are the combination of three positions to neutralize a fourth, synthetics involve the combination of two positions to replicate a third. Before entering a larger option position (50 to 100 contracts or more) it should be considered whether the outright position or the synthetic is priced better.

The following information is required to calculate the synthetic position price (in each formula, each call and put has the same strike price and expiration):

- Current stock price.
- Option strike price.
- Dividend payment dates and amounts.
- Days to option expiration.
- Cost to carry the synthetic position.

$$\text{Cost to carry} = \text{Applicable interest rate} \times \text{Strike price} \times \text{Days to expiration}/360$$

$$\text{Long stock} = \text{Long call and short put}$$

$$\text{Synthetic long stock} = \text{Strike price} - (-\text{Put price} + \text{Call price} + \text{Cost to carry})$$

$$\text{Short stock} = \text{Short call and long put}$$

$$\text{Synthetic short stock} = \text{Strike price} - (+\text{Put price} - \text{Call price} - \text{Cost to carry})$$

$$\text{Long call} = \text{Long stock and long put}$$

$$\text{Synthetic long call price} = (+\text{Put price} + \text{Stock price} + \text{Cost to carry}) - \text{Strike price}$$

$$\text{Short call} = \text{Short stock and short put}$$

$$\text{Synthetic short call price} = (-\text{Put price} - \text{Stock price} - \text{Cost to carry}) + \text{Strike price}$$

$$\text{Long put} = \text{Long call and short stock}$$

$$\text{Synthetic long put price} = (+\text{Call price} + \text{Strike price} - \text{Cost to carry}) - \text{Stock price}$$

$$\text{Short put} = \text{Short call and long stock}$$

$$\text{Synthetic short put price} = (-\text{Call price} - \text{Strike price} + \text{Cost to carry}) + \text{Stock price}$$

If at option expiration, the underlying stock closes at the strike price of the options used to create a synthetic position, not buying back the short option creates uncertainty. This is because your decision to exercise

TABLE 5.2 Conversions, Reversals, Synthetics		
Synthetic (Formula)	**Closing Synthetic**	**Reversal/Conversion**
+Cn = +P + S	−C	Conversion
+Pn = +C − S	−P	Reversal
−Cn = −P − S	+C	Reversal
−Pn = −C + S	+P	Conversion
+Sn = +C − P	−S	Reversal
−Sn = −C + P	+S	Conversion

Key: C = Call, P = Put, S = Stock, n = Synthetic, + = Long, − = Short

your long option would depend on whether you were going to exercise the short option.

We now have two ways to acquire a building block: We can purchase (sell) the building block directly or purchase (sell) it synthetically. To determine whether to put a position on directly or synthetically, we need to calculate the price of the synthetic position.

Putting on a building block synthetically always involves combining the other building blocks. For calls, this means using puts and stock. For puts, it means using calls and stock; and for stock, it means using puts and calls. The rule is that when puts and stock are combined, they are always either both bought or both sold. When combing calls with either puts or stock, if the call is purchased, then the other leg is sold and vice versa.

Completion of any two sides of the triangle is a synthetic. Completion of all three sides is a reversal or conversion (see Table 5.2).

THE GREEKS AND DELTA VALUE

Delta is the most common of the Greeks and is sometimes referred to as the *hedge ratio factor*. Delta is generally defined as referring to the rate of change that an option will move in relationship to the underlying stock, index, or commodity future. Long call options always have a positive delta because their prices increase as the stock price increases and decrease as the stock declines. Long put options always have a negative delta because the put option price will decrease as the stock price increases, and will increase as the stock price declines.

Position Delta

A strategy may involve one or more options in combination with the underlying security. An easy way of evaluating the basic outlook of the strategy is to determine the net deltas of all the options and the underlying security that make up the strategy. This net number is called the position delta. A position with a positive delta would tend to be bullish and a position with a negative delta would tend to be bearish. A position with little or no delta, also known as *flat delta*, would tend to be neutral as to stock direction.

Delta measures how much an option's price is expected to change for a $1 change in the price of the underlying stock. Each share of stock always has a delta of 1. So, if an option has a delta of 75, it could be expected to move 75 cents for every single-dollar move in the underlying stock or index. Every call option has a delta value ranging from 0 to 100; every put option, from 0 to −100. Options that are very near-the-money carry a delta value of about 50, meaning they will move about 50 cents for every single-dollar move in the underlying security. The deeper ITM the option, the greater its delta value. A deep-in-the-money put or call could have a delta value of 85 to 95, and it could even approach 100 if it gets very-deep-in-the-money. However, we all know that options have time value associated with them, so it is most unlikely that any option in reality will have a 100-delta value.

The delta is also an approximation of the probability that an option will finish in the money. When the security moves, whether fractionally or significantly, at-the-money options seem to move only at a percentage as fast as the security itself. As the index moves upward, the option, depending on how deep-in-the-money, will move proportionally to the security based on its underlying delta.

Put options have a negative delta because their value increases as the underlying security falls. Hence, an option with a delta of −25 would increase in value by about 25 cents if the underlying security falls by $1. The importance of delta in regard to put options is its use in determining the hedge ratio. The hedge ratio determines the number of put options needed to protect against an adverse move in the price of the underlying security. You would need four put options with a delta of 25 to fully hedge the purchase of 100 shares of stock. When the security falls, the value of a put increases because a negative number is being divided by a positive number. So we end up with a delta that has a negative number. This difference between negative and positive deltas becomes important when combining spread positions.

A delta position is a directional position. To reduce the risk of a delta position, sell or buy the opposite delta position. This is called a hedge (see Table 5.3).

Gamma

The gamma of an option tells you how much the delta of an option changes as the underlying security changes. Every option has a delta, but the value

TABLE 5.3 Delta and Hedge Positions

Delta Position	Hedge Position
Long stock	Sell call
	Buy put
Short stock	Buy call
	Sell put
Long call	Sell call
	Buy put
	Sell stock
Short call	Buy call
	Sell put
	Buy stock
Long put	Sell put
	Buy call
	Buy stock
Short put	Buy put
	Sell call
	Sell stock

of that delta changes as the security changes. As the security goes up or down in value, the delta also changes.

A 50-delta call that is near ITM would become a 60- or 70-delta call, were the stock to rise, making the call deeper-in-the-money. Gamma tells us the rate at which the option delta will increase or decrease as the underlying stock moves up or down. If the stock's 100-strike call had a gamma of three, this would mean that the delta could be expected to rise 3 percent for every single-point rise in the stock. With the stock trading at $100 and options carrying a delta of 50, with a gamma of 4, a $5 rise in the stock would be expected to push the option price to $6 and the delta to 52. If the security were to rise another 5 points to 110, the option would go up to 9⅛, and the delta of 52 would rise to 54. In general, gamma is highest when the option is at-the-money, decreasing as it gets further OTM.

By calculating gamma, traders can determine how much their position delta will change, allowing them to adjust as necessary. Professional traders do this constantly, but it is less of a concern to the small trader. It is useful in any case to know about deltas and gammas, since the construction of hedges and the risk management of multiple-option positions rely significantly on such knowledge.

Position Gamma

Position gamma is the measurement of the position's curvature—that is, how much one's position deltas will change for each one-point move in the underlying security.

Long/Positive Gamma

This is the same as long curvature. The position needs directional movement to gain rewards. Long gamma is known in the trade as *backspreading*. Backspreaders are looking for swings in the underlying security and for increasing volatility.

Short/Negative Gamma

This is the same as short curvature. The position is a neutral outlook and requires no directional movement. Short gamma is known in the trade as *frontspreading*. Frontspreaders are premium sellers, looking for a decrease in volatility and speculating on low to no movement of the underlying security. Long option contracts will create long gamma. Short option contracts will create short gamma. Stock has no gamma.

Omega

Leverage refers to the ability to control more stock than you could acquire outright with your own funds. This is achieved either by borrowing money to acquire stock (e.g., purchasing stock on margin), or through purchase of an option. Payment of the option price allows you to control the shares for a fraction of their market price for a limited time. The option leverage ratio, or elasticity, is a useful tool for determining which options to purchase, given the expectation of movement in a stock. Omega is simply the percentage of change in an option's value over a given percentage of change in the underlying stock: Underlying price/Option price × Option delta = Omega. Higher omega numbers equal higher leverage but require a larger and faster move in the underlying stock to be profitable.

Vega

Vega is a measurement of change in volatility. The vega is noted in theoretical point changes for each 1 percent change in option volatility. Vega tells us how much an option will increase in value as the volatility increases. As the volatility of an option changes, the premium you pay for it will increase. Volatility changes are critical because of their impact on option premium levels. Vega directly addresses this concern. Vega tends to decrease with the approach of expiration, so the fewer days remaining until expiration, the less important the changes in volatility become. To look at it from another perspective, the more vega decreases, the lower the risk of volatility changes. Vega may not be emphasized nearly as much as delta or gamma, but it is important when viewed in relationship to all the Greeks.

Theta

All option traders know that time erodes the value of options with the approach of expiration. The rate at which time decay erodes an option's value is defined by theta. Depending on whether you are long or short, theta will work for or against you.

Premium buyers should hold low theta options, since time decay will then be less significant. On the other hand, if you are shorting options for premium income, you want to sell high-theta puts and calls, since profits there of will accrue relatively faster.

Theta is expressed as a negative number to reflect the erosion of time value. It tells us how much premium erosion will cost in a single day. Short sellers of options will have a positive theta, meaning he or she would make money from time decay, with all other variables remaining constant.

SUMMARY

This chapter has covered trading vehicles other than stock. Futures contracts permit great leverage—what traders would call "lots of bang for the buck." The ideal vehicle for trading futures is the E-mini contract, which was tailor-made for the small trader who wants to work from home or a trading room. The E-mini S&P contract and the E-mini Nasdaq contract are the most active vehicles, and both provide excellent liquidity as well as plenty of price movement. Always keep in mind, however, that leverage cuts both ways—the losses sustained in futures contracts can be just as spectacular as the gains we sometimes hear about.

Exchange-traded funds are an excellent vehicle if you are not comfortable with the risks of futures contracts, even when mini-sized. Put and call options, too, give you the ability to limit risk and to craft positions so that you can profit not only from a move up or down in the underlying security, but from a wide variety of outcomes related to its price as of a certain date. Again, a caveat is in order. Although it is true that, if you buy a call option on a stock for $2, the most you can lose is that $2, keep in mind that losing it would represent a 100 percent loss on the trade.

TheMarketWatch Options Trader, edited by David Nassar and Larry McMillan, is a weekly newsletter that provides detailed analysis of option trades each week in an educational format. For a small fee, the options newsletter provides a tremendous amount of value. You can subscribe to it at www.marketwatch.com.

CHAPTER 6

Trading Strategies

In this chapter, we study strategies you can employ to increase your odds of becoming consistently profitable.

First we explore trading systems that are embedded in the Profiler. These thoroughly tested long and short systems are designed for the active swing trader who wants to commit a portion of their assets to a systematic approach to trading rather than a more arbitrary or discretionary approach, which requires a higher degree of research, discipline, and experience.

A second strategy we explore employs trading options. While many believe the professional options trader has a significant edge over the average retail customer, our approach will sweeten the odds for those that follow it with discipline. Although it is impossible to achieve a perfectly level playing field in options trading, you can come closer using a few relatively simple techniques.

There are hundreds, if not thousands, of strategies that can enhance your trading odds, the important thing to understand is that even the simplest tactics can increase your profitability if you take the time to learn them well and implement them in a disciplined way. It is not strategies in themselves that ensure success, but your patience and diligence in observing how a stock, index, option, or future moves in price relative to what we anticipate by using a strategy.

Before we dig into these strategies—a word on discipline. The simple fact is that almost any method for gaining an edge is anchored by discipline.

Perhaps discipline is easier to achieve if you remember that we must suspend what we believe should happen and trade only what we observe. For example, suppose one observes that stocks that gap higher by more than 5 percent tend to experience a low-volume consolidation of those gains, and then typically restart and continue their ascent over the next month of trading. This simple observation can be a highly profitable strategy for a disciplined trader, provided that they do not expect perfect results each time the event shows itself. One person may observe the exact same pattern and make money while another lets his emotions get in the way, and loses. It may seem difficult to understand how one can win and one can lose on the same market move, but this is possible depending on how you let emotions interfere with what is real and objective.

Therefore, regardless of whether you choose to implement the strategies laid out here or if you come up with your own unique methods, the most important trait that you can possess is the ability to let go of a trade that isn't working. Do not underestimate the advantage of self-control in the markets; it is often the only difference between success and failure.

That stated, we begin with the MarketWise Profiler, which has been referenced throughout this manual. As you likely inferred, we are firm believers in the use of technology to assist us in finding the stocks that meet our criteria for prevailing market conditions. The following discussion begins to explain how we use the Profiler to gain a market edge.

The basis of Profiler is *Trend Following*. If we believe the market is in a bullish uptrend, we will use the Profiler to isolate the stocks that have the best chances of moving higher in concert with the market—those stocks are found in the Stage 2-1 (Strong Mark-Up). Conversely, if we believe the market may be transitioning from distribution to a bear market we would search for stocks in Stage 3-3 (late distribution), or 4-1 (strong decline). In this regard, we would seek stocks in Stage 3-3, defined as stocks that have undergone at least a couple of months of distribution and now potentially on the verge of a break down into a strong decline.

Once trend is defined, there are many different ways of searching the market for trading ideas within the trend—while also incorporating ones own personality and interests. Many strategies also exist to implement ideas depending on; perceived financial risk of putting the trade on; anticipated time in a trade; capital resources available; and your level of patience to name a few.

For instance, if you interpreted a market that was declining, you might choose to focus on Stage 4-1 stocks with the idea of shorting the market, which is pretty straightforward. We could then add another dimension to this market condition—such as earnings. Many participants like to follow earnings and there is no reason not to if this interests you. Suppose it is the beginning of the quarterly earnings season, and some of the most widely followed stocks in the market just appeared on Profiler to have entered Stage 4-1 (before earnings). One might think it would be a good time to have exposure to the short side of the market based on Profiler, but also fear a rally if the company were to surprise and report good earnings. In the case, the trader could easily be conflicted. Earnings reports are often a catalyst for large price movements and if the company you have chosen to sell short reports earnings that are better than what was expected by the analysts, you might find yourself in the very uncomfortable position of being on the wrong side of the market as your stock surges higher. Being short a stock that is rallying can bring about fearful buying as it opens the door to potentially unlimited losses (see Chapter 4 for more on selling short). This scenario is obviously not one you want to find yourself in.

One simple strategy worth exploring to help limit exposure to losses while still participating in the trend if the stock declines as expected, would be to purchase put options instead of shorting the equity. As explained in Chapter 5, the only money you can lose when you purchase options is the premium you paid, while if the stock were to drop sharply your gain on the options position could be several hundred percent! The point is, choosing a particular strategy to implement can sometimes be just as difficult as finding the right stock. This is why we have created actual trading systems in the Profiler that allow you to focus on proven results in trading with the trend, whether it is bullish or bearish, without the conflict often associated with news, earnings, upgrades, and so on.

The searches that one chooses to focus on may be very different than what other traders or investors may be focusing on, but that is what makes the customizability of the Profiler invaluable. It allows one to hone in on the opportunities that meet *your own* criteria, without being hypnotized by news and current events that often obscure good analysis.

If you are unsure of which strategies to implement once you have found an idea, or you are unable to narrow your focus, then the Market-Wise Profiler will supply you with actual trading ideas including actual entry and exit price levels. These ideas are found in the "Trading Systems" section of the Profiler (see Figure 6.1) and they are given to you each day for stocks that meet the stringent criteria we have coded into our algorithms for the long and short systems. The stocks that meet our potential trade executions have coded contingent buy (or short sale) entries along with initial protective stop orders and profit targets. While there may be as many as a dozen or so ideas presented on a given day, the actual number of trades that are actually entered the next day is usually about a third of the potential ideas listed, and this is based on these profiled stocks actually meeting our price entry targets. While we will not divulge the actual criterion that goes into the stock selection, we will give you some general parameters so you can have confidence in the robustness of our systems.

FIGURE 6.1　The Trading Systems tab allows you to see algorithmically generated trade set-ups.

Therefore, regardless if you choose to use the Profiler to find your own ideas based on your scanning ideas, or you use our systems, the Profiler is an invaluable tool. Let's take a look.

THE PROFILER'S-SYSTEMS TRADING

The first thing to recognize is that the algorithms for our systems are based on the principles laid out in this book with the cornerstone being Foundational Analysis. The first criterion of the long system is that the stock must be in a strong uptrend (Stage 2-1). Based on the principle that "a trend, once established, is more likely to continue than reverse" we have back tested each of the three substages of the Markup phase and found that the Stage 2-1 stocks consistently outperform the stocks that are in Stage 2-2 or 2-3, which is why we start our system with stocks in Stage 2-1. The next parameter for sorting stocks in our long system requires a minimum average daily volume of at least 600,000 shares; this eliminates stocks that may be too illiquid. Next, stocks under \$5/share are eliminated from consideration as many traders utilize margin and stocks under \$5 cannot be margined.

We then look for a healthy breather in the stock since one of the most important aspects of finding the lower risk entries in the long system is to find stocks that have recently consolidated after a sharp move higher. The candidates that have made it this far in our process of elimination are highly charged stocks that have experienced first a strong move higher then either; a pullback in price or a consolidation through time. The consolidation period for these stocks must have occurred on decreasing volume (relative to the volume as the stock advanced); this volume action can be interpreted as a lack of aggressive sellers, which makes continued upside movement more likely.

In simplistic form, these are the general search criteria for stocks in our long system; look to Figure 6.2 to see what the results look like on a given day. Looking at the "Current Orders" section represented in Figure 6.2 you will notice the column headings that indicate:

- *Symbol:* This is the list of stock symbols for stocks with potential entries for the next day.
- *Quantity:* This is the number of shares to be traded based on a $10,000 commitment per idea (if you change the system to trade an equal number of shares, such as 1,000 shares per trade, your results will vary dramatically from the back tested results).

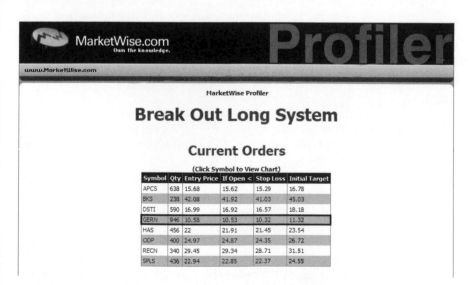

MarketWise Profiler

Break Out Long System

Current Orders

(Click Symbol to View Chart)

Symbol	Qty	Entry Price	If Open <	Stop Loss	Initial Target
APCS	638	15.68	15.62	15.29	16.78
BKS	238	42.08	41.92	41.03	45.03
DSTI	590	16.99	16.92	16.57	18.18
GERN	946	10.58	10.53	10.32	11.32
HAS	456	22	21.91	21.45	23.54
ODP	400	24.97	24.87	24.35	26.72
RECN	340	29.45	29.34	28.71	31.51
SPLS	436	22.94	22.85	22.37	24.55

FIGURE 6.2 This table shows the current orders section which lists symbols of stocks meeting the long system requirements along with order execution strategies.

- *Entry:* This is the price at which you should enter the stock only if the stock meets the parameters in the next column.
- *If open <:* This indicates that the stock should only be purchased if the stock opens for trading at a price less than the number indicated. What we are attempting to accomplish here is to avoid chasing stocks that gap higher, and instead look for stocks that open slightly lower in which buyers then regain control of the momentum.
- *Stop loss:* This is the initial protective stop, it is meant to limit our losers by exiting positions that either move against us more than 2.5 percent or trade below the prior days low, whichever is less. This initial stop loss price is automatically adjusted each day so that if the position is held overnight you have a new stop price that trails the stock higher, allowing you to lock in much higher profits.
- *Target:* The target price is the level we expect the stock to trade up to over the next 1 to 10 trading sessions, this target is approximately 7 percent above entry price. History shows that up to 20 percent or more of the stocks that are entered go on to meet their target price before getting stopped out (think Newton's first law of gravity). When a stock attains its target level we suggest that you only start to "act like a seller," but not necessarily be a seller. This means that trailing your stops will allow for further upside should the rally continue. We also exit only 50 percent of the position, allowing a nice profit on a portion of the position but still leaving room for further upside with the remaining half position. The remaining position will continue to be updated in the open positions section until the stock is closed out via a stop order. It is important to leave this partial position open to attain greater profits, the system actually had one stock meet its target price, only to continue higher by another $11.00/ share over the next 4 trading sessions, and this was on a $27 stock!

Not only are the potential trade ideas listed in the table, but they are also shown graphically on our proprietary charting software, which includes the order details written out as well as being visually displayed with bars on the chart itself (see Figure 6.3). On the top segment of the chart where the price candles are displayed, there is a green horizontal line, which closely represents the anticipated purchase price. Just below the entry line is another horizontal line, which is colored red, this line indicates where the initial protective stop should be placed. The final horizontal line, colored black, indicates the initial price target where you should enter trailing stops and exit half of your position with a profit. The middle segment of the price chart shows you the primary and substage of each stock. For our long system, all the stocks will be Stage 2-1. Below the stage segment, volume is represented along with its own vertical scale. Being

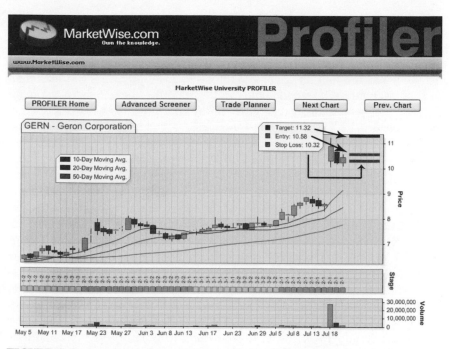

FIGURE 6.3 The chart of Geron Corporation visually shows where to buy, set stops, and begin to takes profits (target).

able to see the actual trade setup along with the anticipated movement allows you to visualize what a move would look like if it trades as anticipated and attains our objective.

Once a trade has met the entry parameters, the Profiler will continue to automatically update the positions at the end of each day in the "Open Position" section. Seen in Figure 6.4, the Open positions section contains

Open Positions
As of Close on Wednesday, July 20, 2005
(Click Symbol to View Chart)

Symbol	Qty	Size	Entry Date	Entry	DaysIn	Prev Close	Open P/L	Closed P/L	Target	Trailing Stop
AKAM	684	Full	7/19/2005	14.66	2	14.84	$123.12	$0.00	15.69	14.65
ALKS	355	Half	7/15/2005	14.12	4	15.82	$603.50	$351.45	Target Hit 07/20	15.42
CHRS	864	Full	7/20/2005	11.58	1	11.77	$164.16	$0.00	12.39	11.48
CVTX	370	Full	7/20/2005	27.09	1	27.71	$229.40	$0.00	28.99	27.02
INTU	204	Full	7/20/2005	48.98	1	48.94	($8.16)	$0.00	52.41	48.68
NTGR	466	Full	7/20/2005	21.51	1	22.13	$288.92	$0.00	23.02	21.58
PLAY	203	Half	7/19/2005	24.64	2	26.9	$458.78	$349.16	Target Hit 07/20	26.23

FIGURE 6.4 The "Open Positions" shows details for where a position has been entered.

some useful information for managing your trades until the position has been closed out. The symbol and quantity of shares purchased are shown just after the symbol (once again assuming a commitment of $10,000/position). The "size" column indicates how many shares are currently open, if the stock has not met its price target it will state "full" and if the stock has met its price target it will indicate "half." To better keep track of the positions the entry date and the number of days the position has been open is also indicated. The next column indicates the closing price for the latest session, followed by the open and closed profit and loss (P/L). The open P/L indicates the total unrealized profit or loss for any shares that are still held long. The closed P/L indicates the total amount of profit taken when the stock has met its price target. The target column serves as a reminder of where we think the stock can go. If a stock has attained its initial target, this column will indicate the date the profit target was hit. The final column is the most important because it addresses the topic of money management. Too many traders start to become complacent once they have a stock position that has reached profitability, only to see their profits evaporate in the event selling pressure ensues—this we consider unforgivable.

This complacency is fueled by phrases like "winners take care of themselves." Successful traders know that winning trades need to be managed and by continually raising your stop (trailing stops) as the stock continues its ascent is an unemotional way of allowing your winners to run. The final column is labeled "trailing stop" because the stop is automatically adjusted higher as the stock attains greater levels of profitability.

Looking now at the second opened position in Figure 6.4, ALKS, we can click on the symbol to view a chart (see Figure 6.5), just as we did when the stock was in the "current orders" section. Notice in Figure 6.5, the chart shows more detail than Figure 6.3 because a position has been taken (note Figures 6.3 and 6.5 show different stock symbols—the point is to see the added detail). Notice the box located in the middle of the top section of Figure 6.5, we can see that a position was entered on July 15, and the current number of shares held is 355. "Days in trade" refers to how long the position has been held (in this case four days). This stock has both an open and closed P/L because, as indicated, the initial target was hit on July 20. The open profit of $603.50 is the current profit on the 355 shares currently held, while the closed P/L indicates a profit of $351.45 on 50 percent of the initial position—taken July 20 as the stock reached its initial price target. You will also notice on Figure 6.5 that the green line (located at $14.12 for this chart) indicates where the stock was purchased while the red line ($15.42) represents the location of the stop on the remaining shares still held long.

The first question that most people have is: "How profitable are these systems?" and here again we need to disclose that actual trading results will very greatly between the users of any system, including ours. In Figure

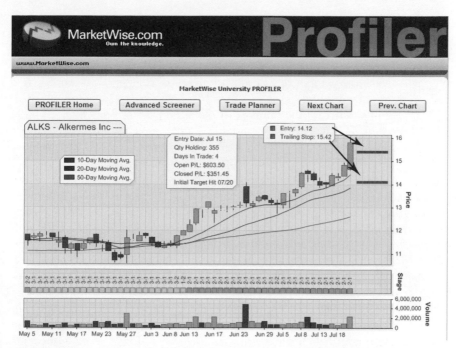

FIGURE 6.5 The chart for open positions hold some key information for managing the trade once a systems trade has been opened.

6.6 we present some of the back tested results for the long system over a 15-month period (April 2004 to June 2005). We begin our assessment of performance with what might appear to be a negative, which is the Win/Loss ratio. Over this test period, the system generated 406 trades, of which 175 were winners and 231 were losers. In percentage terms, our system won just 43 percent of the time. To the untrained eye, this system would seem to be one not worth further consideration, however when we look at the profitability of the winners versus the losers, we quickly realize the net P&L is what matters—not winning percentage. In fact, like baseball, most traders and systems have less than a 50 percent batting average, and this should come as a source of relief, given most people expect they must be right more than wrong to make money—not so! As long as we can make more while right than we lose while wrong, trading will be profitable and this is the end goal. Based on our back-test results as of the writing of this book, our model portfolio had results of $35,088.10. It is clear there is more to the story than the Win/Loss ratio.

We started out the chapter stressing the importance of discipline and money management. It is these principles that support the system. The size of the average winner was $407.51, while the average loser saw a drawdown

Break Out Long System Summary
April 2004 through June 2005

Month	Trades	Profit/Loss	Winners	Losers	Avg. Profit of Winners	Avg. Loss	Max Open
April, 2004	26	$3,594.60	9	17	$758.73	($190.23)	10
May, 2004	10	$300.45	5	5	$202.02	($141.93)	4
June, 2004	8	$1,859.48	6	2	$339.09	($87.54)	3
July, 2004	23	($2,806.74)	5	18	$191.08	($209.01)	3
August, 2004	7	($602.32)	1	6	$7.32	($101.61)	3
September, 2004	33	$2,435.38	16	17	$344.89	($181.35)	15
October, 2004	38	$133.72	15	23	$267.75	($168.81)	17
November, 2004	72	$8,377.12	36	36	$365.96	($133.26)	17
December, 2004	46	$2,172.44	16	30	$402.27	($142.13)	7
January, 2005	10	($438.56)	4	6	$147.42	($171.37)	3
February, 2005	26	$6,592.54	16	10	$506.59	($151.29)	7
March, 2005	31	$4,674.62	13	18	$533.13	($125.34)	10
April, 2005	17	$275.10	5	12	$362.19	($127.99)	4
May, 2005	18	$4,005.45	8	10	$669.78	($135.28)	7
June, 2005	41	$4,514.82	20	21	$426.87	($191.55)	5
	406	$35,088.10	175	231	$407.51	($156.82)	17

FIGURE 6.6 This table shows the results of the long system over a 15-month period.

of just $156.82. This means the winners were 2.61 times larger than the losers over this 15-month back-test period, and that is a winning formula that speaks to the often-stated cliché "cut your losers and hold the winners." For a complete view of all the trades that accompany Figure 6.6, please refer to the Profiler website where you can view the actual entry and exit prices for each of the trades.

The short system is not nearly as active in a bull market as the long system, just as we would expect the long system to be less active in a bear market. In fact, over the same 15-month period of time there were just 60 trades entered on the short side for a total profit of $9,524.33 (see Figure 6.7). While not nearly as profitable as the long system on a dollar basis, the short system does have a greater degree of accuracy with its 50 percent win/loss ratio and the average winner is 3.79 times greater than the losers which results in solid overall performance numbers.

Always keep in mind that the prior example of systems trading using Profiler was based on a block of time, but the concepts are timeless. For the purposes of demonstrating a living system, I used actual performance examples for this time period, but this system is based on age-old principals

Break Out Short System Summary
April 2004 through June 2005

Month	Trades	Profit/Loss	Winners	Losers	Avg.Profit of Winners	Avg.Loss	Max Open
April, 2004	3	($130.92)	0	3	$0.00	($43.64)	3
May, 2004	5	$973.01	3	2	$405.46	($121.68)	2
June, 2004	2	($238.08)	1	1	$15.72	($253.80)	3
July, 2004	2	$1,942.06	2	0	$971.03	$0.00	2
August, 2004	8	$4,878.65	7	1	$732.56	($249.24)	7
September, 2004	1	$487.72	1	0	$487.72	$0.00	0
October, 2004	1	$88.00	1	0	$88.00	$0.00	1
November, 2004	6	($792.98)	1	5	$15.24	($161.64)	3
December, 2004	0	$0.00	0	0	$0.00	$0.00	0
January, 2005	4	$275.53	1	3	$594.11	($106.19)	2
February, 2005	6	$164.74	2	4	$244.72	($81.18)	2
March, 2005	4	($9.84)	2	2	$125.82	($130.74)	1
April, 2005	6	$127.96	2	4	$252.80	($94.41)	3
May, 2005	11	$1,889.56	7	4	$313.37	($76.00)	6
June, 2005	1	($131.08)	0	1	$0.00	($131.08)	0
	60	$9,524.33	30	30	$430.91	($113.43)	7

FIGURE 6.7 This table shows the results of the short system over a 15-month period.

of the market. Therefore, while the exact entry, exit, and stop rules of the trading systems featured in the Profiler may evolve and adjust as market conditions change, the basic premise of the system is once again—timeless.

PRICING PUTS/CALLS—A STRATEGY YOU CAN USE

If you're a typical options trader, you've probably seen far more of your puts and calls expire worthless versus double or triple in value. Therefore, we are going to shed some light on improving your odds, but first it will help to know why it is so difficult for the retail trader to win in the options market. To make this point, let us take a brief step back to 1973.

It is no coincidence that many of the traders who bought seats on the Chicago Board Options Exchange (CBOE) when it opened for business in 1973 came from the Las Vegas casinos. These blackjack players and professional gamblers often lived a nerve-wracking existence since a pit boss existed to look over every table—seeking players who consistently beat the house (see *Bringing Down the House*, by Ben Mezrich, New York: Free Press, 2002). For winning at this game was not (and still is not) easy work, since even the most sophisticated card-counting systems yielded profits of no more than $2 or so for every $100 the player could shove out on the table. One such card system was legendary and marketed under the name: "Revere Hi-Opt II"—and anyone capable of using this relatively complex system successfully probably had the brains to make a comfortable living playing poker, backgammon, gin rummy, or just about any other game where the odds can be bent in one's favor by applying considerable IQ-power to the problem.

So it was natural that, when the CBOE opened its doors in 1973, some of America's top blackjack professionals high-tailed it from the Nevada desert to the Loop District of Chicago. It was not just the prospect of making a living without some casino goon breathing down their necks that brought the card-counters to the Windy City, but the main attraction was the odds. Compared to hustling at blackjack, winning on the options floor was as easy as pitching stones into a pond. It was a seller's game back then, and the premium income a market maker typically received for selling naked puts and calls was so juicy that disciplined sell-side players almost couldn't lose. For many of them, in fact, the application of relatively simple strategies sufficed to produce the kind of income that, for a while, made options market makers the envy of the trading world.

Unfortunately for these insiders, the gravy train bogged down as more and more savvy speculators found their way to the options floor. The efficient market prevailed and the more traders who arrived on the floor, the more efficient it became. Over time, option premium levels decreased to the point where they no longer fully reflected the volatility risk in the underlying stocks. Under the circumstances, selling naked puts and calls below their fair value was like selling cheap burglary insurance to store-owners in a bad neighborhood. In the end, the sellers faced a much tougher game, and many had their incomes reduced significantly, because they were effectively under pricing risk.

The trend has continued to this day, requiring the floor pros to come up with increasingly sophisticated strategies to make money. So if professionals have been having a hard time of it, where does that leave the retail customer? The short answer is, not exactly swimming in a sea of opportunity. Swimming in a pool full of sharks would be closer to the truth.

But suppose instead of swimming with the sharks, participants who had trouble trading stock due to higher capital requirements could instead buy options. Buying 400 shares of XYZ that trades at $200 for $80,000 in anticipation of a rally limits many players; therefore, why not buy four call options for, say, $4.00 apiece, putting a total of $1,600 at risk? That would allow many with limited capital or experience to participate with far greater leverage and less risk than if they put up $80,000 to buy the stock. Using this strategy it would not be inconceivable that a move of just 10 percent in the stock—in any stock—could yield a profit of 200 to 300 percent or more of invested capital for holders of out-of-the-money call options.

But there is a downside, and it is this: Most options expire worthless and only a rare few ever produce gains on the order of 200 percent to 300 percent! The reason for this is that the sellers of those options, usually market makers (the sharks) or exchange-floor specialists are adroit handicappers in pricing risk. And even if they were obliged at times to sell puts and calls at relatively depressed levels, over the long haul they were far more skillful at pricing options than the typical retail customer buying them. This is to say, the floor traders enjoyed the "house" edge in setting option prices not unlike the casinos do.

So how does one beat them at their game? First, it must be conceded that no retail strategy can succeed entirely in surmounting the professionals' small but nonetheless crucial edge. Floor pros enjoy far-more-lenient margin requirements, and their transaction fees are practically negligible in comparison with the retail customer's. But with the relatively recent advent of virtual electronic option exchanges such as International Securities Exchange (ISE), the playing field has been leveled somewhat, to the point where some floor traders are asking themselves whether, all things considered, they'd be better off trading from their offices or homes rather than doing battle in the pits every day.

Some of the techniques we are about to show you are borrowed from the market makers and shaped over years of trading options. Here is a short list of essential edge-building tactics, each of which will be explained below in greater detail that will allow you to better swim with the sharks as opposed to being eaten by them:

1. Use of contingency-type orders that tie the purchase or sale price of an option to the price of the underlying stock
2. Accurate identification of "swing points" where a stock's trend is likely to reverse
3. Use of cheap options (i.e., under $2.00) for increased leverage
4. Calculation of "fair value" for puts and calls before buying them
5. Reduction of premium risk by selling options against those already owned

Let's look at the first item—use contingency-type orders—since this is vital to any option trader's success. In the old days, before direct-access trading platforms existed, such orders were conveyed to one's broker over the phone. An example of a contingency order would be as follows: "Buy one July 45 call for $2.20 (i.e., $220 per contract) or better, contingent on the XYZ stock trading at 44.30 or higher." A slightly modified version might read, "Pay $2.20 for one July 45 call so long as XYZ stock is bid 44.30 or higher." Similarly, we might instruct a broker to "bid 2.60 for one July 45 put, as long as XYZ stock is offered for 46.30 or less." The reason for using contingency orders should be apparent to anyone who has traded options through a retail broker. Have you ever placed an order to buy a call option for a certain price, only to get filled when you no longer wanted to be filled (i.e., as the stock began to fall)? In the first example, one might have calculated that $2.20 would be a great price for the July 45 call option if the stock were trading around 44.30. But it would be a poor price if the stock were trading lower—say, around 43.70.

We use contingency-type orders to avoid overpaying, since over time, buying options at bargain prices is one of the most significant ways to build an edge. The idea is to be profitable on a trade from the get-go—to enter the trade, that is, with the wind behind us. And the best way to do so is to make certain we have not paid too much for a put or call. Remember, the edge in the options game is measured in nickels and dimes, and if we are to expect success, we can't afford to give up even a penny here or a penny there every time we trade. Market makers make millions picking up nickels and dimes with bulldozers! The good news is that electronic trading platforms give you direct access to the real-time bids and offers of market makers and other traders participating in options markets. Whereas there have never been more than a handful of retail brokers willing to bother with contingency-type orders, this capability is intrinsic to such electronic-access platforms as RealTick®'s Turbo Options, and is relatively easy to use.

But finding put and call bargains still requires doing a little preliminary work, much as we would compare prices and models when shopping for a car. Let's look at an example of the steps we take to implement an option strategy.

If an underlying stock (XYZ) were trading in a three-point range from the low teens after falling steeply from near 30 earlier in the year, how might we price the option? (See Figure 6.8.)

With the stock seemingly consolidating in the range between $14 and $15, it seemed plausible that it might rally at least a few points over the next several months. Accordingly, the July 17.50 call options were targeted for purchase. Keep in mind that this particular strategy was employed to leverage the *vague* expectation that the stock would trend higher over a period of several months, not that it would move sharply higher over the very near-term to a specific target.

With the stock oscillating between $14 and $15, the best time to buy calls would have been when it was trading toward the low end of that range, near $14. So how can we determine how much to pay for call op-

XYZ Corp

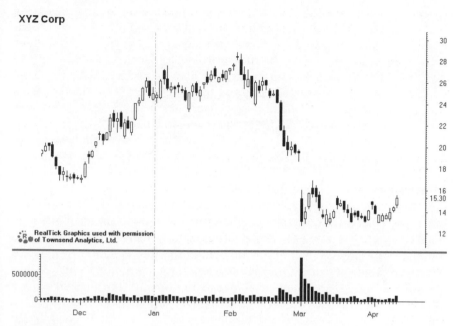

FIGURE 6.8 XYZ stock from the *Wise Idea Newsletter.*

tions if the stock eases down to $14? First, let's see how expensive the out-of-the-money calls were at the time, as indicated by their implied volatilities. Implied volatility is simply a measure of how much risk premium is being factored into put and call options. Options on a stock that has fluctuated between $20 and $22 for a month might carry an implied volatility of 17, a relatively low number that suggests the stock has not been moving around much. But if bullish rumors were to cause the stock to surge several points in just a few days, call options would increase in value as well, for two reasons. First, the stock will have moved to a higher price level, and second, option volatility (a.k.a. "risk premium") will also have increased as price action in the stock got wilder. One might think of this risk premium like an insurance company would (i.e., as the threat of risk becomes more likely), the premium one pays reflects the risk. In the case of options, because market makers act like insurance companies by selling premium, they face the risk of call buyers having their options expire "in the money." The risk of this occurring increases with volatility—hence implied volatility.

In fact, as we see in the Turbo Option table from RealTick in Figure 6.9, option volatilities were sky-high, ranging from about 63 to 70. (This compares with a typical implied volatility of 20 to 30 for a "dull" stock.) The item of particular interest in this table is labeled Vbid—short for bid

Ticker	Delta	Open	High	Calls Low	Bid	Ask	VBid	Last	Trade Volume	
	1.00	14.69	15.28	14.41	15.14	15.15	15.00	15.15	1000	
										☐ Apr '03
										☐ May '03
										▣ Jul '03
+MJQGB	1.00	0	0	0	5.40	5.70	66.60	4.40	0	10.000
+MJQG\	0.99	3.50	3.50	3.50	3.50	3.90	65.18	3.50	6	12.500
+MJQGC	0.57	1.95	2.25	1.95	2.30	2.45	70.36	2.25	5	15.000
+MJQGW	0.04	1.20	1.30	1.10	1.25	1.45	65.22	1.30	5	17.500
+MJQGD	0.00	0	0	0	.70	.80	64.90	.50	0	20.000
+MJQGX	0.00	.35	.40	.35	.35	.40	62.94	.40	10	22.500

FIGURE 6.9   XYZ call options. (Used with permission of RealTick.)

volatility. This is the price that buyers of these options were actually willing to pay when the stock was trading at $15.15. Since, like the pros, we aim to buy options on the bid (wholesale) rather than the offer (retail), we want to use bid-side volatilities to calculate bargain prices for call options. We see that 65.22 is the actual volatility for July 17.50 calls, but cheapskates that we are, we will try to buy them only if they come down to super-bargain levels—say, a 62 volatility.

So, assuming we want to buy July 17.50 calls at a 62 volatility or lower, how much, in theory, should the call sell for with the stock trading down near $14? To answer that question, we need to use an option valuation calculator. Such calculators are available for free at numerous Web sites, but we prefer the very-easy-to-use software sold by friend and options expert Larry McMillan. Figure 6.10 represents a sample screen from his calculator, into which I have plugged the following variables:

1. Underlying price of XYZ, $14.00
2. Strike price and expiration of July 17.50 calls (the option I want to buy)
3. Implied option volatility of 62—a target level that would dictate a good price for the calls
4. Expiration date in July, to calculate values for the July options
5. The date when the options would be bought—assume April 11 for this example (this factor is necessary because options shed value over time)

With these variables plugged in, the calculator spits out 77 cents as what one should hope to pay for a July 17.50 calls, if XYZ shares fall to $14 on April 11. The actual calculator screen is shown in Figure 6.10.

The theoretical price of 77 cents sounds just about right, since we can buy a dozen of them for under a thousand dollars, commissions included. Many option pros will tell you that buying "cheap" options is a losing strat-

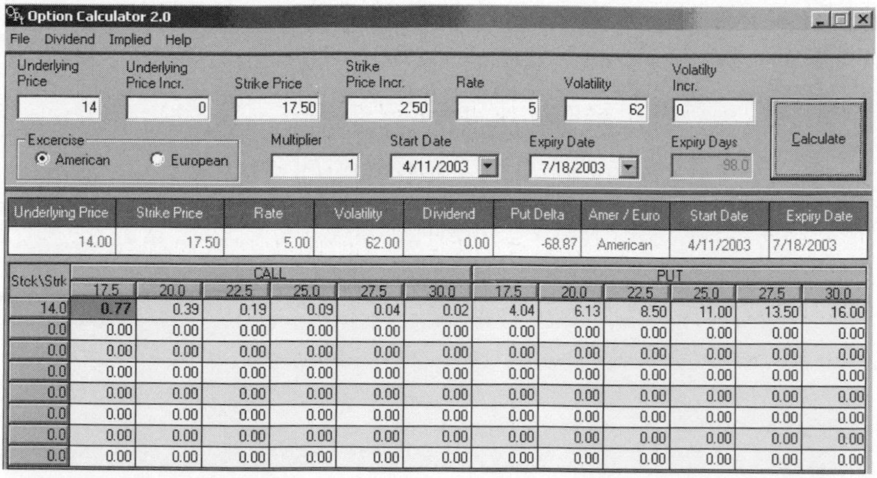

FIGURE 6.10 XYZ options calculations. This can be found at www.optionstategist.com.

egy, but we say it depends on how well you play the game. By employing this kind of good analysis, we can compete with the pros by not paying too much for risk premium. While many option trades such as this may not yield a profit, the loss is limited to a cheap premium paid. When the trades do work, the winners tend to be dramatic, overshadowing many small losses that may have come prior. If this sounds familiar, think of the strategy we employ with trading equities, that is, cutting losses quickly and letting profits run. As you can see, the principals remain the same, but the tactics using options require some understanding. It is this little knowledge and understanding that build a tremendous edge over the average member of the public. As I stated many times prior, it is only a small edge that the casinos have that builds billion dollar pyramids in the desert—so don't think you need a gigantic edge to win at trading. Most participants understand very little about the market and treat it as a form or entertainment or gambling. These participants would do better in Vegas, for at least they may get a free show and dinner! In the market, those with a little knowledge can go a long way.

By emulating this strategy and many more that you will discover on your own through the infinite possibilities of options, you will be building an edge into your trading much the way professional floor traders do it: one step at a time.

CHAPTER 7

Indicators
and Oscillator

T echnical analysis involves more than just recognizing chart formations. Technicians take their analysis a step further by using tools
such as indicators and oscillators as a means of confirming and supporting what message prices in the market may be sending.

As securities fluctuate, much of the price change can be attributed to
overreactions from the collective market, and this is where indicators and
oscillator shine. By using these tools in conjunction with trend analysis,
we begin to see greater detail within trend that contributes to timing. I
like to think of trend analysis as a decision process to go long or short,
while I think of indicators and oscillators as timing tools of when to act on
the decision.

Oscillators and indicators are also particularly useful in determining
trading ranges or trend reversals. An oscillator will, by way of its name,
produce readings that can only oscillate between some fixed boundaries.
You might think of these boundaries as flexible guard rails that post on the
charts. Indicators and oscillators are normally charted in a separate window below the actual stocks price chart, and there is much to be said
about them. In fact, entire books are written on the subject. There are literally hundreds of them, but always remember, they are all derivatives of
the foundational variables we spoke about—price, time, volume, and velocity. We will touch on the ones that we believe carry the greatest value
such as: Stochastic, Relative Strength Index (RSI), the Arms Index (TRIN),
and Fibonacci Retracement.

As you become familiar with the use of indicators and oscillators, it is imperative you treat them for what they are and understand what they are not. Too many traders attempt to use a single indicator or oscillator as a system within itself. The true value of these technical studies is to confirm the decisions you should have already made during trend analysis and the foundational variables noted. The purpose is once again intended to improve the timing of your entry or exit strategy, but not replace trend analysis. Use them to reinforce your conviction and even adjust stops, but don't get caught in the trap of using these indicators as a standalone trading system.

STOCHASTICS

George Lane created the Stochastics indicator and it has stood the test of time for decades as a useful tool for traders. Stochastics measure the relationship of the closing value of stocks relative to the range of price during a given time period being studied. For instance, if we are measuring Stochastics on a daily time frame, it measures where the stock closed that day in relation to the high and low for that same day. The fundamental premise of the Stochastics indicator is that a strong stock or commodity will tend to close each period of time at the upper end of the range while a weak security will tend to close at the lower end of the range.

The Stochastisc indicator will be rising when closing prices occur near the upper end of the daily range (or time frame being measured) and the Stochastics indicator will be falling when closing prices occur near the lower end of the range. Stochastics are graphically represented by two lines that are plotted against each other on a scale of 0 to 100; these lines are known as %K and %D. (See Figure 7.1.)

Stochastics readings are used primarily to define what are known as overbought and oversold conditions. Simply stated, the term *overbought* means the stock has reached a level of buying that is unlikely to continue and that a consolidation or reversal becomes more likely. Oversold is just the opposite, it implies that a stock has moved to the downside at a rate which is unlikely to continue and that makes a stabilization or reversal to the upside more likely.

Stochastics—Interpretation

The Stochastics oscillator is represented as two lines (%K and %D) which are charted between fixed endpoints of 0 to 100. Measurements above 80 are classically defined as overbought, while measurements below 20 are defined as oversold. When a stock reaches overbought or oversold, traders should be alert for signs of a potentially tiring trend. For instance, when a

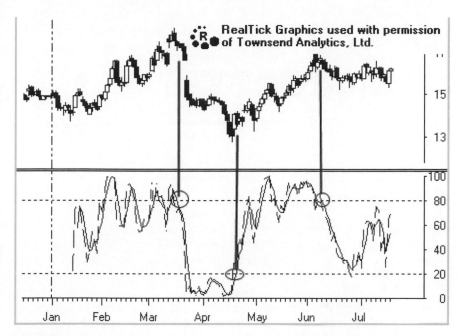

RealTick Graphics used with permission of Townsend Analytics, Ltd.

FIGURE 7.1 This chart shows the %K and %D Stochastics plotted on a scale of 0 to 100. The 20 and 80 levels are also drawn in to assist in easy identification of overbought and oversold conditions.

stock that has been rallying for some time, ultimately begins to show signs of being overbought as measured by Stochastics, it makes sense to tighten stops and be alert to any potential weakness. It is equally important to know that just because a stock exhibits signs of "overbought" via Stochastics, it does not mean the stock will immediately reverse. It is prudent is recognize that emotionally driven markets will often stay "overbought" for sometime, which can allow for even greater profitability, therefore, the real lesson is to be aware of the indication without reacting too soon.

Remember, other components of analysis will also need to be considered. Just because the Stochastic moves into overbought or oversold territory, does not mean the stock is ready to change trend. Many consider the levels above 80 overbought and the levels below 20 oversold, but this is far from absolute. Stochastics is merely indicating that price action is beginning to show initial signs of reversal, whereby current prices may not be able to sustain themselves. But until a true break in trend occurs, the benefit of the doubt belongs to the current trend. The astute trader should be aware of Stochastics, but wait for a true price break in trend (bullish or bearish) before reacting.

The mathematical formula for Stochastics is given next, but it is of less importance than understanding what the math seeks to measure. The Stochastics indicator is plotted as two lines: the %K line and the %D line:

$$\%K = 100\left[\frac{\left(C - L21\ \text{close}\right)}{\left(H21 - L21\right)}\right]$$

where C = The most recent close
   L21 = The lowest low for the last 21 trading periods
   H21 = Highest high for the same 21 trading periods

%D is a smoothed version of the %K line, usually using 3 trading periods. The %D equation is as follows:

$$\%D = 100 \times \left(\frac{H3}{L3}\right)$$

where H3 = The 3 period sum of (C − L21)
   L3 = The 3 period sum of (H21 − L21)

From this equation, the values are plotted on a chart from 0 to 100—known as the oscillator. A %K reading of 62 percent or 62 tells us that the most recent close was in the 62nd percentile of the high/low range over the number of periods being measured. The oscillator works the same way as a bell curve—illustrating when the trading range has extended far outside the average or mean. The concept is based on the premise that once a given stock trades far enough from the mean (80 percent for bullish range and 20 percent for bearish), the stock price will regress back toward the mean—hence a reversal.

Once the %K is calculated, the %D is usually then just a 3 period moving average of %K, also reflected on the oscillator. Essentially, like a moving average on stock prices, the %D seeks to smooth the volatile nature of the faster moving %K line. Not unlike how the moving average of price will move slower than price itself.

The Stochastics formula can be used for any time frame, from monthly charts all the way down to one-minute charts.

Another popular way of using Stochastics is to identify when relative movement of the indicator fails to coincide with the price action for which it measures. This is known as a divergence. An example of a divergence would be when a stock in a downtrend makes a lower low while the Stochastic instead makes a higher low. This divergent action indicates the buyers are becoming more aggressive and that a reversal to the upside

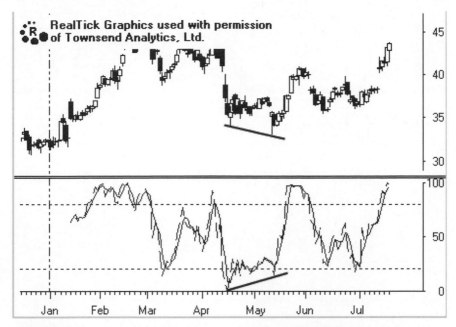

FIGURE 7.2 This chart shows a bullish divergence between price and the Stochastic. The April low in the stock occurred close to $34 while the Stochastic made a low near the zero line. The stock then made a lower low near $32.50 in mid-May while the Stochastic made a higher low near the 20 line. Divergences (bullish divergence) like this one often precede a short-term change in trend.

could be nearby. (See Figures 7.2 and 7.3.) Divergences between price action and an indicator such as Stochastics can be an early clue of a forthcoming reversal in trend.

Stochastics, in essence are a momentum indicator that can warn of strength or weakness in price based on mathematically calculating change in trading range. The idea is to anticipate in advance of the ultimate turning point, but as stated, not all overbought and oversold conditions cause an immediate turn.

Like all technical tools, Stochastic indicators are best learned through patient observation. You can read a book about them and feel like you understand the subject pretty well, but nothing will multiply the value of what you have learned as quickly as watching how the indicators play out in an actual market. While much more can be said about Stochastics, this basic understanding is all that you really need to know at this point. As experience grows, the divergences referenced above will become clearer, and your "radar" will go off much more frequently as a result.

FIGURE 7.3   This chart shows a bearish divergence between price and the Stochastic. As the stock made higher highs, the Stochastic made a series of lower highs. The divergence foreshadowed the subsequent decline.

RELATIVE STRENGTH INDEX

The Relative Strength Index (RSI) is a momentum indicator that is similar to stochastics in that it measures the closing prices over a given time period. The biggest difference between RSI and stochastics is that the RSI does not measure the range of the instrument being studied. It simply measures closing prices. Developed in 1978 by Welles Wilder, the RSI has stood the test of time as a popular and useful indicator. The purpose of RSI is to measure the relative internal strength of a stock. Its strength or weakness is not compared to other stocks, sectors, or indices—but only measured against its own price history.

The RSI should not be confused with the concept of Relative Strength which is a popular way of measuring a stocks strength or weakness compared to a larger universe of stocks.

The RSI measures the relative changes between higher and lower closing prices, and provides us with a way of determining if a stock is gaining or losing momentum. To determine overbought or oversold conditions, the oscillator is plotted on a vertical scale from 0 to 100. Unlike Stochastics

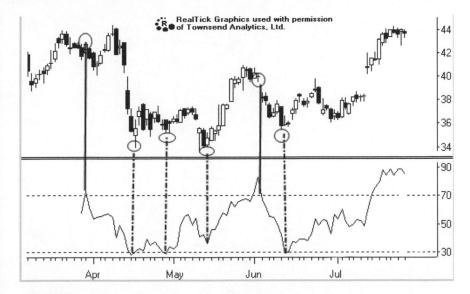

FIGURE 7.4 The RSI is an excellent indicator for spotting potential reversals. Notice how the stock moved lower after readings were above 70 and how the stock also turned higher after reaching levels below 30.

where we use 20 and 80 to define overbought or oversold, the 70 percent and 30 percent levels are used to warn us of conditions being overdone when using the RSI—but once again, these are simply guides and not literal levels that are absolute.

Essentially, the RSI is a tool we use in foundational analysis because it measures velocity and momentum. The indicator shows a potential slow-down in trend when the velocity starts to reach extreme conditions. Like Stochastics, it is important not to literally define overbought with a sell signal or oversold as a buy signal. These levels are merely reference points to alert us to a probability that prices may be near a reversal point. The proper way to utilize this oscillator is to be alert for a situation to sell a long position (or go short) when the oscillator is above 70 percent and be prepared for a potential buy (or cover a short) when the oscillator dips below 30 percent. (See Figure 7.4.)

Besides being useful for determining overbought or oversold levels, the RSI is commonly used for identifying what Welles Wilder referred to as "failure swings." A failure swing is basically a divergence between price and the RSI that leads to a price reversal. In order to receive a buy signal with a failure swing, the stock must trade down to a level that brings the RSI below 30 percent, followed by short-term recovery in price and then another drive lower where the stock price matches the prior low (or makes

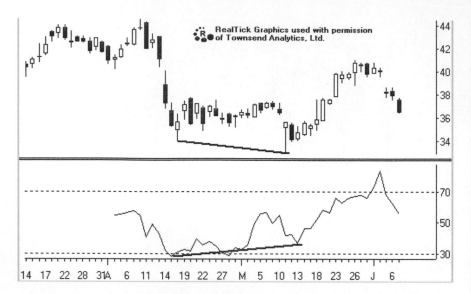

FIGURE 7.5   Notice how the RSI made a higher low while the stock was still declining. This bullish setup often foretells a price reversal back to the upside.

a lower low), while the RSI makes a higher low. Seen in Figure 7.5, these divergence patterns can lead to high confidence reversal situations.

A bearish divergence is a setup that provides traders with an opportunity to sell short a stock that is running out of upside strength. In order for a bearish divergence to occur, the stock needs to trade to a new high relative to a time frame it is being measured against, which brings the RSI up through the 70 percent line. After making a new high, the stock will experience what appears to be normal profit taking followed by another drive to either match the old high or make a higher high. If during the second rally higher, the RSI fails to reach the 70 percent level—we have a bearish divergence (see Figure 7.6). It is important not to sell short until the price starts turning lower again as a divergence will not always lead to a reversal. Divergence trades can be very rewarding, however they are considered high risk, given it is predicting a reversal of trend. Therefore, be sure to honor your stops, otherwise you could find yourself holding a large loser.

ARMS INDEX

The ARMS Index was created by Richard Arms Jr. The primary function of the ARMS Index is to measure excessive market behavior as defined by volume (another foundational variable). The Arms Index is also known as the Trading Index (TRIN).

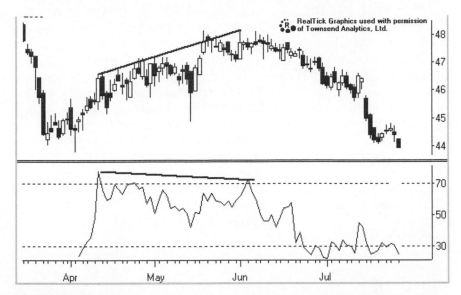

FIGURE 7.6 Notice how the RSI made a lower high while the strength persisted in the stock price. The RSI divergence indicates there is a potential reversal coming to the upside.

The TRIN allows us to look beyond simple price action, and instead measure the emotional intensity level of its participants through volume. Important facts about the TRIN include:

- There exist at least two TRINs in the marketplace. A TRIN based on the NYSE, which is the one most commonly thought of and referenced, and TRIN for the Nasdaq Composite Index. We will focus on NYSE TRIN, but the formula applies identically if looking at the Nasdaq. The behavior of these two TRINS on any given day can be quite different, and often act independently of each other.
- The numerator of the TRIN formula measures the number of advancing stocks divided by the number of declining stocks to form a ratio. The denominator of TRIN measures the cumulative volume for advancing stocks divided by the cumulative volume of the declining stocks.

$$TRIN = \frac{\left(\dfrac{\text{Advancing issues}}{\text{Declining issues}} \right)}{\left(\dfrac{\text{Advancing volume}}{\text{Declining volume}} \right)}$$

Mathematically, TRIN is a broad market indicator (NYSE or Nasdaq) that measures when volume, in association with direction, accelerates to a point where the move is likely to exhausts itself. We have stated several times that stocks and markets move the most (have the most velocity) on the least volume and then peak with high volume. This price/volume relationship shows up most frequently during high-velocity news related events. As volume grows to frenzied levels we must realize that the market crowd becomes aligned (meaning most participants are net long or net short) and that leaves conditions ripe for a reversal. When greed and fear run rampant, price/volume ratios reflect the markets collective emotion. For example, if the number of advancing stocks is twice the number of declining stocks (two to one) while the volume associated with advancing stocks is also twice the volume of declining stocks (two to one), we have a neutralized situation, and things are as they should be (the market is in a sustainable rally):

$$TRIN=\frac{\left(\frac{2}{1}\right)}{\left(\frac{2}{1}\right)}=1.0 \text{ par}$$

But if the market becomes emotionally charged and pushes the ratio of advancing stocks over declining stocks to the point of four to one while volume remains at two to one, we will have a volatile rally on relatively lower proportionate volume. This type of rally is one that should be closely watched because while most stocks are moving higher; it occurs on less volume. Therefore, a move like this (think FOMC news, GDP, etc) is considered reactionary and often over soon after it starts. In essence, this type of ratio causes this rally to be less trusted because it lacks the necessary fuel (volume) to sustain itself:

$$TRIN=\frac{\left(\frac{4}{1}\right)}{\left(\frac{2}{1}\right)}=2.0$$

In this scenario we have a TRIN of 2.0, but this number can mean more than one thing. For example, in a bear market, decliners could be leading advancers with high volume, resulting in another high TRIN, but a much different signal than the previous example:

$$\text{TRIN} = \frac{\left(\frac{1}{2}\right)}{\left(\frac{1}{4}\right)} = 2.0$$

In this example, sellers are firmly in control. Not only are the number of declining stocks twice as large as the number of advancing stocks, but the downside volume is also four times greater than the volume in the stocks that are advancing. In this case, TRIN acts like the classic sentiment indicator and interprets this as oversold which makes the market ready for a potential reversal.

This exercise demonstrates why no indicator (including TRIN) can be read literally, given both of the examples come up with the same value, but mean different things. Therefore, we once again remind ourselves the importance of understanding what the indicator or math seeks to measure. To literally interpret TRIN or any indicator without understanding it, is akin to blindly following the advice of others. In order to avoid traps like this, let's return to the first example.

When markets turn, they often exhibit a rapid rally on light volume (e.g., four to one ratio divided by two to one). The advancing stocks show strength, but the volume has yet to catch up. As the market follows through, volume of advancing shares will tend to rise, thereby exhibiting a healthier trend than the low volume rally. As volume improves, TRIN will naturally retrace (4/1)/(3/1) confirming a lower risk long position. Knowing what stage the market is in will also help you to separate what may be a classic bear market rally from an emerging new bullish trend. (See Figure 7.7.)

Using the TRIN

The Contrarian Approach When the overall market trades into an area of supply (resistance), accompanied by extreme low TRIN; look for opportunities to sell short. Conversely, when the market trades into an area of demand (support), accompanied by extreme high TRIN, look for stocks to go long.

Using TRIN for Confirmation When the overall market is in a solid trend, TRIN can help confirm the momentum of that trend. For instance, if a new move has been ignited into an area of supply or demand, and TRIN is now confirming the direction of the move—look to follow the trend, not fade it. For example, an extreme low TRIN (below 0.50) will commonly accompany a bullish reversal once the move is underway. Vice versa, an

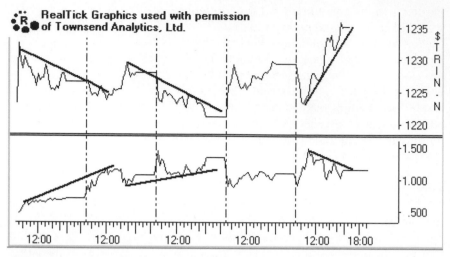

FIGURE 7.7 The top chart is an intraday chart of the S&P 500 and the bottom chart shows the TRIN. A ratio of 1 indicates the market is in balance. A TRIN above 1 it indicates more volume is coming into declining stocks, while a TRIN below 1 indicates that more volume is coming to stocks that are advancing.

extreme high (greater than 2.0) TRIN will commonly accompany a bearish reversal once the move is underway. These extreme readings should be considered confirmation the new move is underway.

Like all indicators and oscillators, the TRIN is not a trading system by itself, it is merely an objective measure of the conviction of buyers and sellers for the overall market on a given day. Rather than focusing solely on the absolute TRIN reading, traders should pay more attention to the trend of TRIN over several days and even weeks for potential trade setups.

FIBONACCI RETRACEMENTS

Fibonacci, or more formally Leonardo Pisano of Pisa, was an Italian mathematician from the thirteenth century who has had a profound impact on the world. Fibonacci was able to show degrees of order within seemingly random and chaotic mathematical sequences, which have an undeniable correlation to many physical properties within the universe, science, art, architecture, and yes . . . the stock market. Is this to say that there is some mystical intelligence beyond our comprehension that explains some of life's secrets? No, not really. In our estimation, the real value of Fibonacci retracement relates to the perception value of many market technicians who follow it. For this reason, the sequence we are about to study offers a path or structure that many believe influence market behavior. In the end, we will leave it to the philosophers of the world to debate Fibonacci's influence within the universe—it is our interest to follow the impact his work has had on traders and the footprints his math leaves behind.

Because so many market technicians perceive and trade price swings based on Fibonacci retracements, one could say that his sequencing has created a self-fulfilling prophecy—and we subscribe to this camp. Those who are believers of Fibonacci have applied his work to gain insight on potential order within the financial markets. Fibonacci was a leading thinker in his day and in his book Liber abaci (A.D. 1202), he pondered:

> *A certain man put a pair of rabbits in a place surrounded on all sides by a wall. How many pairs of rabbits can be produced from that pair in a year if it is supposed that every month each pair begets a new pair which from the second month on becomes productive?*

His results yielded a sequence of numbers in which two consecutive numbers when added together produce the third, that is, 1, 1, 2, 3, 5, 8, 13, 21, 34, 55, and so on. This has come to be known as the Fibonacci sequence. Since the thirteenth century, scholars have attempted to apply this sequence of numbers in many other fields as stated.

Chaos theory, a twentieth-century system of mathematics, finds its roots in Fibonacci's work, as it purports to find order in random samples of data. Mountains, clouds, streams and many other natural phenomena are now being looked at differently in an attempt to find patterns. What Fibonacci found was that patterns in seemingly random numbers begin to form after eight reverberations or successive iterations.

Take any two random numbers and add them together and that result is added to the former sum in a particular pattern. After eight reverberations we can divide the former number into the latter number and find a definable pattern. Let's start with two random numbers 12 and 17:

$$\text{Reverberation 1: } 12 + 17 = 29$$

$$\text{Reverberation 2: } 29 + 12 = 41$$

$$\text{Reverberation 3: } 41 + 29 = 70$$

$$\text{Reverberation 4: } 70 + 41 = 111$$

$$\text{Reverberation 5: } 111 + 70 = 181$$

$$\text{Reverberation 6: } 181 + 111 = 292$$

$$\text{Reverberation 7: } 292 + 181 = 473$$

$$\text{Reverberation 8: } 473 + 292 = 765$$

Now divide the seventh reverberation by the eighth:

$$\left(\frac{473}{765}=0.618\right)$$

Where the Fibonacci sequence becomes fascinating is when you try different random numbers for the first two addends. No matter what two numbers are chosen, the result after eight reverberations will have the same ratio—0.618. Over the years, this ratio has become known as the *Golden Mean.*

It is fairly recently that Fibonacci analysis has been applied to trading and its popularity as an analysis tool has become mainstream. Since computer technology has advanced and made what was once complicated analysis much easier, technicians apply Fibonacci analysis to swings in the market across all time frames, although longer time frames seem to get more attention. The most common usage for Fibonacci is looking for potential support/resistance levels as a market retraces a move in either direction. The theory is that if a stock experiences a pullback of greater than 61.8 percent of the recent trend, that the stock is no longer experiencing a pullback, instead it tells us of a trend failure.

Besides the 61.8 percent level, two other levels are closely watched by Fibonacci traders; 38.2 percent (which is equal to 1 − .618) and 50 percent. Looking at Figure 7.8 to understand this concept better, we will apply Fibonacci levels to the move that occurred from $14.45 (labeled point A) to just under $17.50 (labeled point B). This move of just over two points higher experienced a pullback that saw the price come down quickly to the 38.2 percent retracement level, where the stock experienced some buying which stabilized the stock for a couple of days. Apparently the sellers were not done at the 38.2 percent level because the stock then came down to find intraday support at the 50 percent level. Once the 50 percent level held as support, buyers rushed in and continued to push the stock back up past the old high. If the 50 percent level had not held as support, the next potential level of support would have been found at the 61.8 percent level near $15.50. If this level failed to act as support it would be inferred that buyers did not have sufficient interest in the stock and that the sellers had gained control. As we know markets do not head straight up or straight down and normal pullbacks are necessary for stocks to regain their upward momentum.

Fibonacci levels assist traders in trying to determine if swings in the market are natural retracements or if the market has retraced too much and a reversal is at hand. The ratios that define these retracements are highly monitored by institutional firms and retail traders alike, therefore,

FIGURE 7.8 This chart shows the Fibonacci levels overlaid on price.

they do have significance. The value of knowing these levels should not be downplayed because Fibonacci analysis can reveal to us how market participants may be approaching the market. Just as it would be important to know if a major market maker had a large institutional buy or sell order, it is also valuable to know where buyers and sellers may step in based on Fibonacci levels. If one can determine a primary uptrend where many market players sentiment will be to try to buy dips, Fibonacci levels can provide us with levels of support that may not be revealed by simply looking at traditional price support on a chart.

Many newer traders often wonder why Fibonacci analysis seems to work. Is it because of some mystical force of nature that buyers show up at a certain percentage retracement levels? Or is it because enough participants decide not to sell at the 61.8 percent level while other participants decide to buy at the 61.8 percent level, thus making it a self-fulfilling prophecy? Whatever you want to believe, the mere observance of these levels does cause an imbalance in supply and demand and there are often many very profitable trades to be entered at these levels, and that should be a good enough reason to follow these levels. The important thing with

Fibonacci and any of the other indicators and oscillators we have studied is to remember they are not trading systems but analysis tools that assist us in identifying potential entry and exit points. At the end of the day, the only thing that pays us is price and that should be our most important determining factor as to whether or not to enter a trade. These indicators and oscillators can be excellent for leading us to a trade, but be sure to make your decision to enter only once price has confirmed what the indicator led you to believe.

CHAPTER 8

Traditional Pivot Analysis

The market is obviously made up of the sum of its participants, and underlying each participant are emotions. The best measure of the market's collected emotion is range. Range can be measured over the course of a day, week, year, or any time frame for that matter. Range simply measures the extent of bullishness (greed), bearishness (fear), and even complacency. Prices settle into areas where we have consensus, a word that describes where most agree. Therefore, when prices close the day at a given price level, we could say that the price consensus was based on the collective group who participated in trading for a given financial instrument. Volume, as we know is another way of measuring the depth of that consensus, and the more participants or shares that trade at a given price, the more we can surmise that the market agrees with that price level. This stated, a form of analysis was developed years ago to mathematically measure this range of emotion and has since evolved into what we now know as *pivot analysis*.

Traders have used this unique and relatively simply form of analysis to find potential pivotal price levels. These price areas, which often act as levels of support and resistance, are called *pivots*, and many times identify important reversal or continuation patterns for the day, week, month, or even the year.

First made popular decades ago by floor traders trading futures at the Chicago Mercantile Exchange (CME), pivot analysis has endured through the years because, when coupled with good discipline, it provides an

TABLE 8.1 The Pivot Formula
Pivot point (P) = (H + L + C)/3
First resistance level (R1) = (2 × P) −L
First support level (S1) = (2 × P) −H
Second resistance level (R2) = P + (R1 − S1)
Second support level (S2) = P − (R1 − S1)

edge. A unique aspect of pivot analysis is that pivots are calculated by a mathematical function, this is a departure from traditional technical analysis—which seeks to find support and resistance levels on charts. Pivot analysis fits more into the category of what is known as quantitative analysis, whereby price action in the market is measured through statistics. The concept here is that humans, when measured statistically, leave clear clues of their collective psychology, and these clues are in the form of price levels. Not unlike the way statisticians can calculate with reasonable accuracy the way people will exit from a burning building or even riot in the streets after a World Series championship—quantitative analysis measures the pivotal price levels left by millions of participants. This allows traders to calculate potential pivotal areas that are not plainly visible to the average investor using fundamental analysis or even traditional technical analysis. Looking at Table 8.1, it is evident that the underlying pivot formula is comparatively simple, while its historical performance is undeniable.

THE PIVOT FORMULA

The pivot formula is most effective when used on heavier volume instruments that have a wide daily range. On a less liquid, narrow range instrument, the pivot levels would be closer together and therefore less effective. It also makes sense that a narrow based volume instrument or stock would not accurately reflect the collective participants as well as a broader sampling.

An ideal instrument to apply pivot analysis is the E-mini S&P 500 futures contract—traded on the CME. The E-mini S&P 500 futures contract, or ES, trades massive volume each day with powerful range—not to mention that it is based on the top 500 publicly traded companies in America—a broad based sampling for sure.

From Table 8.1 notice that the only pieces of information needed to calculate the pivot levels for a particular instrument are the high of the period (H), the low of the period (L), and the close of the period (C). From these three pieces of information, the pivot point, as well as support and resistance levels, can easily be calculated. The most significant piece of information given by the pivot formula is the pivot point (P). The pivot point is often considered to be a focal point for institutional traders, floor traders and even astute retail investors.

The basic concept for pivot trading is quite simple. The idea is to take a bearish position if the pivot point is penetrated from above, meaning prices are falling—and a bullish position if the pivot point is taken out from below (prices rising). Let's explore.

THE PIVOT IN ACTION

To demonstrate the use of pivots, we illustrate the pivot levels on a chart (Figure 8.1), which offers better visual interpretation. Upon examination of the right side of Figure 8.1, buyers take control and push the E-mini S&P 500 Futures contract higher as the daily pivot gets taken out from below

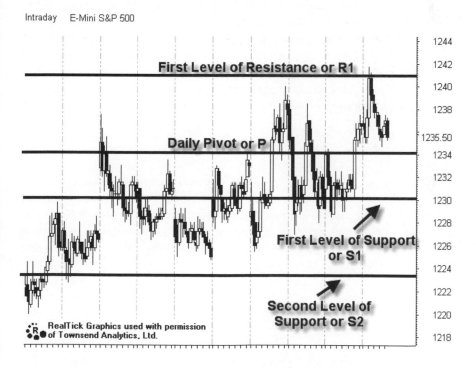

FIGURE 8.1 The traditional pivot levels are plotted on this chart of the E-mini S&P 500 Futures contract. Looking to the right side of the chart, if the contract was able to get above R1 the next area of potential resistance would be R2 (not visible on this chart).

(bullish). This represents the markets greed if you will, and the corresponding rising demand for the S&P's. At this point traders would enter long positions above the daily pivot, expecting the rally to accelerate and move
higher. The natural place to set the stop would be just beneath the daily
pivot level that was just penetrated. Now that we have defined the entry
and stop, we can focus on the initial target. The first target would be called,
R1—meaning the first expected level of resistance. As the ES approaches
R1, traders could do a few things. First, traders could be patient and observe whether R1 gets taken out. If the rally continues past R1, stops would
be moved to just beneath R1 to protect profits. Secondly, traders could exit
one half of the long position and take partial profits, and let the remaining
position ride in the event the market continues to rally. Seems simple
enough and it is, so don't overcomplicate it. Remember, this approach was
developed by floor traders where markets move fast, therefore, they had
little time to react or make the process more complicated than it was intended to be. You would be wise to follow the same approach.

Continuing with Figure 8.1, note that the ES did in fact rally above the
daily pivot to R1 where the contract ultimately ran into resistance and
pulled back to the daily pivot. Astute traders who used trailing stops would
have maximized gains before the contract pulled back to the daily pivot by
resetting the stop just below R1.

Calculating Pivots

Using the pivot formula is easy and you simply need to calculate a few setups for yourself to get comfortable with it. Referring to Table 8.2, we illustrate the actual pivots based on using the formula in Table 8.1.

If the E-mini S&P contract traded within a range from 1218.00 to
1225.25, before closing at 1221.00, the pivot calculation would be as shown
in Table 8.2. Note that in Table 8.2, there is a difference between the calculated pivot levels and the pivot levels that are practical to use while trading.
This is because the E-mini S&P contract only trades in quarter point increments, therefore we round to the nearest quarter point. The ES contract

TABLE 8.2 Pivot Calculations Based on the Pivot Formula in Table 8.1

	Actual Levels	Practical Levels
Second resistance level (R2)	1,228.67	1,228.75
First reisistance level (R2)	1,224.84	1,224.75
Pivot point	1,221.42	1,221.5
First support level (S1)	1,217.59	1,217.5
Second support level (S2)	1,214.17	1,214.25

has a minimum tick increment of a quarter of a point, and without the conversion, it would be difficult to determine where to open and close trades.

Choosing the Right Data for Calculations

The E-mini S&P 500 contract trades from Sunday night at 6:00 P.M. until Monday at 4:15 P.M. Eastern Standard Time (EST), before briefly pausing between the hours of 4:15 to 4:30 P.M. On Monday at 4:30 P.M., the ES contract opens again for trading until 5:30 P.M., where it pauses until 6:00 P.M. The contract technically opens for trading at 4:30 P.M.; therefore, the question often arises—which session should one look to for the high, low, and closing price?

We use the closing price at 4:15 P.M. for the "close" variable, and for the "high" and "low," we take a different approach. Because institutional traders will look to all trading sessions despite relatively light volume in after-hours sessions, we follow the same approach. Some traders will simply use the high and low generated from the time period of 9:30 A.M. until 4:15 P.M.; however, significant back testing has proved this theory to be inadequate. Traders can experiment using different highs and lows, based on whether the relative high or low was set in the overnight session or during "normal" trading hours, but the generally accepted rule-of-thumb is to use the most extreme levels whether it occurs in the overnight session or during normal trading hours. This is very different from after hours trading in stocks, given the liquidity in stocks after hours is dramatically less in comparison to futures.

Even though most of the significant volume occurs between 9:30 and 4:15 P.M., the overnight session cannot be ignored because the direction of the overnight session often sets the stage for the regular trading day. This direction is often influenced by news, which is most often released after the close of the U.S. equities market. Therefore, futures markets are the first markets to respond to the news, hence the reason after hours sessions are so important to futures. (See Figure 8.2.)

THE AREA BETWEEN R1 AND S1

Many times throughout a particular trading session, the session range remains between the first level of support and the first level of resistance (S1 and R1, respectively), as market makers and institutional participants attempt to manage risk within this range. Because these participants are more active and trade in and out of positions within this range, expect much smaller, more violent moves. Their short-term trading horizon often limits range until something truly powerful moves the market. It is only

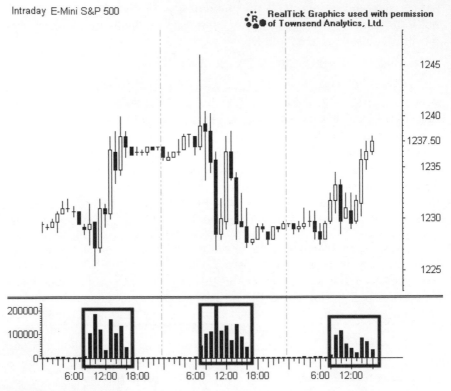

FIGURE 8.2   This intraday chart of the E-mini S&P 500 Futures shows that the volume is much greater from 9:30 A.M. to 4:15 P.M. but it is important to understand that there can be significant price action during the overnight session due to news and other events. Traders calculating pivot levels should use all highs and lows in order to obtain the most relevant pivot information.

when R1 or S1 gets taken out, that we can expect short-term traders are of less influence and the move is more structural or substantial.

During larger moves outside S1 and R1, floor traders are of less influence, and it is the off-floor traders (institutional money such as mutual, hedge and pension funds) that tend to command market direction. These moves can be gauged by velocity (high), and once detected often flag a market that has the propensity to trade toward the second level of support or resistance (S2 and R2).

If there is a large amount of velocity associated with the move, S2 or R2 will often be penetrated, and this is the move that intermediate- and longer-term investors should focus on as opposed to smaller more violent moves within S1 and R1. We suggest learning to trade the larger moves first before trying to compete with the floor traders through day trading the futures. In time, as your skill grows, you may consider more short-term moves associated with S1 and R1.

ILLUSTRATING PIVOT LINES ON REALTICK

It may seem like a lot of work calculating pivots, but in time it becomes easy. For those who prefer having the pivot calculated for them, systems exist that do it for you. Traders taking advantage of the RealTick trading platform can place pivot analysis lines on a particular chart. The five lines of the pivot formula can then be displayed on the chart automatically, and many find this very useful. (See Figure 8.3 for an example.)

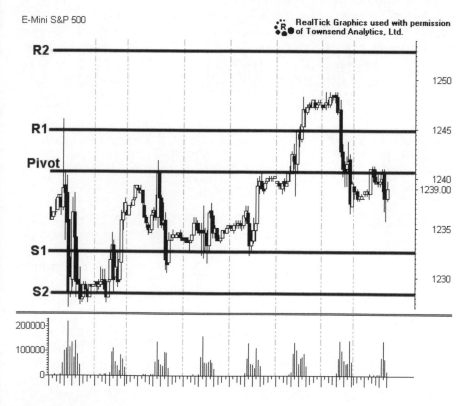

FIGURE 8.3 RealTick pivot lines.

ARCHIVING PIVOT LEVELS

For those that choose to calculate their own pivots (and we suggest you do), the tools available to do so make it really easy. Because of the dynamic nature of the equities markets, many of us want to be aware of key levels within the market, therefore we keep both daily and long-term pivot calculations since we know institutions are doing the same. With the help of Microsoft Excel, the pivot formula can be built into a spreadsheet and will never need to be done again. Systems like RealTick then allow you to automatically upload the daily data into Excel each day. Figure 8.4 shows an example of a spreadsheet, illustrating the range from S2 to R2, giving the trader valuable information to be aware of if the market trades to these levels. Often times, the market will trade to pivot levels within the day and then more radically as a result of institutional programs kicking in, and amateurs can only look to news to find an explanation. The truth is there usually will not be any news to explain it. This is because the media is often just as uninformed as the amateur.

As you can see from Figure 8.4, potential volatility exists for the Dow between S2 and R2, signaling a range of 141 points. This is information you would want to have! Moreover, as column 12 shows, the distance from the *prior days close* to the calculated pivot is a *positive 19 points*. By closing above the next day's pivot, the Dow will have a bullish bias going

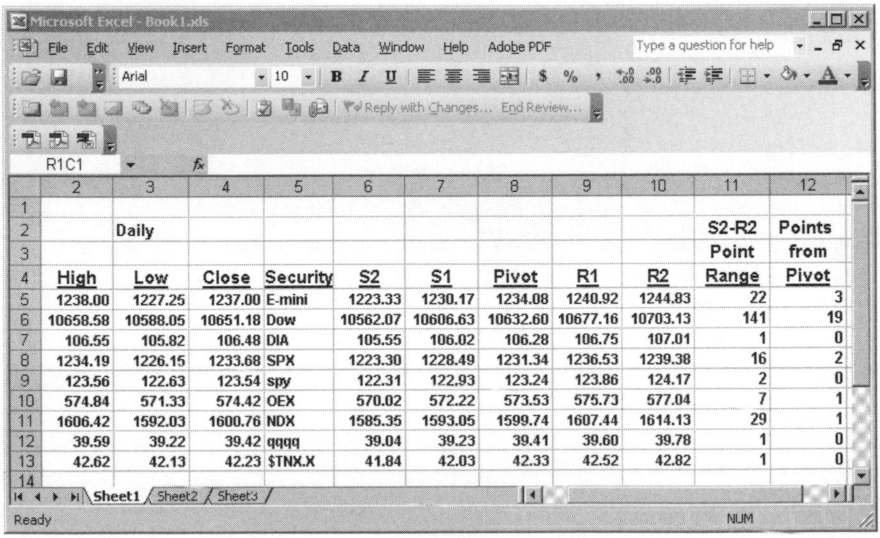

	2	3	4	5	6	7	8	9	10	11	12
1											
2		Daily								S2-R2	Points
3										Point	from
4	High	Low	Close	Security	S2	S1	Pivot	R1	R2	Range	Pivot
5	1238.00	1227.25	1237.00	E-mini	1223.33	1230.17	1234.08	1240.92	1244.83	22	3
6	10658.58	10588.05	10651.18	Dow	10562.07	10606.63	10632.60	10677.16	10703.13	141	19
7	106.55	105.82	106.48	DIA	105.55	106.02	106.28	106.75	107.01	1	0
8	1234.19	1226.15	1233.68	SPX	1223.30	1228.49	1231.34	1236.53	1239.38	16	2
9	123.56	122.63	123.54	spy	122.31	122.93	123.24	123.86	124.17	2	0
10	574.84	571.33	574.42	OEX	570.02	572.22	573.53	575.73	577.04	7	1
11	1606.42	1592.03	1600.76	NDX	1585.35	1593.05	1599.74	1607.44	1614.13	29	1
12	39.59	39.22	39.42	qqqq	39.04	39.23	39.41	39.60	39.78	1	0
13	42.62	42.13	42.23	$TNX.X	41.84	42.03	42.33	42.52	42.82	1	0
14											

FIGURE 8.4 A spreadsheet of pivot levels.

into the next session. This information allows for a better strategy than following the news.

PIVOTAL PSYCHOLOGY

Before trades were entered through traditional pivot analysis, it was important to back test the relatively simple mathematical formula over and over. Traders quickly saw that these mathematically derived levels around the calculated pivot simply outlined a type of standard deviation.

Interesting enough, it was usually levels calculated from pivot analysis that answered the once-challenging question, "I wonder why the market abruptly stopped, instead of moving to the next level?" Further research seemed to point towards investment houses using pivot analysis to control their stock inventory with this simple, yet effective risk management tool. It makes sense to institutions to program the daily pivotal levels into a computer each night in order to hedge inventory risk (holding large positions) during the following session. If a particular portfolio gets too profitable or too risky, computer programs take the emotion out of trading and simply use these levels to manage risk and take profits. This is why this tool is an ideal strategy for institutional traders, and why we like to follow the approach. After all, whom would you rather shadow in the market—institutional money or amateur money?

Paper Trading

It makes sense to practice this approach before committing actual capital. There are certainly advantages to paper trading, but you have to be realistic about emotions (or lack thereof) and price slippage that paper trading cannot simulate. Nonetheless, paper trading is a good idea while learning to pivot trade. The endeavor is especially worthwhile if discipline is a problem for you. Pivot trading offers a well-defined strategy that can control emotions by using only objective price data. If emotional news driven trading has been your nemesis, perhaps pivot trading will be a good alternative to sleepless nights of abnormal heartbeats while imagining a geopolitical event ruining your entire trading account.

Because almost all traders begin with some form of paper trading, try putting on your thinking cap and bringing a pencil and a pad of paper to the computer around 9:00 A.M. (EST). The session will often go something like this: The ES starts trading at 1220.50 and the set-up from the night before has a trader looking to sell short two contracts at 1220.00. The paper trader will note they are short at 1220, but in reality, with a live account, a second of hesitation will more likely have a trader chasing the trader lower. Instead of selling at 1220, the likely scenario could result in a trader selling considerably lower and therefore, *taking on much more risk than first anticipated*. The caution here is that while paper trading, traders always find better liquidity than real trading. Therefore, don't be fooled into believing that paper trading accurately reflects reality. The value here is more about learning to calculate the pivot, while understanding that slippage and emotion will play a big part once real trading begins.

STRATEGY AND MONEY MANAGEMENT

With a significant amount of traders looking at pivots, a question that comes up often is; which pivot level is more valuable—R1 or R2 when gauging resistance, or S1 or S2 when gauging support? The answer is, disciplined traders do not have to have the answer to such questions, since stops should always be there to protect you. As a swing trader, it is extremely important to construct a plan that allows one to closely monitor open positions, while *always having a stop in place* to control risk. The pivot levels are the natural areas to set stops. Notice we state the word— *areas*. This means that a stop should be places near these pivots, not necessarily at the exact pivot. This is important because every trader has their own tolerance for risk and this number is not the same for everyone. The important lesson is that the pivot levels should be used to determine the area in which stops should be set.

For example, looking at Figure 8.5, the ES contract traded outside its calculated R2 level, possibly signaling overbought conditions. If long, a trader would have a stop in place underneath this R2 area, protecting profits. Alternatively, if a trader is looking to open a short position, it would make sense to look for additional weakness before initiating a position. This would come once R2 is cleared (broken) to the downside. If a short position is triggered, the profit objective would be at least R1. As a general rule, a trader who achieves between 2 to 3 points in favorable movement should consider moving the initial protective stop to a trailing stop near breakeven. This will preserve capital while leaving the opportunity for profits to run. Continuing with the short sale example in Figure 8.5, a move underneath R1 would then be a signal for traders to move their stop down to just above R1, to protect profits should the market decide to turn and rally. If the weakness does persist, we would look to the daily pivot as our next level of support where the short may be covered (with a nice profit). Should the market continue lower, we would then see S1 as the next level of support and then S2 after that. If S2 were achieved on this short, we

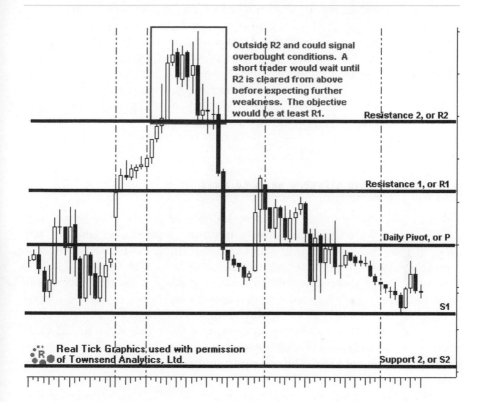

Outside R2 and could signal overbought conditions. A short trader would wait until R2 is cleared from above before expecting further weakness. The objective would be at least R1.

Resistance 2, or R2

Resistance 1, or R1

Daily Pivot, or P

S1

Real Tick Graphics, used with permission of Townsend Analytics, Ltd.

Support 2, or S2

FIGURE 8.5   The S&P E-mini futures contract—penetrating several key levels.

would consider ourselves "outside" the bands (or pivots) for this time frame. Traders would then need to look either at longer-term pivot levels (based on weekly and monthly highs, lows, and close) or other technical analysis tools.

LINING UP LEVELS ON MULTIPLE TIME FRAMES

If short-term pivots are penetrated, it then makes sense to move to a longer-term time frame. While you achieve a solid understanding of the short-term market psychology using the daily pivot, the true structural moves will be seen better by using the weekly and monthly support/resistance levels. To calculate pivot levels on longer-term time frames, simply take the prior periods high, low, and close from weekly or monthly charts. Then plug the data into the pivot formula.

TABLE 8.3	Importance of Pivot Time Frames
Time Frame	Importance
Monthly	Very important
Weekly	Very important
Daily	Important
Confluence	Most important

Note that the term *confluence* is a measure of monthly, weekly, and daily.

As we move to this longer-term time frame, it makes sense to discuss the psychological importance of each time frame. See Table 8.3 for a broad definition and weight of each time frame. This should help you focus on its significance relative to trading strategies, that is, how long to stay with a trade.

Looking to Table 8.3, notice that more weight should be placed on the weekly and monthly pivotal levels than on a daily calculation. The most weight should be put on pivotal levels that line up on multiple time frames, which we call "confluence" (e.g., monthly. Weekly, and daily pivots are near the same number).

When confluence zones occur, they strengthen an area of support and resistance as well as boost a trader's confidence about a particular range.

Trading is a business that requires an edge, and traders can increase their edge by using confluence zones to help enter and manage positions. It is not uncommon for an instrument to trade outside the weekly and monthly S2/R2 levels (the widest levels as seen on the chart). When outside the weekly and monthly S2/R2 levels an instrument is considered stretched and ripe for a correction. Take for example the S&P E-mini futures contract. If the ES had a monthly S2 of 1060 (no reference to any figures), S1 of 1070, pivot of 1080, R1 at 1090 and R2 at 1200; and the ES traded from 1060 to 1080 for the month, a trader could gauge the market action for the month as bearish, since the trades that occurred were from S2 to the pivot. This is where confluence is important.

It is equally important to understand at what point daily pivot levels lose their importance. Typically daily pivot levels are only valid for a particular trading day or session (9:30 A.M. to 4:15 P.M.). The importance is only increased if it lines up with a high or low made in the past few sessions. Therefore, as daily pivots line up with longer-term pivots, the importance increases.

TRADING A CONFLUENCE ZONE

When determining an intermediate to longer-term bias, using a confluence of both pivot and Fibonacci analysis is also very helpful. Fibonacci was explored in Chapter 7 and is used for finding support and resistance levels— very different than pivot analysis. Therefore, if Fibonacci levels and pivot levels also agree (another form of confluence), we have a powerful message being sent from the market.

To demonstrate the use of Fibonacci retracement analysis for finding intermediate-term bias, look to Figure 8.6 that shows a weekly chart of XYZ Corp. Notice the right side of the chart where the stock is underneath the 38.2 percent retracement level (bold line near $25.00). The stock is currently still within the bearish trend, but traders should not sell the stock short without confirmation. We can achieve this with both pivot analysis and Fibonacci.

FIGURE 8.6   A weekly chart of XYZ Corp with Fibonacci lines drawn on it.

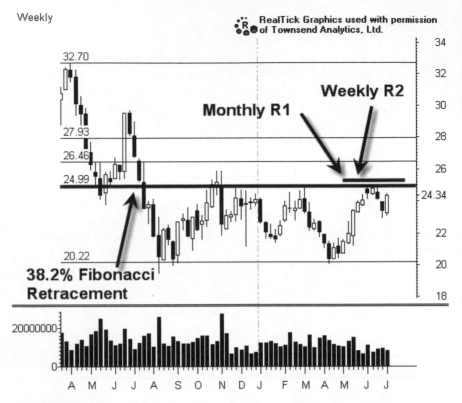

FIGURE 8.7   The construction of a confluence zone using pivot analysis and Fibonacci analysis.

To increase confidence in shorting the stock as it nears the $25.00 level, it is helpful when there is also confluence of the daily, weekly, and monthly pivot as well (see Figure 8.7). In this particular example there is a monthly R1 at $25.14 and a weekly R2 at $25.26 as well as a 38.2 percent Fibonacci retracement at $25.00. Putting it all together, the trader can construct a zone of resistance from $25.00 to $25.26 (the confluence zone). As long as resistance holds at these levels, shorts can be activated, with a protective stop set slightly above the $25.26 level.

To get a closer look at the confluence zone, see Figure 8.8. XYZ Corp managed to rally slightly above the upper bounds of the confluence zone (25.26) for a brief period, but quickly began to move lower, breaking down to the prior Fibonacci level. In this example, the short sellers have a clear entry point within the area of confluence as well as a defined stop (above 25.26). The first target area is calculated using Fibonacci analysis of the recent move higher (Figure 8.8). In this example, the 38.2 percent retrace-

FIGURE 8.8 The confluence zone is clearly identified and easy to calculate, providing the short sellers a low-risk entry, defined stop and profit target.

ment provided support for XYZ Corp and the stock bounced significantly off this level confirming that the 23.50 area was a good target. At 23.50, short-term traders would also consider going long. The point is, confluence provides a formidable edge regardless of which trade one takes.

SWING TRADING WITH CONFLUENCE AREAS

The next example of a swing trade set-up involves the S&P E-mini futures contract (ES). In this case, a swing trader with a bullish long-term outlook can take advantage of confluence zones to trade both with the primary trend and against it. This approach is designed for the more active trader who wishes to trade both from the long and short side of the market within a given trend.

FIGURE 8.9 The E-mini S&P 500 futures contract with various pivot levels drawn.

Looking at Figure 8.9, starting at the left side of the chart, notice that the ES broke solidly above the monthly R2 level. This immediately shows that the ES is having a bullish month. As the ES holds above the monthly R2, it gives a good signal to get long with an objective of weekly R1. After the ES tested monthly R2, the ES moved sideways for several days. At that point, traders using confluence zones could then construct a zone of resistance from 1237.25 to 1242.50 made up of the monthly R2 (1237.25), the weekly R1 (1240.75), as well as the daily R1 (1242.50). This zone could be seen as a potentially significant resistance area. In other words, you would not expect the ES to run through this zone without encountering some sort of increased selling pressure.

As Figure 8.10 shows, the E-mini S&P futures made a brief rally above the confluence zone, and then failed to hold above this zone of resistance. The probabilities are now lined up for a correction against the primary

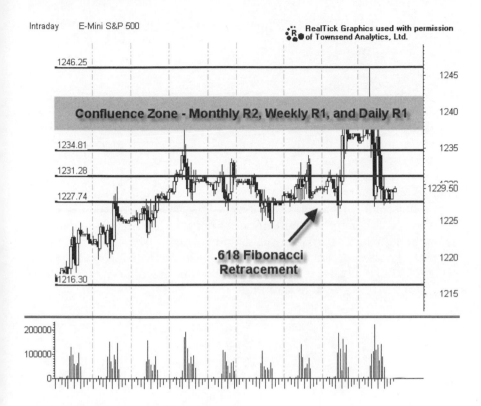

FIGURE 8.10 The E-mini S&P 500 futures chart with confluence zones and Fibonacci lines drawn.

bullish trend. Traders looking to short the ES should enter short positions as the ES rallies through the confluence zone then falls back below the zone. In this example, short positions are initiated as the ES falls below monthly R2. Again, looking to the right side of Figure 8.10 notice the correction that occurs after the ES falls below monthly R2. The first target of the short is at the weekly pivot (1228.00). This level also coincides closely with the 0.618 or 61.8 percent, Fibonacci retracement of the move. At this point, traders are urged to take at least partial profits and closely watch how the ES acts in this area. If continued weakness is observed the second target is near the monthly R1 level.

When learning about confluence zones, it is important to remember that we are not seeking to buy bottoms and sell tops—for this is impossible to do consistently. Instead, we seek to exit the long position at monthly R2 (1237.17), which is below the high of the move. Entering short positions at monthly R2 high is also unreasonable. It is more important to trade with the confluence zones once we break down through monthly R2. This is a much higher probability of trading, and every trader and investor must know that it is impossible to consistently predict highs and lows.

SUMMARY

For highly liquid instruments that trade with a significant daily range, the use of traditional pivot analysis can greatly enhance a trader's confidence and ability to trade profitably regardless of market conditions. Despite such a simple mathematical formula, a significant amount of traders continue to put strong emphasis in these calculations, either to manage inventory, swing trade, or simply scalp a few points out of the marketplace.

The pivot analysis learning curve is not very steep, and traders that embark on the task of archiving calculated levels will gain an edge by seeing clear levels of strength and weakness. On an intraday basis, traders using RealTick will have the ability to show these pivot lines rather effortlessly; thus saving a great deal of time.

CHAPTER 9

Planning and Staying on Track

Short-term trading is a business, just like any other. You will have greater success, faster, if you establish a plan and set goals that give you a clear sense of direction.

The optimum plan is the written one. People who commit their plans to paper usually achieve their goals. Those who merely hold their plans in mind as vague generalities usually achieve a lot less. The mind responds better to specific written ideas, making it easier to follow a strategy.

Planning on paper forces you to make concrete decisions. It also gives you a way to measure your progress and discipline. In fact, a written plan should be a prerequisite to opening an account.

To meet your objectives more quickly, jot down your trading business plan, along with an overview of your trading goals. Next, you can design your personal trading journal, which will evolve into an important part of your trading journey. Early planning will give you a focus and clarity as to your end-point objectives.

You can begin by answering the questions in this chapter.

WHAT IS YOUR TIME COMMITMENT?

First, do you intend to be a full-time or part-time trader? If you intend to tackle the market full time, you may have a large portfolio. Maybe you have been trading part time and want to become fully involved. You may even have the eventual goal of earning your living and providing for your family with a full-time career in trading—a goal that takes a maximum commitment of time and money. To absorb the most knowledge at the fastest rate, research, study, and watch market action whenever possible.

Maybe you prefer to position yourself as a part-time trader to supplement your income. If you would like to trade actively (intraday), you may want to investigate trading the first or last hour of the trading day; those times are usually the most conducive to market swings and volatility.

Swing trading and position trading (holding a position for the duration of an uptrend or downtrend, on a daily chart) also lend themselves well to part-time participation.

Whether you commit to pursuing your goal as a full-time or part-time trader, if you are a novice, you need to dedicate extra time for study and research over and above the hours you apply to actual trading. Keep in mind that you will never know everything there is to know about this business. If you are still trading years from now, you will still be studying years from now.

HOW WILL YOU FUND YOUR TRADING ACCOUNT?

It is important to realize that you must start with enough equity to get you through the learning curve. An account funded with a few hundred dollars will not be adequate. If you intend to trade actively, meaning more than four round trips in any five-day period, an SEC rule states you must have at least $25,000 equity in the account at all times. You also need a cash cushion on top of that amount to protect from losses.

The money in your trading account should be labeled "high risk." It has to be money you can afford to lose. It is unwise to use money intended for your children's' college education, a vacation, or the down payment on a new house. Directly stated, you must not fund your trading account with money that, if lost, will diminish your lifestyle in any way.

WHAT STYLE OF TRADING WILL YOU PURSUE?

Again, commit this information to paper. This helps to remove certain emotions associated with trading. Many traders allow their feelings to regulate the trade instead of just following their game plan. This can be costly: The market is extremely unforgiving when you break the rules, but it can be very rewarding when you follow them. Here, at MarketWise, we have seen many traders with no serious plan attempt to engage the market, only to end up angry, frustrated, and with a lot less money than when they started.

Those with a well thought-out and detailed plan, however, are able to execute trades with confidence.

You have to play two important roles in the trading process:

1. As the planner.
2. As the executor.

Once you have planned your trades, your job then becomes to execute the plan. This does not mean that the intended trades will be profitable. However, they should have low risk/high reward scenarios that increase your chances of success. The market is a dynamic ever-changing environment. Your trading plan should be flexible. If it is not working, then change it!

Here are some sample statements that may help you clarify your personal trading goals:

Example 1: "I plan to trade for the very short term by using intraday scalping methodology and only holding stocks for a few minutes. I will be a specialist when it comes to stock selection, and follow only a handful of stocks. I will not hold any positions overnight."

Example 2: "My approach is to trade intraday, focusing on a momentum approach for my trading style. I plan to hold positions for a few hours so that I do not churn and burn. I will close out all my positions before the market closes each day."

Example 3: "I will only trade semiconductor stocks that are part of the $SOX.X index. I will learn everything there is to know about this sector and the related stocks. I will learn how they trade in every type of market environment. I will not hold positions overnight."

Example 4: "My plan is to be a swing trader and hold positions for one to five days. If the stock is trending in my favor, I may hold the position but I will reduce my share size over the weekend. I will only use technical analysis to determine my entry and exit points. I will take positions in any stock that fits my criteria. I will only trade Stage 2 stocks on the long side and Stage 4 stocks on the short side."

Example 5: "I plan on playing the long-term trend. I will hold stocks 3 to 10 days and use technical analysis as my decision tool. The profits gained will supplement my income."

This is the first step in formulating your trading plan. You may want to attain many other goals, and some of these goals may even require a combination of techniques. Whatever your motivations may be, make sure you have considered your options carefully and know your risk tolerance and personality. As the professionals say, "If you don't know who you are, the market is an expensive place to learn."

WHAT ARE YOUR PROFIT OBJECTIVES?

Now, look at your profit objectives. As a trader, your goal is to match your trading strategies with your investment objectives. If you are trading for supplemental income, then your share size, profit target, and loss limit should be compatible with this objective.

Whatever your goals, your intent should be consistency in your trading style. Daily profit targets should be, at a minimum, double what your maximum loss is. Therefore, if you plan to risk a maximum of $250 a day, then you should plan to make a minimum of $500, giving yourself a minimum risk/reward of 1:2.

HOW WILL YOU MANAGE YOUR PROFITS?

Managing profits is an area that challenges some traders. The question most often asked is, "What do I do when I have reached my profit target for the day?" Answer: Stop trading for the day and analyze what you did to have a profitable day.

Remember, greed kills! At MarketWise, we have witnessed many talented traders who have succumbed to their greed. They have lost a lot of money over the past few years, so this statement cannot be stressed enough.

DO YOU EVALUATE ALL YOUR TRADES?

Most people focus on the trades they made during their losing days, but rarely glance at the trades they completed on their winning days.

Always evaluate your successful trades, so that when they present themselves in the future you can trade them well again. If you are consistently beating your daily profit goals—congratulations! Your next step toward your growth as a trader is to reset your goals higher.

ARE YOU KEEPING A JOURNAL?

One of the most productive steps you can take is to keep a trading journal. You may want to create a special folder, or keep it on your computer. Either way, it is important to keep a record of all your trades. With these facts, you can learn from your mistakes and your victories, as well as measure your personal progress.

The optimum journal has standard pages with areas for this information:

- Trade date, stock symbol, number of shares, entry price, initial protective stop price, initial profit target, exit date, exit price, and profit/loss.
- *Intended style of trade:* (scalp, momentum, swing, position, or intermediate term) and risk/reward ratio (½, ⅓, ⅓+).
- Why did I take this trade? (Sample answer: I entered this trade because the stock had made the first pullback after a strong move up out of a base on the daily chart. The major moving averages were lined up from slowest to fastest. Volume has been strong on positive days, and subdued on pullback days.)
- *Money management—trade progression and result:* (Sample answer: Stock XYZ moved above the high of the pullback day on high volume, and I entered the trade by buying 500 shares. It followed through, coming almost to my initial profit target by 2:30 P.M. As the market looked weak and the stock began to falter, I took my profits at that time.)
- *Chart review:* For this part of your journal, capture intraday or daily charts (SnagIt is a good program for capturing graphics), depending on the time frame of your trades. Then you can draw in the actual progression of your trades from entry to exit. Figures 9.1, 9.2, and 9.3 show sample charts. Trade Logs for these charts might read as follows:

Trade log: On this day, XYZ could not make a new high and broke down below its 10- and 20-period moving averages on a one-minute chart. I sold short at 10:07, as it broke support for a scalp trade. I lowered my stop progressively, until 10:25, when the opening gap was

FIGURE 9.1 Scalp trade.

XYZ Momentum Trade

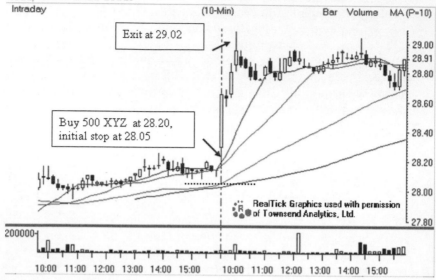

FIGURE 9.2 Momentum trade.

XYZ Swing Trade

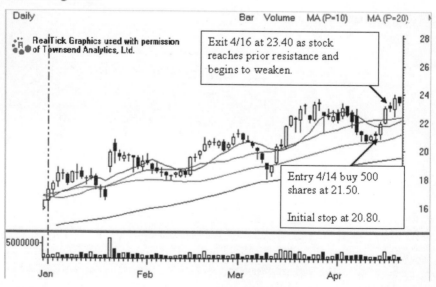

FIGURE 9.3 Swing trade.

nearly filled and Nasdaq futures showed signs of strengthening. I then closed my position for a $0.26 profit (see Figure 9.1).

Trade log: On this day, XYZ gapped up slightly, then moved back to support to fill the gap. I bought 500 shares at 9:35 A.M. at 28.20 for a momentum trade. My stop was at 28.05, just under prior day's close and supporting moving averages. The stock moved up (faster than I thought it would) to 29.08 and reached prior resistance on a daily chart. I sold at 29.02 for an $0.82 profit (see Figure 9.2).

Trade log: On this day, I bought 500 shares of XYZ at 21.50 for a swing trade as it pulled back to support at its 50-day moving average, then bounced. I placed my initial stop at 20.80, under the low of the entry day and at support. As the stock moved up on 4/15, I established a trailing stop of $0.50. The stock closed near the high of the day. On 4/16, I tightened the trailing stop, and as the stock reached prior resistance at 23.45, the stop automatically closed the position at 23.35, for a profit of $1.85 (see Figure 9.3).

To reiterate, have the following preparations in place before you begin trading:

- Write down the commitment of time that you will dedicate to your trading career. Will you be a full-time or part-time trader?
- Assess the capital with which you will fund your trading account. Make sure it is money that, if lost, will not diminish your lifestyle, or that of your loved ones.
- Target the trading style that best fits your lifestyle and establish written guidelines for your end-point objectives.
- Calculate profit objectives and management techniques that align with your risk tolerance and equity.
- Create a trading journal to evaluate your trades. Include text and chart entries that show the actual progression of your trades.

SUMMARY

Make sure your investment objectives are consistent with your trading plan. What requirements must be met for you to enter a trade? What charts and time frames will you use to make trading decisions? Will you trade breakouts, breakdowns, gaps, support and resistance, key moving averages? Know your maximum loss for a day, week, and month, and then never go over those limits.

A trading plan should be dynamic, much like the market. Maybe the plan does not suit your personality. Or it may be too time restrictive for your other commitments. It is *your* plan, and you can adjust and update it to match your needs.

Your plan should also align with the market environment. Take what the market gives you and do not expect anything more. High expectations can bring huge failure and disappointment. You will be much wiser to develop a positive outlook on your trading skills. To make $100,000 per year trading, you need to make $2,000 per week or $400 per day. When you break it down to daily objectives, it does not seem overwhelming.

And remember, trading success is not a destination, but a never-ending journey!

CHAPTER 10

Your Path to Success

This book was designed to help shorten your path to profitable trading, as well as to remove some of the stress from the learning process. The ideas, methods, and techniques in Chapters 1 through 9 represent the distilled knowledge of MarketWise instructors. Over a great many years, and in their combined experience, they have achieved enviable success in nearly every conceivable environment of the stock market. All of them have been through bull markets and bear markets; some are authors of books about trading; and most have traded professionally on the floor of a stock, options, or futures exchange. They have learned not only how to avoid repeating their mistakes, as failed traders are wont to do, but also how to teach what they know. We hope that this fund of information will help you avoid some of the pitfalls that plague all beginners.

Another thing these instructors have in common is that, at one time or another, each experienced a financial setback or two on the road to success. As all serious students must eventually learn, setbacks are not only unavoidable, they are absolutely essential for traders who want to master the psychological challenges of the game. Learning how to lose is not as easily done as learning how to interpret a chart, or how to execute a trade. Although the latter skills are necessary and crucial, and although doing them well is certain to contribute to the edge traders need to profit, they are not by themselves sufficient to achieve that goal. The more difficult part of the learning process entails delving into the "inner game" of trading, for it is in your own mind—and not on the charts—that you win or lose the game.

We have known people who were absolutely brilliant at reading stock charts, but who somehow failed as traders. They had the chart patterns down cold: rising wedges, pennants, head-and-shoulder formations, Fibonacci levels, momentum oscillators, moving averages, and flags. But when their money was on the line, all their expertise seemed to disappear. Either the stock did not do what it was "supposed" to do, or the trader had it pegged right, but exited a winner too early or held a loser too long. Or perhaps the trader was skillful enough to make a little money on most trades, but lost significantly more on the occasional trade gone terribly awry. And then there is the trader who picks great entry points most of the time, but who exits too early to reap the maximum benefit.

These examples illustrate that knowledge by itself is not enough. Two traders might both know a great deal about how short- and long-term moving averages interact, and they both might get perfect scores on a test on that subject. But it is by no means predictable that they would do equally well with their money on the line, since to interpret and use moving averages is not necessarily to succeed with them.

It is crucially important to understand that, no matter how well a systematic approach works, it will not work all the time. If it did, there would be no reason for anyone to read a book about trading, since all we would have to do to make piles of money would be to apply the same method precisely the same way each and every time. Winning with such a strategy is not possible, for no mechanical system or method can deliver consistent profits week after week, month after month, year after year. Many traders do not realize this, and they often waste months or even years experimenting with various trading systems without ever finding one that works.

When we speak of a trading system that works, it implies a system that will do one thing above all—free us from the burden of having to make trading decisions. This is what most traders seek when they experiment with technical tools such as Gann angles, Elliott Wave Theory, Pyrapoint, Andrews Pitchfork, and other widely touted analyticals. Although each of these tools can bolster your timing and make it easier for you to achieve trading profits, none can provide a guaranteed income. There really are no guarantees, and even the best traders will go through periods when losses come all too easily and self-doubts reign. The ability to get through such periods and back to profitability is what separates the dabblers and losers from the true professionals. Being a professional does not necessarily mean working on the floor of the exchange or in a trading room. Rather, it is the way in which you approach the job. Whereas dabblers are apt to let emotions cloud their judgment, true professionals are objective and methodical in recognizing and correcting their mistakes.

WHERE TO NEXT?

You have many resources at MarketWise to help you achieve your goals as a trader. You have already completed the first part of your journey by reading this book. But where to next? Consider making your next stop www .innerworth.com. MarketWise offers this online facility because we recognize the crucial importance of psychological resources to the successful trader. Your confidence, commitment, self-esteem, analytical capability, and emotional control are just some of important inner qualities you can optimize with self-awareness and practice.

Visit this web site and you will find tests designed to improve your mental and emotional fitness. In one section—"Assessments"—each questionnaire focuses on a specific psychological attribute critical for investment success. By completing the exercises, you can increase your awareness of your psychological makeup, identify areas of difficulty, and develop a plan for modifying your behavior to become a more successful investor. These assessments, which take about five minutes to complete, are posted every week. The time spent will pay significant dividends over the long run.

For a fee, the Trader Personality Inventory™ (TPI) can illuminate your psychological strengths and weaknesses in great detail and with precision. The TPI can have long-term implications for your trading success. The comprehensive report generated from the benchmark TPI is nothing less than your own personal manifesto for trading success. It is designed to provide immediate feedback on ways to improve your investing psychology by uncovering the specific strengths and weaknesses of your personality as it relates to the tasks of trading.

Innerworth psychologists and several top traders (all with 20+ years of active trading experience) spent nearly two years working closely with one of the most successful and reputable personality assessment firms, building on their 30 years of expertise. The TPI is the result, a uniquely powerful tool for building and maintaining a mental edge in the markets. Innerworth's leading product, the TPI is probably one of the most powerful analytic tools anywhere on the Web for directly improving your investing success.

This is an excellent starting point for beginners because it gives them a precise idea of the trading style that is best suited to their temperaments. Armed with this knowledge, it will also be easier to pick the courses MarketWise offers that will benefit you most. Innerworth's value is by no means confined to beginners, since results are sufficiently detailed to give experienced traders new insights about their trading practices.

Speaking of experienced traders, one thing most of them have in common is that they had mentors to help them along. Nothing speeds the learning process more effectively than having an experienced guide to show you how to get through the rough spots. All traders who have traveled the path of success have learned from their mistakes. Some traders will even tell you that the best lessons they received resulted from losses, not gains. To the extent this is so, we should wish to keep those losses as small and painless as possible. What better way to trade than under the watchful eye of someone who has made enough mistakes to learn from them? You can gain much wisdom from such a person.

Another form of wisdom is encapsulated in the rules of trading. These rules have evolved over decades—make that centuries—of trading. Take the following trading rules to heart. Each in its own way has helped deflect the pain of taking a loss and converted it to the wisdom of winning.

Some Rules for Successful Trading

- Formulate a trading plan and stick to it. It will help you to relax and exercise good judgment, especially when stress and temptation are greatest.
- Know when to cut your losses. If you are quick to bail out of losers, you should be able to make a good living trading by being right only 40 percent of the time.
- Let your profits run. It is often tempting to exit with a small profit, especially to break a losing streak. But this will never suffice to overcome losses, which typically will be more numerous.
- Use a system and stick with it. *All* systems have the potential to work once you have mastered them through diligent observation and application.
- Manage risk at all times. Traders who learn to do this well can profit even if they are not so good at picking timely entry and exit points.
- Be mindful of the trend. This will help you recognize when to stick with a winning trade and when to exit it.
- Never meet a margin call. If your original profit objective was $500, why put up another $2,000 to salvage a position that has turned against you?
- Do not try to trade too many markets; mastery of just a few is challenging enough.
- Do not trade if you are not in a position to accept losses, for it will limit your options and distort your priorities.
- Do not overtrade. There will always be other opportunities.
- Use charts and other technical tools to impose self-discipline.

- Know before the market opens exactly what you plan to do. This is your best defense against emotional swings.
- Never turn a loss into a straddle. This is worse than locking yourself into a loss: It is more like throwing the key away.
- Accustom yourself to taking small losses and to riding large gains.
- Recognize that emotional swings and lack of trading discipline will cost you more money in the long run than markets that have not gone your way.
- Shun hot tips and rumors. If this proves difficult, try making a list of tips that have made you money versus those that have not.
- Learn to trade from both the short side of the market and the long side. This is as useful as learning to shoot and dribble a basketball with either hand.
- Analyze your bad trades. The most valuable lessons are to be found not in your winning trades, but in the losers.
- Keep an intraday diary, recording market data along with your observations. Reread it occasionally to hone your perceptions.
- Look for divergences in related markets, since such divergences often telegraph trend changes.

SUMMARY

No list of rules can be anywhere near complete, for each of us must ultimately be guided by a set of rules that will be as unique as our individual trading personalities. But in the preceding list, you can find glimmers of light that will help illuminate the path to success. The value of some of these rules is self-evident. We have all heard many times that successful traders know when to cut their losses and when to let their profits run. This seems obvious enough, but that does not necessarily mean it is an easy rule to follow. In fact, it may require adhering to half-a-dozen other rules just to implement the one effectively. Only after much practice and observation will you know which rules work best for you, and which are easiest to implement. That is the road that all traders must travel to succeed, and while there are a few shortcuts, there is no getting around the fact that mastery can come only through patient and disciplined observation over weeks, months, and years.

As proof that this works, we have a friend—now a highly successful trader—who arrived in San Francisco with just $2,000 in his bank account and no job. He drove a cab for a year, then moved up the ladder with a stint as a Realtor. But his interest in trading, inspired by fantasies of wealth, eventually took precedence, and he plunged in, reading every book he could find on the subject. For many newcomers, this might have been the beginning of the end, since all too many of them jump right into trading after reading a book or two. But our friend kept plugging along, shopping online brokers to see which provided the best service, or the cheapest, or the best combination of both. Then he started to hang out in the chat rooms, observing how traders plan their day and execute their plan. He started to trade on his own with help from a half-dozen newsletter gurus. Then he whittled the gurus down to one or two favorites, taking the best that each had to offer and incorporating their best tricks into a style that he could truly call his own. Today, he makes enough money trading just three to four hours a day to support an extravagant lifestyle in San Francisco. The thing to understand is that traders are made, not born. But success does not happen overnight. Getting there can take long months of patient observation, disciplined record keeping and, probably, many simulated trades. MarketWise is here to help you each step of the way. So come join us. And Trade Wise!

MarketWise Tools—Routes to Success

No one has ever mastered the art of trading merely by reading books and going to seminars. Learning from these sources will not be worth much unless you actualize it by trading in real time, with real money. Although this book is designed to provide you with the broadest and firmest learning foundation possible, it comes with no guarantee that you will be able to trade profitably when you try out what you have learned. For you to achieve success will take much diligence, patience, and more practice; there are no shortcuts in these areas.

There is no such thing as a "natural" trader—traders are made, not born. In fact, any trader who has succeeded has done so through hard work, steadfast discipline, and an exceptional desire to achieve psychological self-mastery. In the end, you must conquer your own demons to trade unemotionally—especially when you are losing money, as happens to all traders from time to time.

Since all the instructors at MarketWise have traveled this difficult, frustrating, and sometimes treacherous path, our goal is to offer you the best of what we have learned. We hope to shorten your learning curve while making your progress toward profitability as quick and painless as possible. This chapter describes the tools and learning aids that are available from MarketWise.

Our extensive resources include live classes at our Boulder, Colorado, headquarters and at other locations in the United States and Canada, as well as in virtual space on the Internet. We also publish several newsletters each day that provide specific and detailed strategies for stocks, futures, indexes, and options, and timely analyses of the day's news and events.

To guide active day and swing traders, we also offer Wise-Ex, an interactive, web-based forum where subscribers receive guidance through the trading day, from the opening bell until the close. Other learning aids include psychological testing, books, audiotapes, CDs, and web-based seminars.

Another offering at MarketWise is "Innerworth," which provides lessons and tips each day to those who seek to master the inner game of trading. The site is intended to reveal your strengths and weaknesses as a trader. It begins with a test you can take in 25 minutes to determine your psychological profile in considerable and revealing detail.

All of our services and products are described at our web site, www .marketwise.com. Figure A.1 shows the home page.

FIGURE A.1 Web site for www.marketwise.com.

MARKETWISE WEB SITE RESOURCES

Many resources are available to the trader on this site, including descriptions of our online classes, free seminars, newsletters, educational programs, and research/analysis. Details about these programs can be accessed by clicking on any of the dark gray rectangles near the top of the screen. Our key classroom offering is this flagship course:

- *Foundational analysis:* You will learn all you need to know to begin trading. What are direct-access traders? They are traders who take absolute control over their trading. Besides making all their own trading decisions, direct-access traders handle all the details of executing and tracking orders and performance via a computerized trading platform. Direct-access traders are their own market analysts, trade-pickers (stocks, indexes, futures, or options), and order-desk clerks. All these functions are computerized now, so it is not as difficult as it sounds.

    Here are some of the things you can expect to learn:

    —How to predict the price action of stocks using the foundational ariables of price, volume, velocity, and time.

    —How to protect yourself if you are wrong.

    —How to recognize repetitive cyclical patterns in various time frames to determine entry and exit price levels. The goal is to enter trades at the beginning of trends for low-risk, high-probability trades.

    —How to place stop-loss orders to manage risk and maximize reward.

    —Techniques for controlling emotions and avoiding costly errors.

    —How to plan your trades and trade your plan.

    —Money management techniques.

    —Using the MarketWise Profiler to find the best trading and investing ideas in less than 20 minutes a day. A unique feature we offer all course graduates is a lifetime subscription to the Profiler as long as you maintain a funded account with our brokerage affiliate Terra Nova Trading, LLC.

- *Online courses:* These courses are designed for those who want to learn to trade or to sharpen their technique but who find it difficult to travel to one of our classrooms. The courses are usually conducted over three to four hours and the material continues to evolve. More information on the classes currently being offered can be found at www.marketwise.com.

- *Live online events:* MarketWise offers free online webinars to anyone who registers on our web site home page. These Internet sessions include school instructors trading live markets with real money on a regular basis. You will get a detailed, blow-by-blow account of how trading decisions are made, as well as a glimpse of the trading methodology taught in our classrooms.

Here are some online seminars that MarketWise instructors have offered:

- Using the MarketWise method to analyze the trend of the market and spot trading opportunities during the open.
- An overview of how classical pivot analysis and Fibonacci retracements are used in trading the E-mini contracts.
- How professionals use support (demand) and resistance (supply) to get the low-risk entry and consistently stay on the right side of the market.
- Watch one of our instructors fade the morning gap. By using a professional trading system, the instructor will show you how TICK and TRIN can help target entry and exit points.

TUNING TO THE MARKET INTRADAY

MarketWise offers the following products and services to help traders keep abreast of the markets intraday:

- *Wise Idea Newsletter:* This newsletter was created to provide a timely and concise look at factors affecting the market each day. It is designed to help new traders understand how professionals gain an edge, and to offer in-depth technical analysis of low-risk, actionable ideas.

  In the *Wise Idea Newsletter,* professional traders give you their thoughts about how to trade each day, with special emphasis on the psychology of the market. The newsletter highlights specific stocks, options, and futures ideas and teaches you how to use technical analysis from a short-term trader's perspective. One of the most important factors separating professional traders from those who trade as a hobby (quite often an expensive one) is the detailed analysis performed before committing their hard-earned capital to a position in the market. Each morning, four stocks are analyzed on two different time frames: a daily chart that shows the longer term perspective, and a 45-day chart that takes a look at the shorter term trends of the stock using hourly bars. This breakdown allows you to choose the analysis that best fits your trading plan.

- *Wise-Ex:* This interactive, subscription-based Web forum is designed for those who want to tap into the skills and experience of veteran traders intraday. It is a real-time streaming audio and video service delivering market information, market calls, and educational trading methodology. Subscribers log on daily via the Internet and monitor the pulse of the markets tick by tick, viewing it through the eyes and voice of professional traders. You will see and hear them trade, teach, and explain the natural flow and trend of the daily market. The MarketWise audio-video "Squawk Box" replaces old text-based systems allowing for the continuous dissemination of market information. You will feel as if you are an exchange member—make that a member of *all* the exchanges—at one time in a virtual world. Presenters each day include instructors on the MarketWise staff, trading experts who are affiliated with the school, and active floor traders on the various exchanges.

In the area of continuing education, MarketWise has developed an ongoing program that continually supports our graduates and clients. The *Continuing Education* portion of the web site gives our graduates and clients the ability to access ideas on trading strategies, market commentary, and updates to trading tools at no charge. Here are some of the topics stored in our archives than you can access via a computer:

- Fading the Trade.
- Gap Trading.
- Stock Splits—How to Play Them.
- When Do I Sell?
- Directional Movement Indicator.
- Options Trading Primer.
- Profiting from the Short Squeeze.
- Fair Value.
- A Bear Market Is a Bear Market.
- Your Winning Mind-Set.
- Using Dynamic Trailing Stops.
- Managing a Swing Trade.

The web site also contains specific *Reference Material*, including a detailed set of instructions for writing a trading plan. If you do not know what a trading plan is, or how to construct one, this guide is a great place to start before you sit down to trade with real money on the line.

The Trading Plan section at www.marketwise.com will help you define your goals and find a trading style to match them. It covers the most important concerns of the novice as well as of the more seasoned trader. By the time you have explored this material thoroughly, you will be able to provide answers to the following key questions:

- What is my electronic trading philosophy or style?
- Am I a long-, mid-, or short-term trader?
- What are my trading goals?
- Are they realistic?
- Am I psychologically and financially suited for electronic trading?
- How do I start a trading diary? A database of trades?
- How will I plan to select trades? To close out or offset trades?
- What is my analysis technique?
- What strategies suit my resources?
- Which markets will I trade?

Are you worried about the tax implications of trading? MarketWise .com maintains a library of useful material at the *Tax Center*. Wondering how to find good stocks to trade? Try the *Sectors and Stocks* guide on the web site. It will help you develop a list of industry groups and sectors, and it identifies the most prominent stocks in each group. There is also an *ECN* page with up-to-date information about the virtual electronic exchanges, as well as a separate page with detailed information about brick-and-mortar exchanges such as the New York Stock Exchange, the Chicago Board Options Exchange, the Pacific Exchange, and the Chicago Board of Trade.

MarketWise provides a broader range of services, products, and information designed to ease, quicken, and solidify the learning process. For those who hope to succeed at trading, it is not enough to simply absorb a few classroom lectures, or to dabble with a Level II screen. The road to profits requires patience, persistence, diligence and the willingness to draw on all available resources. Our goal is to provide you with the best information we can find on trading, and to make this information both easy to access and painless to digest. Our tools are at your disposal: We encourage you to visit www.marketwise.com frequently to find and use the ones you need.

Glossary

American-style option   An option contract that may be exercised at any time between the date of purchase and the expiration date. Most exchange-traded options are American-style.

Arbitrage   The simultaneous purchase and sale of identical or equivalent financial instruments or commodity futures in order to benefit from a discrepancy in their price relationship.

Ask   Also called "offer." It indicates a willingness to sell a futures contract at a given price.

Assignment   Notice to the seller (writer) of an option that has been exercised by the buyer.

At-the-money   An option whose *strike price* is equal or very near the market price of the underlying security or futures contract.

Back months   The futures or options on futures months being traded that are furthest from expiration. Also called deferred or distant months.

Bar   A discrete interval on a *chart*. If you are using a five-minute bar chart, each hourly segment of that chart will contain 12 vertical bars. Each of those bars will graphically represent the high, low, opening, and closing prices recorded during a discrete five-minute interval. Similarly, in a daily chart each bar represents a whole day's action.

Basis   The local cash market price minus the price of the nearby futures contract.

Bear   One who believes prices will move lower.

Bearish key reversal   A bar chart formation that occurs in an uptrending market when the day's high is higher, low is lower, and close is below the previous day's close. Can signal an upcoming downtrend.

Bear market   A market in which most prices are falling.

Bear spread   A vertical spread involving the sale of the lower strike call and the purchase of the higher strike call, called a bear call-spread. Also, a vertical spread involving the sale of the lower strike put and the purchase of the higher strike put, called a bear put-spread.

Blowoff volume   An exceptionally high-volume finishing stroke to a rally.

Breakaway gap   A gap in prices that signals the end of a price pattern and the beginning of an important market move.

Broker   A person or firm that executes orders to buy or sell futures contracts, stocks, or options for customers. Full-service brokers provide market information and advice to customers, whereas discount brokers simply execute their orders.

Brokerage house   A firm that handles orders to buy and sell futures, stocks, and options contracts for customers.

Bull   One who expects prices to rise.

Bullish key reversal   A bar-chart formation occurring in a downtrending market where the day's high is higher, low is lower, and close is above that of the previous day. It can signal an upcoming uptrend.

Bull market   A market in which most prices are rising.

Bull spread   A vertical spread involving the purchase of the lower strike call and the sale of the higher strike call, called a bull call-spread. Also, a vertical spread involving the purchase of the lower strike put and the sale of the higher strike put, called a bull put-spread.

Buy-on-Opening   To buy at the beginning of a trading session at a price within the opening range.

Call option   An option contract that gives the holder the right to buy the underlying security or futures contract at a specified price for a certain, fixed period of time.

Call value   At expiration, equal to the futures or stock price minus the strike price of the call.

Carryover   Last year's ending stocks of a storable commodity.

Cash commodity   The actual physical commodity as distinguished from a futures contract.

Cash price   Current market price of the actual physical commodity. Also called "spot price."

Cash settlement   Final disposition of open positions on the last trading day of a contract month. Occurs in markets where there is no actual delivery.

CFTC   Acronym for the Commodity Futures Trading Commission, as created by the Commodity Futures Trading Commission Act of 1974. This government agency currently regulates the nation's commodity futures industry.

Channel   Once a trend line is created either up or down on a *chart*, parallel lines connecting the most obvious tops and bottoms of the oscillations within that *trend* can be drawn to create a channel. It can be a rising, falling, or a sideways channel.

Chart   A graphical representation of price movement plotted over time. There are many types of charts, but the bar chart is the most common.

Chartist   One who employs technical analysis.

Clearing House   An entity responsible for settling trading accounts, clearing trades, collecting and maintaining performance bond funds, regulating delivery, and reporting trading data.

Close   The period at the end of the trading session. Sometimes used to refer to the closing range.

Closing purchase   A transaction by which the purchaser cancels out a short position in a given option, stocks, or futures contract.

Closing range   The high and low prices, or bids and offers, recorded during the period designated as the official close.

Closing sale   A transaction by which the seller cancels out a long position in a given option, stock, or futures contract.

Commission   The fee charged by a broker to cover the trades you make to open and close each position. When trading futures, commissions are payable when you exit the position, completing a "round turn." Commissions on stocks and options are usually half on initiation and half on liquidation.

Commitment   When a trader or institution assumes the obligation to take or make delivery on a futures contract.

Commodity exchange   An incorporated, not-for-profit association of members that promulgates rules and procedures for the trading of futures and options on futures contracts, provides the physical or electronic means to do so, and oversees trading practices.

Contract   Unit of trading for a financial or commodity future. Also, the actual agreement between buyer and seller of a futures or options transaction as defined by an exchange.

Contract month   The month in which futures contracts may be satisfied by making or accepting delivery. Also called the delivery month.

Covered call-writing   A strategy in which one sells *call* options on an equivalent long position in the underlying security or futures contract.

Covered put-writing   A strategy in which one sells *put* options on an equivalent short position in the underlying stock or commodity.

Credit spread   An option spread in which there is a net collection of premium.

Day order   An order that will be filled during the day's trading session or canceled.

Day trader   A trader who establishes and liquidates positions within one day's trading, ending the day with no position in the market.

Debit spread   An option spread in which there is a net payout of premium.

Deferred pricing agreement   A cash sale in which one delivers the commodity and agrees with the buyer to price it at a later time.

Delivery   The tender and receipt of an actual commodity or financial instrument in settlement of a futures contract.

Delta   The rate of change of an option's premium in relation to the change in the underlying futures price. The delta is expressed in percentage terms. Because option's premiums do not always move by the same amount as the underlying futures or stock price, this delta factor is used. Generally, a change in the underlying futures price will result in a smaller change in the option premium. Suppose that an S&P 500 futures price rises by 1.00 point, and a call option on that contract rises by .50 points. It is obvious that the option premium gained only about one-half of what the futures price did. This would indicate that particular call option's delta is 50 percent. If the underlying futures fell in price, delta could help predict a similar loss in the value of the options premium. Deltas range from 0 percent (deep out-of-the-money options) to nearly 100 percent (options that are deep-in-the-money).

At-the-money options have deltas of approximately 50 percent. If an at-the-money call has a delta of 50 percent, it would move only about half as much as the underlying vehicle. However, the deeper-in-the-money the put or call, the higher its delta value.

Demand   The quantity of a commodity that buyers are willing to purchase from the market at a given price.

Derivative security   A financial security whose value is determined in part from the value and characteristics of another, the underlying security.

Double top, bottom   A bar-chart formation signaling a possible trend reversal. It describes a price high or low that has been tested but not penetrated.

Downtrend   A price trend characterized by a series of lower highs and lower lows.

Electronic trading   Trading via computer through an automated, order entry and matching system. Electronic trading systems link markets and customers around the world.

Elliott Wave Theory   A type of technical analysis that studies price wave sequences.

Equity options   *Put* or *call* options on shares of individual common stocks.

European-style option   An option contract that may be exercised only during a specific period of time just prior to its expiration.

Exercise To implement the right under which the holder of a put/call is entitled to buy or sell the underlying stock or futures contract.

Exercise notice A notice tendered by a brokerage firm to the central clearing entity that exchanges an option for a stock or futures contract.

Exercise price The price at which the holder (buyer) may purchase or sell the underlying futures contract. Also called strike price.

Exhaustion gap A gap in prices near the top or bottom of a price move that signals an abrupt turn in the market.

Expiration date The last day that an option may be exercised into the underlying futures contract. Also, the last day of trading for a futures contract.

Expire Letting the expiration date for an option pass without exercising or offsetting the option.

Fast market Term used to define exceptionally busy market conditions.

Fill-or-kill order (FOK) A limit order that must be filled immediately or canceled.

Floor broker An exchange member who is paid a fee for executing orders for clearing members or their customers. A floor broker executing orders must be licensed to do so.

Floor trader An exchange member who generally trades only his or her own account or an account controlled by him or her. Also referred to as a local on commodity exchanges.

Forward contract A private agreement between buyer and seller for the future delivery of a commodity at an agreed price.

Foundational analysis The study of price, volume, time, and velocity to determine which markets to trade and when to trade them.

Fundamental analysis The study of supply and demand information to help project stock or futures prices.

Fundamentalist One who engages in fundamental analysis.

Futures A term used to designate all contracts covering the purchase and sale of financial instruments or physical commodities for future delivery on a commodity futures exchange.

Futures commission merchant (FCM) A firm or person engaged in soliciting or accepting and handling orders for the purchase or sale of futures contracts, subject to the rules of a futures exchange, and who, in connection with solicitation or acceptance of orders, accepts any money or securities to margin any resulting trades or contracts. The FCM must be licensed by the CFTC.

Futures contract   A standardized agreement, traded on a futures exchange, to buy or sell a commodity at a specified price at a date in the future. Specifies the commodity, quality, quantity, delivery date, and delivery point or cash settlement.

Futures option   Option on individual futures contracts.

Gamma   Gamma tells you how much the delta will change when futures prices increase or decrease. For example, assume a call on an S&P futures contract has a delta of 50 percent. This implies that if the futures move up 1.00 point, the option will gain about .50 points. The gamma of the call is 1.2 percent. If futures increase by 1.00 then the delta (not the option premium) will increase by 1.2 percentage points $(50 + 1.2 = 51.2)$ to 51.2. In other words, the option premium will increase or decrease in value at the rate of the gamma.

Gap   A price area at which the market did not trade from one day to the next.

Go long   Acquire a stock, futures contract, or option on same.

Good-till (GT)   An order that remains in effect until it is canceled or the specified date is passed.

Good-till-canceled (GTC)   An order that remains in effect until it is canceled, filled, or the contract expires.

Go short   Sell a stock, option, index, or futures contract that you do not own to start with. Your profits come when you buy back, or "cover" those shorts at a lower price.

The Greeks   The Greeks are essential to determining an option's value. While futures traders deal with two dimensions—the up-and-down movement of a contract—options traders have to work with four dimensions: the futures price and strike price, as well as time decay and changing volatility. For a more detailed discussion of these variables, see listings in this glossary for "Delta," "Gamma," "Theta," and "Vega."

Head and shoulders   A sideways price formation at the top or bottom of the market that indicates a major market reversal.

Hedge   A conservative strategy used to limit risk by effecting a transaction that offsets an existing position.

Hedger   A person or firm who uses the futures market to offset price risk when intending to sell or buy the actual commodity.

Hedging   The purchase or sale of a futures contract as a temporary substitute for a cash market transaction to be made at a later date.

Hedging line of credit   Financing from your lender for hedging the sale and purchase of commodities.

Index options   Options on individual indexes, such as the S&Ps and the Nasdaq 100.

Inflection point, or pivot price   Price level established as being significant by market's failure to penetrate or as being significant when a sudden increase in volume accompanies the move through the price level.

Initial performance bond   The funds required when a futures position (or a short options on futures position) is opened. Previously referred to as initial margin.

Intercommodity spread   A spread trade involving the same month of different but related futures contracts.

Intermarket spread   A spread trade involving same or related commodities at different exchanges. Also called an interexchange spread.

In-the-money   A call option with a strike price less than the underlying futures price, or a put option with a strike price greater than the underlying futures price.

Intraday bar charts   Charts that have time frames varying from one minute to sixty minutes. A three-minute *chart* will have a *bar* for each three-minute interval, with each bar's vertical length determined by the high and low prices achieved during the interval it records.

Intrinsic value   The relationship of an option's in-the-money strike price to the current futures or stock price. If a stock is trading at $63, a call option with a $60 strike price would have an intrinsic value of $3 (anything more than that would be time premium).

Introducing broker (IB)   A firm or person engaged in soliciting or accepting and handling orders for the purchase or sale of futures contracts, subject to the rules of a futures exchange, but not in accepting any money or securities to margin any resulting trades or contracts. The IB is associated with a correspondent futures commission merchant and must be licensed by the Commodity Futures Trading Commission.

Leverage   The use of a small amount of assets to control a greater amount of assets.

Limit move   See "Maximum price fluctuation."

Limit order   An order that can be filled only at a specified price or better.

Liquidation   Any transaction that offsets or closes out a long or short futures or options on futures position.

Margin   A sum, usually smaller than the initial performance bond, that must remain on deposit in the customer's account for any position. A drop in funds below this level requires a deposit back to initial performance bond levels. Previously referred to as the maintenance margin.

Market-if-touched (MIT) A price order that becomes a market order when the market trades at a specified price at least once.

Market-on-close (MOC) A market order filled during the close of a trading session.

Market order An order filled immediately at the best price available.

Market sentiment A measure of the percentage of advisory services and traders who are bullish on the index, stock, or commodity.

Mark-to-market The daily adjustment of performance bond accounts to reflect profits and losses.

Maximum price fluctuation The maximum amount the contract price can change up or down during one trading session, as stipulated by exchange rules.

Minimum price fluctuation The smallest increment of price movement possible in trading a given contract, often referred to as a tick.

Moving average chart A chart recording moving averages (3-day, 10-day, etc.) of market prices.

Moving averages A type of technical analysis using the averages of settlement prices.

National Futures Association (NFA) A self-regulatory organization for the commodity futures industry comprising firms and individuals that conduct business with the public. Overseen by the Commodity Futures Trading Commission.

Nearby The nearest active trading month of a futures or options on futures contract. Also referred to as the lead month.

Nonserial options Options for months for which there are existing futures contracts of the same months.

Not-held (NH) A discretionary note on an order stating that the floor broker will not be held accountable if the trade is executed outside the requirements of the order. Gives the broker discretion on getting the order filled.

Offer Indicates a willingness to sell a futures contract at a given price.

Offset Selling if one has bought, or buying if one has sold, a futures or options on a futures contract.

Offsetting a hedge For a short hedger, to buy back futures and sell a commodity. For a long hedger, to sell back futures and buy a commodity.

Offsetting a long option Selling a put with the same strike price to offset a put; selling a call with the same strike price to offset a call.

Opening The beginning of the trading session.

Opening range   The range of prices at which the first bids and offers were made or first transactions were completed. Must be initiated by at least one trade.

Open interest   Total number of futures or options on futures contracts that have not yet been offset or fulfilled for delivery.

Open order   See "Good-till-canceled."

Open outcry   The method of trading publicly so that each trader has a fair chance to buy or sell.

Option   The right, but not the obligation, to sell or buy the underlying security or futures contract at a specified price within a specified time.

Option assignment   The random selection of an option writer to take a position when an option is exercised.

Order-cancels-other (OCO)   An order that includes two orders, one of which cancels the other when filled. Also referred to as one-cancels-other.

Out-of-the-money   An option with no intrinsic value. A *call* option is out-of-the-money if the *strike price* is greater than the market price of the underlying security or futures contract. A *put* option is out-of-the-money if the strike price is less than the market price of the underlying security or futures contract.

Out-trades   A situation that results when there is some confusion or error on a trade (e.g., when both traders think they are buying).

Overbought/Oversold   A condition in which buying or selling has been excessive relative to a previously established benchmark. Trading vehicles can remain overbought or oversold for an extended period. Some of the indicators that measure the degree to which they have become so include a 10-day moving average of the advances and declines in the market, *stochastics*, the McClellan oscillator, William's percentR, Upside and Downside volume, short interest ratio, and the *put/call* ratio, to mention just a few.

Overvalued/Undervalued   There are many different methods to judge the value of a stock, index, or a future. One can use price/earnings ratios, dividend yield, book value, production cost, historical prices, seasonal prices, supply/demand factors, or a multitude of other benchmarks.

Performance bond   Funds that must be deposited by a customer with his or her broker, by a broker with a clearing member or by a clearing member with the clearing house. The performance bond helps to ensure the financial integrity of brokers, clearing members, and the Exchange as a whole. Previously referred to as margin.

Performance bond call   A demand for additional funds to bring the customer's account back up to the initial performance bond level whenever adverse price movement has caused the account to go below the maintenance. Previously referred to as a margin call.

Point and figure chart   A graph of prices charted with x's for price increases and o's for price decreases, used by the chartist for buy and sell signals.

Position   An interest in the market, either long or short, in the form of open contracts.

Position trader   A trader who takes a position in the market that he or she may hold for a long time.

Premium   The competitively established price that the buyer of an option contract pays to the seller for the rights conveyed by the contract. Premium-based trading strategies are employed by most professionals, but estimating future changes in premium levels is the most difficult task of the options trader. *Premium* and *volatility* are often used interchangeably, since the premium in an option ultimately reflects the estimated (and potential) volatility of the underlying vehicle. The options of "crazy" stocks usually trade at very high volatilities.

Price order   An order to sell or buy at a certain price or better.

Pure hedger   A person who places a hedge to lock in a price for a commodity. He or she offsets the hedge and transacts in the cash market simultaneously.

Put option   An option granting the right, but not the obligation, to sell a futures contract at the stated price prior to the expiration of the option.

Put profit/loss   For a long put, equal to the put value minus the premium. For a short put, equal to the premium minus the put value.

Put value   At expiration, equal to the strike price minus the futures price.

Rally   An upward movement of prices following a decline. The opposite of a reaction.

Range   The high and low prices or high and low bids and offers recorded during a specified time.

Registered representative   A person employed by, and soliciting business for, a commission house or futures commission merchant.

Relative strength   A percentage measure of the price change in a stock, index, or future over a specified interval, with more weight given to the most recent period. The time frame may vary, based on cycles.

Relative Strength Index (RSI)   A Relative Strength Index has values ranging from 0 to 100. While this indicator follows the movements of closing prices on *bar* charts, the RSI can warn when a market is near a top or bottom. In an uptrending market with prices making new highs, an RSI climbing above 70 warns of a *trend* reversal if the RSI peaks below its previous high. This is called bearish divergence.

Resistance line A price level above which prices tend not to rise due to selling pressure.

Retracement A price move in the opposite direction of a recent trend.

Round turn See "Commission."

Runaway gap A gap in prices after a trend has begun that signals the halfway point of a market move.

Scalp To trade for small gains. Scalping usually involves initiating and closing a position quickly, sometimes within just a few minutes or less.

Seasonality and cyclicality Most indexes and futures have their own personalities. Some tend to repeat certain patterns and others act erratically. Seasonality occurs in both indexes and futures. There is usually a Christmas rally, and markets are generally expected to rise into holidays. Indexes often rally into option-expiration deadlines on Fridays. The Monday after such expirations, the market usually goes in the opposite direction. Toy stocks rally from July to November. Heating oil prices rise as winter approaches, unleaded gas rises as summer approaches, and frozen orange juice rallies as winter approaches. These are things that occur a high percentage of the time, though not always.

Selective hedger A person who hedges only when prices appear likely to move against him or her.

Selling climax An extraordinarily high volume occurring suddenly in a downtrend signaling the end of the trend.

Serial options Options for months for which there are no futures contracts. The underlying futures contract for a serial option month would be the next nearby futures contract.

Settlement price A figure determined by the closing range that is used to calculate gains and losses in futures market accounts, performance bond calls, and invoice prices for deliveries.

Short One who has sold a futures contract to establish a market position and who has not yet closed out this position through an offsetting procedure. The opposite of long.

Short cash Describes a trader who needs and plans to buy a commodity.

Short hedge The sale of a futures contract in anticipation of a later cash market sale. Used to eliminate or lessen the possible decline in value of ownership of an approximately equal amount of the cash financial instrument or physical commodity.

Sideways trend   Seen in a bar chart when prices tend not to go above or below a certain range of levels.

Speculator   One who attempts to anticipate price changes and through buying and selling stocks, futures, or options aims to make profits. A speculator does not use the market in connection with the production, processing, marketing, or handling of a product.

Spot Price   See "Cash price."

Spread   The price difference between two contracts. Holding a long and a short position in two related futures or options on futures contracts, with the objective of profiting from a changing price relationship.

Spread order   An order that indicates the purchase and sale of futures contracts simultaneously.

Spread trade   The simultaneous purchase and sale of futures contracts for the same commodity or instrument for delivery in different months or in different but related markets. A spreader is not concerned with the direction in which the market moves, but only with the difference between the prices of each contract.

Stochastic Indicator   Like the *Relative Strength Index (RSI)*, a stochastic is an oscillator used to judge price momentum. Stochastics are a popular technical tool.

Stop close only order   A stop order that is executed only during the closing range of the trading session.

Stop-limit   Similar to a stop-loss order, except that your order is executed as a limit order when the specified price is touched. If a stock is trading at 110 and you want to buy it if and when it touches 110.70, a 110.70 buy-stop limit would require your broker to bid 110.70 for the stock or futures contract if that price is touched. If it touches 110.70 but keeps going higher, your order might not get filled.

Stop-limits and certain other types of special orders are "not held," meaning that your broker can use discretion in exercising them and is not responsible for failing to execute the order as given.

Stop-limit order   An order that becomes a limit order only when the market trades at a specified price.

Stop-Loss   When purchasing or shorting a stock, option, or future, a stop-loss is the price at which you will bail out of the position if you are wrong. It is a strategy used to limit losses, and the order itself is executed as a market order when your price is touched.

Stop order   An order that becomes a market order only when the market trades at a specified price.

Stop with a price limit   A stop order with a specified worst price at which the order can be filled.

Straddle   The purchase of a put and a call, in which the options have the same expiration and same strike price, called a long straddle. Also, the sale of both a put and a call in which the options have the same expiration and same strike price, called a short straddle.

Strangle   The purchase of a put and a call, in which the options have the same expiration and the put strike is lower than the call strike, called a long strangle. Also the sale of a put and a call, in which the options have the same expiration and the put strike is lower than the call strike, called a short strangle.

Strike price   The price at which the option buyer may purchase or sell the underlying futures contract on exercise. See "Exercise price."

Supply   The quantity of a commodity that producers are willing to provide to the market at a given price.

Symmetrical triangles   A price formation that can either signal a reversal or a continuation of price movement.

Synthetic call option   A combination of a long futures contract and a long put, called a synthetic long call. Also, a combination of a short futures contract and a short put, called a synthetic short call.

Synthetic futures   A combination of a put and a call with the same strike price, in which both are bullish, called synthetic long futures. Also, a combination of a put and a call with the same strike price, in which both are bearish, called synthetic short futures.

Synthetic option   A combination of a futures contract and an option, in which one is bullish and one is bearish.

Synthetic put option   A combination of a short futures contract and a long call, called a synthetic long put. Also, a combination of a long futures contract and a short call, called a synthetic short put.

Target   The price objective for a particular trade.

Technical analysis   The study of historical price patterns to help forecast futures prices.

Theta   The derivative that measures how much an option will lose in value due to the passage of time. Simply put, it measures time-decay. We know options are wasting assets—they lose a little bit of time-value every day (good for the option writer, bad for the buyer). Theta quantifies how much an option will lose as each day passes. If a call option selling for, say, 14.4, has a theta of 1.03, it means that by tomorrow, the call will lose 1.03 points (assuming there are no changes in any other input) and will be worth only 13.37 points (14.4 − 1.03 = 13.37). Remember too, that time decay is not linear. It accelerates as expiration draws closer. Put another way: If there are 100 days until expiration and one day passes, how much time premium has eroded? About $\frac{1}{100}$th. Suppose there are 10 days to expiry and one day passes? In this case, $\frac{1}{10}$th of the time has eroded.

Tick   A reference to a change in price, either up or down. See "Minimum price fluctuation."

Time value   The portion of the option *premium* that is attributable to the amount of time remaining until the expiration of the option contract. Time value is whatever the option has in addition to its *intrinsic value*.

Trader   A member of the exchange who buys and sells futures and options on the floor of the exchange.

Trailing stop   When a position is established and is moving in the direction anticipated, a trailing stop is the price at which you will exit the position in the event of a retracement against the *trend*. The stop "trails" the price movement of the underlying vehicle, and its size can be adjusted according to the risk requirements of the trader. The strategy is used to ensure a profitable exit on an adverse move while allowing you to participate in further price movement with the trend.

Trend   The general direction of the market.

Uptrend   A price trend characterized by a series of higher highs and higher lows.

Uptrend/Downtrend   The direction in which a trading vehicle is moving. There are *trends* within trends, and it is possible to trade an uptrend that exists within a larger downtrend, or vice versa.

Vega   Sometimes called zeta or kappa, vega is the amount by which an option's theoretical value can be expected to change, in theory, if volatility changes by 1 percent. For example, assume a call with a 20 volatility has a theoretical value of 14.4. Its vega is .72 points. If volatility were to advance to 21 percent, the call would gain .72 points. Obviously, higher volatility works against options writers and in favor of options buyers. If volatility dropped from 20 percent to 19 percent, the call would lose .72 points. Vega gives you an idea of how sensitive an option is to perceived changes in market volatility.

Vertical spread   The purchase of a call/put and the sale of a call/put, where the options have the same expiration and different strike prices.

Volatility   A annualized measure of the fluctuation in the price of a futures contract. Historical volatility is the actual measure of futures price movement from the past. Implied volatility is a measure of what the market implies it is, as reflected in the option's price.

Volume   The amount of shares traded or number of transactions in futures or options made during a specified period.

Window   The price range within which a trading vehicle is to be bought or sold, or within which you are anticipating a tradable high or low to form.

With discretion   A discretionary note on an order telling the floor broker to use his or her own discretion in filling the order.

Writer   An individual who sells an option.

Bibliography and Exchange Contact Information

Appel, Gerald. *Winning Market Systems: 83 Ways to Beat the Market.* New York: Traders Press, 1991.

Bass, Thomas A. *The Predictors.* New York: Henry Holt and Company, 1999.

Bernstein, Peter L. *Against the Gods: The Remarkable Story of Risk.* New York, John Wiley & Sons, 1998.

Cohen, Bernice. *The Edge of Chaos.* New York: John Wiley & Sons, 1997.

Colby, Robert W. *The Encyclopedia of Technical Market Indicators.* New York: McGraw-Hill, 1988.

Cramer, James J. *Confessions of a Street Addict.* New York: Simon and Schuster, 2002.

Douglas, Mark. *The Disciplined Trader.* New York: New York Institute of Finance, 1990.

Edwards, Robert D., and John Magee. *Technical Analysis of Stock Trends.* 7th ed. New York: St. Lucie Press, 1998.

Elder, Alexander. *Trading for a Living.* New York: John Wiley & Sons, 1993.

Elder, Alexander. *Come into My Trading Room.* New York: John Wiley & Sons, 2002.

Filer, Herbert. Understanding Put and Call Options New York: Crown 1959.

Gleick, J. *Chaos.* New York: Penguin Books, 1987.

Hirsch, Yale, and Jeffery A. Hirsch, eds. *Stock Trader's Almanac 2002.* 35th ed. Old Tappan, NJ: The Hirsch Organization Inc., 2001.

Kiev, Ari. *Trading to Win.* New York: John Wiley & Sons, 1998.

LeFevre, Edwin. *Reminiscences of a Stock Operator.* New York: George H. Doran Company, 1923.

Lerman, David. *Exchange Traded Funds and E-Mini Stock Index Futures.* New York: John Wiley & Sons, 2001.

Lukeman, Josh. *The Market Maker's Edge.* New York: McGraw-Hill, 2000.

Lynch, Peter. *One up on Wall Street.* New York: Simon and Schuster, 1989.

Mackay, C. *Extraordinary Popular Delusions and the Madness of Crowds.* New York: Harmony Books, 1980.

Malkiel, B. G. *A Random Walk down Wall Street.* New York: W. W. Norton & Company, 1973.

McMillan, Lawrence G. *Options as a Strategic Investment.* 4th. ed. New York: New York Institute of Finance, 2002.

Murphy, John J. *Technical Analysis of the Financial Markets.* Englewood Cliffs, NJ: Prentice-Hall, 1999.

Nassar, David S. *How to Get Started in Electronic Day Trading.* New York: McGraw-Hill, 1998.

Nassar, David S. *How to Get Started in Electronic Day Trading Home Study Course.* New York: McGraw-Hill, 2000.

Nassar, David S. *Rules of the Trade.* New York: McGraw-Hill, 2001.

Nassar, David S. *Electronic Direct Access Trading Course.* Boulder, CO: MarketWise, 2002, 2003, 2004, 2005.

Nassar, David S. *How to Get Started in Active Trading and Investing.* New York: McGraw-Hill, 2004.

Nassar, David S. and William Lupien. *Market Analysis and Evaluation for Swing Trading.* New York: McGraw-Hill, 2004.

Nison, Steve. *Japanese Candlestick Techniques.* New York: New York Institute of Finance, 1991.

Peters, Edgar E. *Chaos and Order in the Capital Markets.* New York: John Wiley & Sons, 1991.

Prechter, Robert R., Jr. *Conquer the Crash,* New York: John Wiley & Sons, 2002.

Prechter, Robert R., Jr., and A. J. Frost. *Elliott Wave Principle.* 6th ed. New York: New Classics Library, 1990.

Schumpeter, J. A. *Business Cycles.* New York: McGraw-Hill, 1939.

Schwager, Jack D. *Market Wizards.* New York: HarperBusiness, 1990.

Schwager, Jack D. *The New Market Wizards.* New York: HarperBusiness, 1992.

Schwartz, Martin S. *Pit Bull: Lessons from Wall Street's Champion Trader.* New York: HarperCollins Publishers, 1999.

Shannon, Brian. *The Technical Analysis Course.* Boulder, CO: Market-Wise, 2002.

Vaga, T. *Profiting from Chaos.* New York: McGraw-Hill, 1994.

White, E. N. *Crashes and Panics: The Lessons from History.* Homewood, IL: Business One Irwin, 1990.

Wilder, J. Welles, Jr. *The Adam Theory of Markets or What Matters Is Profit.* McLeansville, NC: Cavida Ltd., 1987.

Wilder, J. Welles, Jr. *New Concepts in Technical Trading Systems.* Greensboro, SC: Trend Research, 1976.

EXCHANGE CONTACT INFORMATION

American Stock Exchange (AMEX)
Derivative Securities
86 Trinity Place
New York, NY 10006
(800) 843-2639
www.amex.com

Archipelago Holdings Inc. (AX)
100 South Wacker Drive, Suite 1800
Chicago, IL 60606
(312) 960-1696
www.archipelago.com

Chicago Board Options Exchange (CBOE)
LaSalle at Van Buren
Chicago, IL 60605
(800) 678-4667
www.cboe.com

Pacific Exchange (PCX)
Options Marketing
115 Sansome Street, 7th Floor
San Francisco, CA 94104
(800) 825-5773
www.pacificex.com

Philadelphia Stock Exchange (PHLX)
1900 Market Street
Philadelphia, PA 19103
(800) 843-7459
www.phlx.com

International Securities Exchange (ISE)
60 Broad Street
New York, NY 10004
(212) 943-2400
www.iseoptions.com

The Options Clearing Corporation (OCC)
440 South LaSalle Street, Suite 2400
Chicago, IL 60605
(800) 537-4258
www.theocc.com

Index